SPECIAL TOPICS IN ANALYSIS

by

K. O. Friedrichs

Notes by K. O. Friedrichs
and H. Kranzer

New York University
1953-1954

Table of Contents

Part A

Periodic Solutions of Ordinary Differential Equations and their Bifurcations

Table of Contents

Part B

Asymptotic Integration of Differential Equations

SPECIAL TOPICS IN ANALYSIS

Part A

Periodic Solutions of Ordinary Differential Equations and their Bifurcations

The theory of periodic motion was developed by Poincaré before 1890 in connection with the famous problem of three bodies and presented in his treatise on New Methods in Celestial Mechanics. In later years these methods were adapted by a number of authors to problems of "terrestrial mechanics" and of electrical oscillations. Terrestrial problems seem to offer a remarkable variety of possibilities owing to the presence of resistance; for the same reason, terrestrial problems are in many respects more manageable than problems of celestial mechanics.

It is not intended to give a historical account of the work of Poincaré and of later researchers, nor to show how this work has been used in handling specific problems. It is merely intended to describe an approach to a general theory of periodic motion which has grown out of Poincaré's original work.

1. Continuation Problem

The theory is concerned with the change in time of a number of physical quantities $u_1(t),\ldots,u_n(t)$ subject to a law of interaction which can be formulated as a system of first order ordinary differential equations of the form

$$\frac{du_i}{dt} = f_i(u_1,\ldots,u_n,t) \quad , \qquad i = 1,\ldots,n \quad . \tag{1.1}$$

It is convenient to use the single letter u to denote the set of quantities $\{u_1,\ldots,u_n\}$, and similarly to let f stand for the set $\{f_1,\ldots,f_n\}$; u and f may be regarded as column-vectors, or better still as simply columns as they need not represent physical vector quantities. For such columns we on occasion use the "absolute values"

$$|u| = [u_1^2 + \dots + u_n^2]^{1/2} \quad , \quad |f| = [f_1^2 + \dots + f_n^2]^{1/2} \quad .$$

In terms of "columns" the differential equation system (1.1) takes the form of a matrix equation:

(1.2) $$\frac{du}{dt} = f(u,t) \quad .$$

We shall be concerned with functions of t which are periodic in t with a definite period T. Hereafter, whenever we speak of a periodic function, we shall mean a function which has this definite period T. We assume that the f is periodic in t:

(1.3) $$f(u,t+T) = f(u,t) \quad \text{for all } u \text{ and } t,$$

and we seek periodic solutions u(t) of the differential equation (1.2). Geometrically speaking, we may consider the column $u_1, \dots, u_n$ as representing a point in n-dimensional space; a periodic solution of (1.2) will then correspond to a closed curve, a single circuit of which is traveled through in the time T.

It seems that Poincaré was the first who realized that the perturbation method of solving nonlinear differential equations can be successfully applied to this problem. The perturbation method requires us to consider, instead of one definite differential equation, an entire manifold of differential equations in which the original equation is embedded. Specifically, one considers periodic right members f which depend on a parameter μ:

(1.4) $$f = f(u,t,\mu) \quad .$$

One assumes that for a certain value of the parameter, say for $\mu = 0$, one knows a periodic solution

(1.5) $$u = \overset{\circ}{u}(t) \quad ,$$

called the <u>generating solution</u>, of the corresponding differential equation, and one seeks to establish the existence for small values of the parameter μ of periodic solutions which approximate $\overset{\circ}{u}(t)$. Geometrically, to a closed curve in u-space which is traversible in the time T, we seek neighboring closed curves which become traversible in the same time if the law governing the motion is slightly changed. The problem may thus be said to concern the <u>continuation of periodic solutions</u>.

Intuitively, one might not at first expect this continuation problem to have a solution; for even neighboring solutions of a periodic solution of the <u>same</u> differential equation need not be periodic. However, it will be seen that the variability of μ and the fact that we only ask for <u>one</u> periodic solution of each equation allows us to solve this problem in general, though not in all cases.

2. The Variational Equation

A simple condition can be given under which the continuation problem always has a solution. To formulate this condition we must introduce the <u>variational equation</u>, a linear homogeneous differential equation

(2.1) $$\frac{d}{dt}\,\delta u = A(t)\,\delta u$$

for a new unknown function $\delta u = \{\delta u_1, \ldots, \delta u_n\}$ of t. A(t) is here an $n \times n$ matrix whose components A_{ij} are given by

(2.2) $$A_{ij}(t) = \frac{\partial}{\partial u_j} f_i(\overset{\circ}{u}(t), t, 0) \quad ;$$

this definition may be abbreviated by writing

(2.3) $$A(t) = \frac{\partial}{\partial u} f(\overset{\circ}{u}(t), t, 0) = f_u(\overset{\circ}{u}(t), t, 0) \quad .$$

Clearly $A(t)$ is periodic in t, since f and $\overset{o}{u}$ are. Thus we are led to ask whether the homogeneous linear differential equation (2.1), which can evidently be obtained from (1.2) by formal differentiation with respect to u, has periodic solutions which are not identically zero.

It is clear that the solution $\delta u(t)$ of equation (2.1) depends linearly on the initial values $\delta u(0)$ of δu. Accordingly, there is for each time t a matrix $Y(t)$ such that

$$\delta u(t) = Y(t)\delta u(0) \quad . \tag{2.4}$$

In particular,

$$\delta u(T) = Y(T)\delta u(0) \quad . \tag{2.5}$$

Thus if δu is periodic, the initial values satisfy the relation

$$Y(T)\delta u(0) = \delta u(0) \quad . \tag{2.6}$$

In other words, the column $\delta u(0)$ is an eigencolumn of the matrix $Y(T)$ with the eigenvalue 1. Clearly, then, equation (2.1) has a non-zero periodic solution if and only if the number 1 occurs among the eigenvalues of $Y(T)$. Whether or not this is the case depends intimately on the special nature of the matrix $A(t)$; in general, of course, it will not be so, as each of the n eigenvalues of $Y(T)$ could be made to take on any arbitrary value by choosing $A(t)$ appropriately.

The condition of Poincaré referred to above, under which continuation is possible, is simply that the variational equation (2.1) have no periodic solution, i.e., no solution which has the same period as the generating solution, except zero. If this condition is satisfied we say that the problem of the continuation of the generating solution $\overset{o}{u}(t)$ is non-degenerate. The first result of Poincaré may then be expressed as the

<u>Continuation Theorem 1:</u> Suppose the problem of the continuation of the generating solution is non-degenerate. Then this problem can be solved for sufficiently small values of μ. Specifically, there is a number $\mu_o > 0$ such that to every value of μ with $|\mu| \leq \mu_o$ a periodic solution $u(t,\mu)$ of the differential equation $u_t = f(u,t,\mu)$ exists which depends continuously on μ and reduces to $\overset{o}{u}(t)$ for $\mu = 0$.

3. Regular Continuation

Before proving the Continuation Theorem we must formulate its assumptions and statement more precisely. The assumptions may be grouped into two hypotheses:

<u>Hypothesis I</u> (Generating Solution): There exist positive numbers T, μ_1, ω_1, a (column-) function $\overset{o}{u}(t)$ defined in the interval $0 \leq t \leq T$ and having a continuous derivative $\overset{o}{u}_t(t)$ there, and a continuous function $f(u,t,\mu)$ of the column u and the numbers t, μ which is defined in the domain $|u - \overset{o}{u}(t)| \leq \omega_1$, $0 \leq t \leq T$, $|\mu| \leq \mu_1$ and has a continuous derivative $f_u(u,t,\mu)$ with respect to u. Further, the function $\overset{o}{u}(t)$ satisfies the differential equation

$$\overset{o}{u}_t(t) = f(\overset{o}{u}(t),t,0) \quad \text{for} \quad 0 \leq t \leq T \tag{3.1}$$

and the periodicity condition

$$\overset{o}{u}(T) = \overset{o}{u}(0) \quad . \tag{3.2}$$

<u>Hypothesis II</u> (Non-degeneracy): The only continuous and continuously differentiable column-function $\delta u(t)$ which satisfies the variational equation

$$\frac{d}{dt}\, \delta u(t) = f_u(\overset{o}{u}(t),t,0)\,\delta u(t) \quad \text{for} \quad 0 \leq t \leq T \tag{3.3}$$

and the periodicity condition

$$\delta u(T) = \delta u(0) \tag{3.4}$$

is the function $\delta u(t) \equiv 0$. Here $f_u(\overset{\circ}{u}(t),t,0)$ is an $n \times n$ matrix identical with the previously defined $A(t)$, cf. (2.2).

The contention of Theorem 1 is now that Hypotheses I and II imply the following

<u>Conclusion:</u> There exists a positive number $\mu_o \leq \mu_1$ and a continuous function $u(t,\mu)$ defined in the domain $0 \leq t \leq T$, $|\mu| \leq \mu_o$ and there possessing a continuous t-derivative $u_t(t,\mu)$ with the following properties: It satisfies the condition

$$|u(t,\mu) - \overset{\circ}{u}(t)| \leq \omega_1 \tag{3.5}$$

--insuring that $f(u(t,\mu),t,\mu)$ is defined--the differential equation

$$u_t(t,\mu) = f(u(t,\mu),t,\mu) \quad , \tag{3.6}$$

and the periodicity condition

$$u(T,\mu) = u(0,\mu) \quad ; \tag{3.7}$$

it reduces to the generating solution for $\mu = 0$:

$$u(t,0) = \overset{\circ}{u}(t) \quad . \tag{3.8}$$

The proof of this statement is easily derived from basic facts concerning the solutions of ordinary differential equations, combined with the implicit function theorem.

We proceed by first constructing solutions of the equation

$$\frac{du}{dt} = f(u,t,\mu) \tag{3.9}$$

with initial values $u(0,\mu)$ which lie close to $\overset{\circ}{u}(0)$, i.e. we shall construct curves (not necessarily closed) neighboring the curve given by the generating solution at the point $t = 0$, and then try to find for each μ an initial value for which the corresponding solution will be periodic. The deviation of the initial value from that of the solution $\overset{\circ}{u}(t)$ will be denoted by $v = \{v_1,\ldots,v_n\}$.

In the theory of ordinary differential equations it is proved that the solution of an equation of the type (3.9) depends continuously on the parameter μ and in a continuously differentiable manner on the initial value v provided f is continuous in μ and satisfies a Lipschitz condition in u. Since in our case the Lipschitz condition is implied by the continuity of f_u, we can state

Lemma 1: Under Hypothesis I, formulated above, there exist positive numbers $\mu_* \leq \mu_1$, $\omega_o \leq \omega_1$, and a continuous column-function $u(t,\mu,v)$ of t, μ, and the column v, defined in the domain $0 \leq t \leq T$, $|\mu| \leq \mu_*$, $|v| \leq \omega_o$, with continuous derivatives u_t, u_v, u_{vt}, and satisfying the condition

$$(3.10) \qquad |u(t,\mu,v) - \overset{o}{u}(t)| \leq \omega_1 \quad ,$$

the differential equation

$$(3.11) \qquad u_t(t,\mu,v) = f(u(t,\mu,v),t,\mu) \quad ,$$

and the initial condition

$$(3.12) \qquad u(0,\mu,v) = \overset{o}{u}(0) + v \quad .$$

In addition,

$$(3.13) \qquad u(t,0,0) = \overset{o}{u}(t) \quad .$$

Furthermore, the derivative u_v satisfies the differential equation obtained from (3.11) by formal differentiation with respect to v:

$$(3.14) \qquad u_{vt}(t,\mu,v) = f_u(u(t,\mu,v),t,\mu)u_v(t,\mu,v) \quad ,$$

with the initial condition

$$(3.15) \qquad u_v(0,\mu,v) = 1$$

obtained by differentiation of (3.12). [Note that (3.14) and (3.15) are equations between $n \times n$ matrices; the right side of (3.15) is the identity-matrix.]

For a proof of Lemma 1 we refer to the standard texts on the theory of ordinary differential equations, where corollaries to the basic existence theorem will be found which in substance, if not literally, contain the statements of this lemma.

In order to prove Theorem 1, we try to find a deviation v of the initial values, depending on μ, such that the solution $u(t,\mu,v)$ is periodic, i.e. such that the relation

$$u(T,\mu,v) = u(0,\mu,v) \tag{3.16}$$

holds. To this end we shall use the implicit function theorem in the following form:

Lemma 2: Suppose the continuous column-function $g(\mu,v)$ of the parameter μ and the column v, defined for $|\mu| \leq \mu_*$, $|v| \leq \omega_0$, and possessing a continuous derivative $g_v(\mu,v)$, vanishes for $\mu = 0$, $v = 0$:

$$g(0,0) = 0 \quad , \tag{3.17}$$

and has a non-vanishing Jacobian there:

$$\det g_v(0,0) \neq 0 \quad . \tag{3.18}$$

Then there exist a positive number $\mu_0 \leq \mu_*$ and a continuous function $v(\mu)$ defined for $|\mu| \leq \mu_0$ such that

$$g(\mu,v(\mu)) = 0 \quad , \tag{3.19}$$

and

$$v(0) = 0 \quad . \tag{3.20}$$

Instead of condition (3.18) we may just as well say that the equation

$$g_v(0,0)b = 0 \tag{3.21}$$

for a column b has b = 0 as its only solution.

We apply Lemma 2 to the function

$$g(\mu,v) = u(T,\mu,v) - u(0,\mu,v) \quad . \tag{3.22}$$

From relations (3.13) and (3.2) it is seen that condition (3.17) is satisfied. Equation (3.21) is equivalent to the equation

$$u_v(T,0,0)b = u_v(0,0,0)b \quad . \tag{3.23}$$

Thus in order to verify condition (3.18) we need only verify that the equation (3.23) has no solution except $b = 0$.

To this end we consider the column

$$\delta u(t) = u_v(t,0,0)b \tag{3.24}$$

and deduce from relation (3.14), stated at the end of Lemma 1, that the function $\delta u(t)$ satisfies the variational equation (3.3) of Hypothesis II. Furthermore, the periodicity condition (3.4) is implied by (3.23), so that Hypothesis II gives us $\delta u(t) \equiv 0$. For $t = 0$, in particular, $u_v(0,0,0)b = \delta u(0) = 0$, from which relation we can conclude $b = 0$ since (3.15) the matrix $u_v(0,0,0)$ is the identity matrix. The non-vanishing of the Jacobian (3.18) is thus established as a consequence of the hypothesis of non-degeneracy.

We are therefore permitted to apply the implicit function theorem and to conclude that a continuous function $v = v(\mu)$ exists such that the function

$$u(t,\mu) = u(t,\mu,v(\mu)) \tag{3.25}$$

satisfies the periodicity condition (3.7). Conditions (3.5), (3.6), and (3.8) are satisfied because of (3.10), (3.11), and (3.13) and (3.20) respectively; the requisite continuity and differentiability properties follow from Lemma 1. Thus the Continuation Theorem is proved.

It may be noted that nowhere in the statement or proof of Theorem 1 have we assumed that f is periodic in T. By the same token, however, the theorem in the form stated does not insure the periodicity of the solution $u(t,\mu)$ or even of the generating solution $\overset{0}{u}(t)$ when considered as defined for all real t and not merely in the interval $0 \leq t \leq T$. We now make the further assumption that f is indeed periodic:

$$f(u,T,\mu) = f(u,0,\mu) \quad , \tag{3.26}$$

and extend the definition of f to all t by the relation

$$f(u,t+T,\mu) = f(u,t,\mu) \quad ; \tag{3.27}$$

then <u>the solution $u(t,\mu)$ of the differential equation (3.6), is a periodic function of t</u> for all t.

To see this, we need only recall the basic uniqueness theorem of ordinary differential equations, which states that the solution $u(t,\mu)$ of a first order equation of the type (3.6) is uniquely determined once the initial values $u(0,\mu)$ are fixed. We apply this theorem to the function

$$w(t,\mu) = u(t+T,\mu) \quad ; \tag{3.28}$$

w has the same initial values as u in virtue of (3.7), and satisfies the equation (3.6) because of the condition (3.27) on f. Thus w = u, or in other words

$$u(t+T,\mu) = u(t,\mu) \tag{3.29}$$

for all t and μ, so that u is periodic in t.

The validity of Theorem 1 is certainly very satisfactory, but its scope is nevertheless limited. Indeed, the condition of non-degeneracy is not satisfied in most of the significant continuation problems of mechanics and electricity. The study of degenerate continuation problems is therefore our main task.

There is nevertheless one important class of problems which are non-degenerate, namely those arising from non-resonant forced vibrations. As an example we shall consider the differential equation

$$(3.30)\qquad \frac{du}{dt} - i\omega_0 u = \mu g(u, \omega t) + Fe^{i\omega t}$$

for a system possessing the natural frequency ω_0 which is excited by an external force of frequency ω. We assume that ω_0 is not an integral multiple of ω, and we seek solutions u which are periodic with the same period $T = \frac{2\pi}{\omega}$ as the exciting force. The function $g(u, \Theta)$ is assumed continuous with a continuous derivative g_u and periodic in Θ with period 2π; F is a complex constant.

The generating solution of (3.30) is a pure sinusoidal vibration

$$(3.31)\qquad \overset{o}{u}(t) = \overset{o}{a} e^{i\omega t} \quad ,$$

where

$$(3.32)\qquad \overset{o}{a} = \frac{F}{i(\omega - \omega_0)} \quad .$$

The variational equation takes the form

$$(3.33)\qquad \frac{d}{dt}\delta u - i\omega_0 \delta u = 0 \quad ,$$

the non-zero solutions $\delta u = Ae^{i\omega_0 t}$ of which are all periodic with the period $T_0 = \frac{2\pi}{\omega_0}$, but not with period T unless $\omega_0 = m\omega$ for some integer m, a possibility which we have explicitly ruled out. Hence the continuation problem for (3.30) is non-degenerate, and we can find periodic solutions $u(t,\mu)$ for small $|\mu|$.

Specifically, one can find these solutions in the form of a power series in μ:

$$(3.34)\qquad u(t,\mu) = \overset{o}{u}(t) + \mu \overset{1}{u}(t) + \mu^2 \overset{2}{u}(t) + \dots \quad .$$

Assuming the possibility of such a power-series expansion, we proceed to determine the coefficient $\overset{1}{u}$. We substitute (3.34) into (3.30). After dividing by μ and letting μ approach zero we find that $\overset{1}{u}$ satisfies the equation

$$(3.35) \qquad \frac{d}{dt}\overset{1}{u}(t) - i\omega_0 \overset{1}{u}(t) = g(\overset{0}{a} e^{i\omega t}, \omega t) \quad ,$$

a linear first order differential equation which can be solved explicitly. The general solution is

$$(3.36) \qquad \overset{1}{u}(t) = e^{i\omega_0 t}\left[C + \int_0^t e^{-i\omega_0 s} g(\overset{0}{a} e^{i\omega s}, \omega s)ds\right] \quad ;$$

the constant C can be determined from the condition that $\overset{1}{u}$ be periodic of period $T = \frac{2\pi}{\omega}$, and hence is given by

$$(3.37) \qquad C = \left[1-e^{i\omega_0 T}\right]^{-1} e^{i\omega_0 T} \int_0^T e^{-i\omega_0 s} g(\overset{0}{a} e^{i\omega s}, \omega s)ds \quad .$$

Note that C is finite because $e^{i\omega_0 T} \neq 1$, since $\omega_0 T = 2\pi \frac{\omega_0}{\omega}$ is not equal to $2\pi m$.

Similarly the term $\overset{2}{u}(t)$ could be found by solving the equation

$$(3.38) \qquad \frac{d}{dt}\overset{2}{u}(t) - i\omega_0 \overset{2}{u}(t) = \overset{1}{u}(t)\; g_u(\overset{0}{a} e^{i\omega t}, \omega t) \quad ,$$

and likewise the higher-order terms provided only that g is sufficiently many times differentiable with respect to u.

4. Degenerate Continuation Problems

If the variational equation for $u = \overset{0}{u}$, $\mu = 0$ possesses periodic solutions we say that the continuation problem is degenerate. The number s of linearly independent periodic solutions will be called the "degree of degeneracy". Since the equation (2.1) is of order n, it has a total of exactly n linearly independent solutions; consequently $s \leq n$. If $s = 1$ we say the continuation problem is <u>simply degenerate</u>; if $s > 1$, we call it <u>multiply degenerate</u>. A problem in which $s = n$ is called <u>totally degenerate</u>.

Various possibilities may occur in degenerate cases. It may happen that a continuation of the generating solution does not exist, or it may happen that there are one, two, or more such continuations. If there are several continuations one usually speaks of "bifurcation" of the manifold of periodic solutions. We shall find it convenient to use this term quite generally to refer to the continuation of periodic solutions if the problem is degenerate. Thus we may say that all the significant phenomena of nonlinear oscillations which are deduced from Poincaré's theory are revealed by investigating the bifurcation of periodic solutions.

There are many ways in which bifurcation phenomena can be investigated. Each individual problem may be treated in a specific manner according to its own particular difficulties; however, we do not intend to discuss such special treatments. Instead, we shall outline a general approach which, in principle, covers all cases. The specific treatments by which individual problems have been handled, although frequently shorter than this general approach, are nevertheless essentially only variants of it.

In this general approach to the bifurcation problem one imbeds the differential equation in question in a manifold of "modified" problems which depend on additional parameters. This modification will be so chosen that each modified problem has a solution. Under favorable circumstances the manifold of these new solutions will contain periodic solutions of the original differential equation.

Such a modification can be carried out in different ways. We choose a method in which the modified problem also requires us to find a periodic solution of a differential equation with a periodic right member. The number of new parameters that will be introduced in this procedure is equal to the degree of degeneracy, s. In the following we first restrict ourselves to cases of simple degeneracy, so that one new parameter should be introduced. Later we shall indicate how the theory which we shall develop for simple degeneracy can be carried over to the case of multiple degeneracy; in fact, this can be done nearly literally (see pp. 18-19).

We denote the new parameter by κ. We then try to introduce a function $f(u,\kappa,t,\mu)$ which is periodic in t and which reduces to the unmodified right member for $\kappa = 0$:

$$f(u,0,t,\mu) = f(u,t,\mu) \quad . \tag{4.1}$$

How one may construct such a modified function will be indicated below. After having done this one will ask for periodic solutions u(t) of the differential equation

$$\frac{du}{dt} = f(u,\kappa,t,\mu) \quad . \tag{4.2}$$

The important feature of the modified problem is that the parameter κ is to be considered a new dependent variable, just as the functions u(t). That means that, in addition to the function $u(t,\mu)$, a function $\kappa(\mu)$ is to be found such that $\kappa(0) = 0$ and $u(t,0) = \overset{o}{u}(t)$. Naturally, then, an additional condition must be imposed on the dependent quantities $\{u(t), \kappa\}$.

Most conveniently, one imposes a condition on the initial value u(0) of the function u(t). One might, for example, prescribe one of the n components $u_1(0),\ldots,u_n(0)$. More generally, one may introduce a linear form

$$\ell \cdot u = \ell^1 u_1 + \ldots + \ell^n u_n \tag{4.3}$$

with appropriate constants $\ell^1,\ldots,\ell^n$, and then impose the condition

$$\ell \cdot u(0) = \alpha \quad , \tag{4.4}$$

in which α is a given number. Later on the number α will be restricted to be sufficiently near to the number

$$\mathring{\alpha} = \ell \cdot \mathring{u}(0) \tag{4.5}$$

determined by the generating solution $\mathring{u}(t)$.

Suppose any function $f(u, \kappa, t, \mu)$ has been selected which is continuous and has continuous derivatives f_u, f_κ in a domain $0 \leq t \leq T$, $|u-\mathring{u}(t)| \leq \omega_1$, $|\kappa| \leq \kappa_1$, $|\mu| \leq \mu_1$, and which satisfies (4.1). Further suppose a linear form ℓ has been selected. Then a modified problem is defined. It consists in finding, for each value of μ and α, a periodic function $u(t)$ and a number κ which satisfy the pair of equations

$$\frac{du}{dt} = f(u, \kappa, t, \mu) \quad , \tag{4.6}$$

$$\ell \cdot u(0) = \alpha \quad . \tag{4.7}$$

The existence of a solution of this modified problem again depends on the non-existence of a periodic solution of the associated variational equation. This <u>modified variational equation</u> actually consists of two equations,

$$\frac{d}{dt}\,\delta u = A(t)\delta u + B(t)\delta\kappa \quad , \tag{4.8}$$

$$\ell \cdot \delta u(0) = 0 \quad , \tag{4.9}$$

for the unknown function $\delta u(t)$ and the unknown number $\delta\kappa$. Here $A(t)$ is the same matrix as before, given by (2.2) or (2.3), while $B(t)$ is a column given by

$$B(t) = f_\kappa(\mathring{u}(t), 0, t, 0) \quad . \tag{4.10}$$

A solution $\{\delta u(t), \delta\kappa\}$ of this variational equation will be called <u>periodic</u> if the function $\delta u(t)$ is periodic.

We now say that <u>the modified problem is non-degenerate</u> if the modified variational equation has no periodic solution except $\delta u(t) \equiv 0$, $\delta\kappa = 0$. Using this notion we state the

<u>Continuation Theorem 2</u>: Suppose the modified problem of the continuation of the generating solution $\{\overset{\circ}{u}(t), 0\}$ is non-degenerate. Then this modified problem has solutions for sufficiently small values of μ provided the number α is sufficiently near to the number $\overset{\circ}{\alpha}$ given by (4.5). Specifically, there exist numbers $\mu_o > 0$ and $\alpha_o > 0$ such that for every μ and α with $|\mu| \le \mu_o$, $|\alpha - \overset{\circ}{\alpha}| \le \alpha_o$ a periodic solution $\{u(t,\mu,\alpha), \kappa(\mu,\alpha)\}$ exists which depends continuously on μ and α and reduces to $\{\overset{\circ}{u}(t), 0\}$ for $\mu = 0$, $\alpha = \overset{\circ}{\alpha}$.

Note that in addition to the new dependent parameter κ we have introduced α as a new independent parameter.

Theorem 2 can be proved by a modification of the same arguments that were used to prove Theorem 1. First we consider the parameter κ as a function $\kappa(t)$ of the time t which satisfies the equation

$$\frac{d\kappa}{dt} = 0 \tag{4.11}$$

Then we may consider the system of equations (4.6), (4.11) as one equation of the type (3.6) for the system of functions $\{u, \kappa\}$ instead of for u. Clearly, Hypothesis I, with $\{\overset{\circ}{u}(t), 0\}$ in place of $\overset{\circ}{u}(t)$, is satisfied for this new system. Therefore we may use Lemma 1 with $\{v, \kappa\}$ instead of v. Accordingly, we know that a solution $u(t,\mu,v,\kappa)$ of equation (4.6) exists with continuous derivatives u_t, u_v, u_κ, u_{vt}, $u_{\kappa t}$ satisfying the equations

$$u_{vt} = f_u(u(t,\mu,v,\kappa), \kappa, t, \mu)u_v \quad , \tag{4.12}$$

$$u_{\kappa t} = f_u(u(t,\mu,v,\kappa), \kappa, t, \mu)u_\kappa + f_\kappa(u, \kappa, t, \mu) \quad , \tag{4.13}$$

which are obtained by writing down the matrices of order n+1 corresponding to the extended system of differential equations. Further this solution satisfies the initial condition

$$u(0,\mu,v,\kappa) = \overset{\circ}{u}(0) + v \tag{4.14}$$

and the condition

$$u(t,0,0,0) = \overset{\circ}{u}(t) \quad . \tag{4.15}$$

The periodicity equation

$$u(T,\mu,v,\kappa) = u(0,\mu,v,\kappa) \tag{4.16}$$

is to be satisfied by appropriate choice of the functions $v = v(\mu,\alpha)$, $\kappa = \kappa(\mu,\alpha)$, subject to the condition

$$\ell \cdot v = \alpha - \overset{\circ}{\alpha} \quad . \tag{4.17}$$

Clearly the conditions (4.16), (4.17) are fulfilled for $\mu = 0$, $\alpha = \overset{\circ}{\alpha}$, $v = 0$, $\kappa = 0$. Thus we can use the implicit function theorem to insure the existence of $v(\mu,\alpha)$, $\kappa(\mu,\alpha)$ for sufficiently small $|\mu|$ and $|\alpha-\overset{\circ}{\alpha}|$ provided that the Jacobian of the system (4.16), (4.17) with respect to $\{v,\kappa\}$ as independent variables does not vanish at $\{v,\kappa\} = \{0,0\}$, $\mu = 0$, $\alpha = \overset{\circ}{\alpha}$. But the non-vanishing of this Jacobian is equivalent to the condition that the system of equations

$$\begin{aligned} u_v(T,0,0,0)b + u_\kappa(T,0,0,0)\beta \\ = u_v(0,0,0,0)b + u_\kappa(0,0,0,0)\beta \quad , \end{aligned} \tag{4.18}$$

$$\ell \cdot b = 0 \tag{4.19}$$

for a column $b = \{b_1,\ldots,b_n\}$ and a number β have $b = 0$, $\beta = 0$ as its only solution.

In order to prove that this condition is satisfied, we consider the system

$$\dot{\delta u}(t) = \dot{u}_v(t,0,0,0)b + \dot{u}_\kappa(t,0,0,0)\beta \tag{4.20}$$

$$\delta\kappa = \beta \quad , \tag{4.21}$$

formed with any column b and number β. Equation (4.18) can then be written in the form

$$\delta u(T) = \delta u(0) \quad . \tag{4.22}$$

Since

$$\dot{u}_v(0,0,0,0) = 1 \quad , \tag{4.23}$$

$$\dot{u}_\kappa(0,0,0,0) = 0 \quad , \tag{4.24}$$

as follows from relation (4.14), we have

$$\delta u(0) = b \quad . \tag{4.25}$$

Equation (4.19) can then be written in the form

$$\ell \cdot \delta u(0) = 0 \quad . \tag{4.26}$$

From relations (4.12), (4.13), (4.26) we infer that the system $\{\delta u(t), \delta\kappa\}$ given by (4.20), (4.21) satisfies the variational equations (4.8), (4.9). It follows from the assumed non-degeneracy of the modified problem that $\delta u(t) \equiv 0$ and $\delta\kappa = 0$. The latter relation yields $\beta = 0$ by (4.21); the former relation for $t = 0$ yields $b = 0$ by (4.25). Thus it is seen that $b = 0$, $\beta = 0$ is the only solution of equations (4.18), (4.19). The implicit function theorem is therefore applicable and the statement of Theorem 2 follows.

The notions introduced in this section can be carried over to the case of multiple degeneracy, $s > 1$. Instead of one new parameter we must introduce s parameters $\kappa_1, \ldots, \kappa_s$; the set of these s parameters will then be denoted by κ:

$$\kappa = \{\kappa_1, \ldots, \kappa_s\} \quad . \tag{4.27}$$

Instead of one condition (4.4) we must introduce s such conditions

$$(4.28)\qquad \ell^{(1)}\cdot u(0) = \alpha^{(1)},\ldots,\ell^{(s)}\cdot u(0) = \alpha^{(s)} \quad ,$$

involving s linearly independent forms $\ell^{(1)},\ldots,\ell^{(s)}$ and s numbers $\alpha^{(1)},\ldots,\alpha^{(s)}$. We combine these s numbers into one entity

$$(4.29)\qquad \alpha = \{\alpha^{(1)},\ldots,\alpha^{(s)}\} \quad ;$$

then we may write the s conditions (4.28) in the form (4.4) by letting ℓ stand for the s forms

$$(4.30)\qquad \ell = \{\ell^{(1)},\ldots,\ell^{(s)}\} \quad .$$

The statement of Theorem 2 and its proof then carry over literally, provided the abbreviations

$$(4.31)\qquad u_\kappa = \{u_{\kappa_1},\ldots,u_{\kappa_s}\} \quad ,$$

$$(4.32)\qquad \beta = \{\beta^{(1)},\ldots,\beta^{(s)}\} \quad ,$$

and

$$(4.33)\qquad u_\kappa \beta = u_{\kappa_1}\beta^{(1)} + \ldots + u_{\kappa_s}\beta^{(s)}$$

are used; the quantity $B(t)$ of (4.10) now becomes an $n \times s$ matrix.

5. The Modified Problem

The question now arises whether or not the original degenerate problem can always be so modified that it becomes non-degenerate. The answer is that it can:

Lemma 3: To every degenerate problem there exists a non-degenerate modified problem.

Indeed, we can always find a modified right member f in the form

$$(5.1) \qquad f(u,\kappa,t,\mu) = f(u,t,\mu) + \kappa q(t) \quad ,$$

in which

$$(5.2) \qquad q(t) = \{q^{(1)}(t),\ldots,q^{(s)}(t)\}$$

stands for a set of s periodic functions so chosen that the non-homogeneous equation

$$(5.3) \qquad \frac{dw}{dt} - A(t)w = \gamma q(t)$$

possesses no periodic solution w(t) for any set of numbers $\gamma = \{\gamma_1,\ldots,\gamma_s\}$ not all zero. We have used here the self-evident abbreviations $\kappa q = \kappa_1 q^{(1)} + \ldots + \kappa_s q^{(s)}$, $\gamma q = \gamma_1 q^{(1)} + \ldots + \gamma_s q^{(s)}$, and in addition the word "function" to describe a column of n functions. As we shall show below, such functions q(t) can always be found if, as assumed now, the degree of degeneracy s is at least one.

It will also be shown that the linear form ℓ --or rather the set of forms (4.28)--can be so chosen that the only periodic solution p(t) of the equation

$$(5.4) \qquad \frac{dp}{dt} - A(t)p = 0$$

for which

$$(5.5) \qquad \ell \cdot p(0) = 0$$

is the function $p(t) \equiv 0$.

The variational equations of the problem so modified are

$$(5.6) \qquad \frac{d}{dt}\,\delta u = A(t)\delta u + q(t)\delta\kappa \quad ,$$

$$(5.7) \qquad \ell \cdot \delta u(0) = 0 \quad .$$

Suppose these equations had a periodic solution $\{\delta u(t), \delta\kappa\}$. If $\delta\kappa \neq 0$, the function $w(t) = \delta u(t)$ would be a solution of the equation $\frac{dw}{dt} - Aw = \gamma q$ with non-vanishing γ, which is assumed not to exist. Hence $\delta\kappa = 0$, and consequently $p = \delta u$ is a solution of $\frac{dp}{dt} - Ap = 0$ with $\ell \cdot p(0) = 0$. Thus $\delta u \equiv 0$, and the problem so modified is non-degenerate.

In order to construct the functions $q(t)$ we consider the matrix $Y(t)$ which transforms the initial value $\delta u(0)$ of a solution δu of equation (2.1) into its value at the time t,

$$\delta u(t) = Y(t)\delta u(0) \quad ; \tag{5.8}$$

cf. (2.4). It is well known that this matrix has an inverse for every value of the time t, for otherwise there would exist an initial value $\delta u(0) \neq 0$ such that $\delta u(t_0) = Y(t_0)\delta u(0) = 0$ for a certain time $t = t_0$, in contradiction to the uniqueness statement that $\delta u(t_0) = 0$ implies $\delta u(t) = 0$ for all t. The inverse of $Y(t)$ will be denoted by $Y^{-1}(t)$. The general solution of equation (5.3) is then given by

$$w(t) = Y(t)w(0) + Y(t)\int_0^t Y^{-1}(\tau)\,\gamma q(\tau)d\tau \quad , \tag{5.9}$$

as may be verified by direct substitution; the uniqueness theorem insures that there are no further solutions.

The condition that none of these solutions $w(t)$ be periodic is seen to be equivalent to the condition that the equation

$$[1 - Y(T)]b = \gamma j = \gamma_1 j^{(1)} + \dots + \gamma_s j^{(s)} \tag{5.10}$$

has no solution b for arbitrary $\gamma = \{\gamma_1, \dots, \gamma_s\} \neq 0$, where the columns $j^{(\sigma)}$ are defined by

$$j^{(\sigma)} = Y(T)\int_0^T Y^{-1}(t)q^{(\sigma)}(t)dt \quad , \quad \sigma = 1, \dots, s \quad . \tag{5.11}$$

Otherwise we would obtain a periodic solution w by setting $w(0) = b$.

Since by assumption the problem is degenerate of order $s \geq 1$, the rank of the matrix $1 - Y(T)$ is

$$r = n - s \quad , \tag{5.12}$$

for the relation (2.6) is then satisfied for exactly s linearly independent columns $\delta u(0)$. Consequently, there are s linearly independent rows

$$\chi^{(1)} = \{\chi_1^{(1)}, \ldots, \chi_n^{(1)}\}, \ldots, \chi^{(s)} = \{\chi_1^{(s)}, \ldots, \chi_n^{(s)}\} \tag{5.13}$$

such that

$$\chi^{(1)} \cdot \gamma j = 0, \ldots, \chi^{(s)} \cdot \gamma j = 0 \tag{5.14}$$

whenever the equation (5.10) has a solution. Then we can find s columns $j^{(1)}, \ldots, j^{(s)}$ such that the $s \times s$ matrix

$$\begin{pmatrix} \chi^{(1)} \cdot j^{(1)} & \ldots\ldots & \chi^{(s)} \cdot j^{(1)} \\ \cdot & \cdot\ \cdot\ \cdot\ \cdot & \cdot \\ \chi^{(1)} \cdot j^{(s)} & \ldots\ldots & \chi^{(s)} \cdot j^{(s)} \end{pmatrix}$$

is non-singular. Clearly for such columns $j^{(\sigma)}$ equation (5.14) has no solution for $\gamma \neq 0$.

Having chosen such columns $j^{(\sigma)}$, we may define the functions $q^{(\sigma)}(t)$ by

$$q^{(\sigma)}(t) = T^{-1} Y(t) Y^{-1}(T) j^{(\sigma)} \quad , \tag{5.15}$$

so that, evidently, relation (5.11) holds. For this choice of the functions $q^{(\sigma)}(t)$, therefore, equations (5.14) have no solution $\gamma \neq 0$ and hence equation (5.10) has no solution b. Consequently, for $q(t) = \{q^{(1)}(t), \ldots, q^{(s)}(t)\}$ none of the solutions of equation (5.3) is periodic with period T.

It is also easy to choose the forms $\ell^{(1)}, \ldots, \ell^{(s)}$ such that the relations

$$\ell^{(1)} \cdot p(0) = \ldots = \ell^{(s)} \cdot p(0) = 0 \tag{5.16}$$

do not all hold for a periodic solution $p(t)$ of equation (5.4) unless $p(t) \equiv 0$. For, since there are s linearly independent periodic solutions $p^{(1)}(t),\ldots,p^{(s)}(t)$ of this equation, we only need choose the forms $\ell^{(1)},\ldots,\ell^{(s)}$ such that the matrix

$$\begin{pmatrix} \ell^{(1)}\cdot p^{(1)}(0) & \ldots\ldots & \ell^{(s)}\cdot p^{(1)}(0) \\ \cdot & \cdot\;\cdot\;\cdot\;\cdot\;\cdot\;\cdot\;\cdot\;\cdot\;\cdot\;\cdot\;\cdot\;\cdot\;\cdot\;\cdot & \cdot \\ \ell^{(1)}\cdot p^{(s)}(0) & \ldots\ldots & \ell^{(s)}\cdot p^{(s)}(0) \end{pmatrix}$$

is non-singular. Obviously this is always possible, since by the uniqueness theorem the columns $p^{(1)}(0),\ldots,p^{(s)}(0)$ must also be linearly independent.

Thus the statement of Lemma 3 is established.

By virtue of this lemma, one can always substitute a solvable non-degenerate problem for the degenerate problem whose solvability is doubtful. It should be emphasized that a modification of the form (5.1) is rather special. As will be seen in subsequent sections, other modifications may be preferable under certain circumstances.

If one wishes, one may shift one's interest from the original to the modified problem and consider the problem essentially solved after having insured that it is non-degenerate. If, however, one remains interested in the original problem, one may ask whether or not solutions of the original problem are contained among the solutions of the modified problem.

Clearly, a solution $u(t,\mu,\alpha)$, $\kappa(\mu,\alpha)$ of the modified problem is at the same time a solution of the original problem if the values of the independent parameters μ and α are so chosen that the new dependent parameter κ has the value zero; for the modified right member then reduces to the original one. Thus if the condition

$$\kappa(\mu,\alpha) = 0 \tag{5.17}$$

is satisfied, a solution of the original problem is found. This condition now appears as an equation for the quantity α as a function of the quantity μ. If it has a solution $\alpha = \alpha(\mu)$ which depends continuously on μ and satisfies the condition

$$\alpha(0) = \overset{\circ}{\alpha} = \ell \cdot \overset{\circ}{u}(0) \qquad (5.18)$$

the function

$$u(t,\mu) = u(t,\mu,\alpha(\mu)) \qquad (5.19)$$

is a periodic solution of the original problem.

To be sure, the bifurcation problem has not been solved by the procedure indicated; it has only been reduced to the solution of the bifurcation equation. Nevertheless, this reduction frequently enables one to solve the original problem, for one is usually able to solve the bifurcation equation, which involves only a finite number, s, of unknowns.

It is not obvious a priori that all periodic solutions of the original equation in the neighborhood of the generating solution can be determined by the procedure outlined if one uses only one particular modified problem. We leave as an open question whether or not this is so.

6. A Simply Degenerate Problem

The significance of the artificial parameter κ and the role of the bifurcation equation may perhaps be seen more clearly from the discussion of a single special example, which involves only one quantity u (so that n = 1) and in which the differential equation reduces to a linear one for $\mu = 0$. Specifically, we consider the differential equation

$$\frac{du}{d\theta} - iu = \mu g(u,\theta) \qquad (6.1)$$

in which the function $g(u,\theta)$ has the period 2π in θ. We ask for complex-valued solutions--also with the period 2π --which for $\mu = 0$ reduce to the generating solution

(6.2) $$\overset{\circ}{u}(\theta) = \overset{\circ}{\alpha} e^{i\theta} \quad .$$

Here the "amplitude" $\overset{\circ}{\alpha}$ is any complex number. Since the variational equation

(6.3) $$\frac{d}{d\theta}\,\delta u - i\delta u = 0$$

has the periodic solution $\delta u = e^{i\theta}$ (and essentially no others), the problem is simply degenerate.

As modified differential equation we choose

(6.4) $$\frac{du}{d\theta} - iu = \mu g(u,\theta) - \kappa e^{i\theta} \quad ,$$

and as additional condition we choose

(6.5) $$u(0) = \alpha \quad .$$

It is easily verified that the modified variational equations

(6.6) $$\frac{d}{d\theta}\,\delta u - i\delta u = -e^{i\theta}\,\delta\kappa \quad ,$$

(6.7) $$\delta u(0) = 0$$

have no periodic solution except $\delta u \equiv 0$, $\delta\kappa = 0$, for it is known that the non-homogeneous equation

(6.8) $$\frac{dw}{d\theta} - iw = e^{i\theta}$$

has no periodic solution, while the only periodic solution $p(\theta)$ of

(6.9) $$\frac{dp}{d\theta} - ip = 0$$

for which $p(0) = 0$ is $p(\theta) \equiv 0$. Accordingly, periodic solutions $u(\theta,\mu,\alpha)$, $\kappa(\mu,\alpha)$ of the modified problem exist if $|\mu|$ and $|\alpha-\overset{\circ}{\alpha}|$ are sufficiently small.

One may illuminate the situation by the following observation. As is known, the equation

(6.10) $$\frac{du}{d\theta} - iu = h(\theta) = \sum_{n=-\infty}^{\infty} a_n e^{in\theta} \quad ;$$

in which h is a periodic function of period 2π admitting a Fourier expansion, has as its solution

$$(6.11) \qquad u(\theta) = \sum_{n\neq 1} \frac{a_n}{i(n-1)} e^{in\theta} + a_1 \theta e^{i\theta} \quad .$$

This solution will be periodic if and only if the first Fourier coefficient

$$(6.12) \qquad a_1 = \frac{1}{2\pi} \int_0^{2\pi} e^{-i\theta} h(\theta) d\theta$$

of $h(\theta)$ vanishes. Consequently, the equation

$$(6.13) \qquad \frac{du}{d\theta} - iu = h(\theta) - a_1 e^{i\theta}$$

always has a periodic solution. If the function $h(\theta)$ depends on the solution to be determined, as in the problem above, the Fourier coefficient a_1 is not known a priori but must be determined. Thus the artificial parameter κ may be interpreted as the Fourier coefficient of the right member $\mu g(u,\theta)$, which is to be determined in the process of solution.

Since the modification procedure employed in the present case simply consists of subtracting an appropriate term in the Fourier series of the right member, this procedure appears to be quite natural. When the general modification procedure described earlier is regarded as a generalization of this subtraction of a Fourier term, it may appear to be less artificial than before.

We proceed to investigate whether or not the bifurcation equation

$$(6.14) \qquad \kappa(\mu, \alpha) = 0$$

has solutions $\alpha = \alpha(\mu)$. To this end we observe that the solution of the modified problem can easily be given in terms of expansions in powers of μ. As solution of equations (6.4), (6.5) one finds

$$(6.15) \qquad u(\theta,\mu,\alpha) = \alpha e^{i\theta} + \mu \int_0^{\theta} e^{i(\theta-\theta')} g(ae^{i\theta'},\theta')d\theta' - \mathcal{K}(\mu,\alpha)\theta e^{i\theta} + \dots ,$$

indicating by ... terms of higher than first order. The condition that this solution be periodic gives

$$(6.16) \qquad \mathcal{K}(\mu,\alpha) = \mu\Phi(\alpha) + \dots ,$$

with

$$(6.17) \qquad \Phi(\alpha) = \frac{1}{2\pi}\int_0^{2\pi} e^{-i\theta} g(\alpha e^{i\theta},\theta)d\theta .$$

The bifurcation equation (6.14) thus attains the form

$$(6.18) \qquad \mu\Phi(\alpha) + \dots = 0 ,$$

or

$$(6.18)' \qquad \Phi(\alpha) + \dots = 0$$

where ... now signifies terms which approach zero with μ. If this equation has a continuous solution $\alpha = \alpha(\mu)$ with $\alpha(0) = \overset{\circ}{\alpha}$, the amplitude $\overset{\circ}{\alpha}$ satisfies the condition

$$(6.19) \qquad \Phi(\overset{\circ}{\alpha}) = 0 ,$$

to which we shall refer as the "bifurcation condition". Conversely, if $\overset{\circ}{\alpha}$ satisfies the latter condition and if in addition the derivative $\Phi_\alpha(\overset{\circ}{\alpha})$ does not vanish,

$$(6.20) \qquad \Phi_\alpha(\overset{\circ}{\alpha}) \neq 0 ,$$

the desired solution $\alpha = \alpha(\mu)$ of the bifurcation equation exists by virtue of the implicit function theorem.

If $\overset{\circ}{a}$ is not a solution of the equation $\Phi(\overset{\circ}{a}) = 0$, no periodic continuation of the generating solution is possible. If $\overset{\circ}{a}$ is a solution of this equation, but $\Phi_a(\overset{\circ}{a}) = 0$, the problem of solving the bifurcation equation may be said to be degenerate. In this case similar procedures involving new additional parameters may be used in order to solve this equation.

The example just discussed is somewhat unrealistic. Problems of mechanical or electrical oscillations are always of at least second order, i.e. involve at least two quantities ($n \geq 2$). Also the degree of degeneracy of these problems is mostly equal to two, or certainly not less than two, i.e., $s \geq 2$. We shall discuss such problems in Section 8.

7. Natural Modifications

The introduction of the additional parameter κ is a rather artificial device. Still, in certain cases one is led quite naturally to using such a parameter. Such a case arises if the right member f does not depend explicitly on the time; in other words, if autonomous or free vibrations are investigated, governed by an equation of the form

$$\frac{du}{dt} = f(u,\mu) \quad . \tag{7.1}$$

A problem of free vibrations is always degenerate unless the generating solution is a constant. For, as is easily verified, there is always a non-zero solution of the variational equation, namely the function

$$\delta u(t) = \frac{d}{dt}\overset{\circ}{u}(t) \quad , \tag{7.2}$$

provided $\overset{\circ}{u}(t)$ is not a constant. Clearly, in such a case one cannot expect in general that the oscillations which belong to positive or negative values of the parameter μ have the same period as the generating oscillation which belongs to $\mu = 0$. Consequently, one is forced to consider the varying period as a function of the parameter μ. In order to be able to apply to these cases the approach outlined above, in which a fixed period was assumed, one must reduce the problem to one with a fixed period.

One way to accomplish this is as follows. We use the notation T_0 for the period of the generating solution and denote the varying period by

$$(7.3) \qquad T = (1 + \kappa)T_0$$

Then we introduce the quantity

$$(7.4) \qquad \tau = t/(1 + \kappa)$$

as new independent variable. Considered as functions of τ, the solutions u are then required to have the fixed period T_0. The differential equation now assumes the form

$$(7.5) \qquad \frac{du}{d\tau} = (1 + \kappa)f(u,\mu) \quad ;$$

for $\kappa = 0$ it evidently reduces to the original equation. Thus we are led to the modified problem of finding a periodic solution of equation (7.5) which satisfies a condition

$$(7.6) \qquad \ell \cdot u(0) = a \quad .$$

It should be noted that the modification of the problem thus obtained differs from that indicated in the proof of Lemma 3. In fact, the present modified problem need not always be non-degenerate. If it is non-degenerate, Theorem 2 applies and the existence of free oscillations for sufficiently small values of μ is established. This may be regarded as the desired result although the period of the oscillations varies in general. It would be unnatural to ask for free oscillations with a fixed period; in fact, the bifurcation equation has in general no solution in this case.

A condition insuring that the modified problem is non-degenerate can easily be given. The variational equations of this problem are

(7.7) $$\frac{d}{d\tau}\,\delta u = A(\tau)\delta u + \frac{d}{dt}\,\overset{o}{u}(\tau)\,\delta\kappa \quad ,$$

(7.8) $$\ell\cdot\delta u(0) = 0 \quad ,$$

where the matrix A is given, as before, by (2.3). In terms of the matrix Y(t) introduced in Section 1 the solution of equation (7.7) can be given as

(7.9) $$\delta u(\tau) = Y(\tau)\delta u(0) + \tau\overset{o}{u}_t(\tau)\,\delta\kappa \quad .$$

The condition that this solution is periodic is

(7.10) $$\begin{aligned}[1 - Y(T_o)]\delta u(0) &= T_o\,\overset{o}{u}_t(T_o)\,\delta\kappa \\ &= T_o\,\overset{o}{u}_t(0)\,\delta\kappa \quad .\end{aligned}$$

Let us assume that the equation $\delta u_\tau = A\delta u$ has no periodic solution other than $\overset{o}{u}_t$. Then the rank of the matrix $1 - Y(T_o)$ is n-1, and there exists one row $\chi = \{\chi_1, \ldots, \chi_n\}$ such that the equation

(7.11) $$[1 - Y(T_o)]\nu = j$$

has a solution ν if and only if $\chi\cdot j = 0$. Let us then assume that

(7.12) $$\chi\cdot\overset{o}{u}_t(0) \neq 0 \quad .$$

It follows that equation (7.10), and hence equation (7.7), has no solution unless $\delta\kappa = 0$. Since the only periodic solution of the remaining portion of equation (7.7) is $\delta u(\tau) = c\overset{o}{u}_t(\tau)$ it follows that $\delta u(\tau) \equiv 0$ if

(7.13) $$\ell\cdot\overset{o}{u}_t(0) \neq 0 \quad .$$

In view of (7.12) we may just as well choose χ as our ℓ of (7.6).

If one considers the row χ as a column it satisfies the equation

$$Y'(T_o)\chi = \chi$$

where $Y'(T_o)$ is the transpose of $Y(T_o)$. The column χ may therefore be called "eigencolumn" of the transpose $Y'(T_o)$ with the "eigenvalue" 1.

Thus we see that <u>the modified problem is not degenerate if the equation $\delta u_\tau = A\delta u$ has no periodic solutions other than $c\overset{o}{u}_t(\tau)$ and if, in addition, $\chi \cdot \overset{o}{u}_t(0) \neq 0$ for the eigencolumn χ of the transpose of the matrix $Y(T_o)$ belonging to the eigenvalue 1.</u> Under these conditions then, periodic functions $\kappa(\mu)$ and $u(\tau,\mu)$ exist for which relation (7.5) holds. Hence the function $u(\frac{t}{1+\kappa(\mu)}, \mu)$ is a periodic solution of the original equation (7.1) with a period given by

(7.14) $$T = (1+\kappa(\mu))T_o \quad .$$

Even if the modified problem (7.5), (7.6) is degenerate, one can still treat it by introducing still more parameters as before. These new additional parameters will be truly artificial, and one may hope to be able to eliminate them by solving the new bifurcation equations to which they give rise.

Frequently, one also allows the period to vary in non-free problems; indeed, this is usually done if the bifurcation has no solution. We may, for example, consider the equation

(7.15) $$u_t = i\omega_o u + \mu g(u,\omega t)$$

for one function $u(t)$, in which the function $g(u,\omega t)$ has the period 2π in its second variable

(7.16) $$\theta = \omega t \quad ;$$

solutions $u(t,\mu)$ are sought which are periodic in t with the as yet undetermined period

(7.17) $$T = \frac{2\pi}{\omega} \quad .$$

In terms of the new variable θ and the parameter

(7.18) $$\kappa = 1 - \frac{\omega_0}{\omega}$$

the differential equation assumes the form

(7.19) $$\frac{du}{d\theta} = iu - i\kappa u + \omega^{-1}\mu g(u,\theta) \quad ,$$

which differs for small $|\mu|$ from equation (6.4) only in that $\omega^{-1}\mu$ appears in place of μ and $i\kappa$ in place of κ. Relation

(7.20) $$\kappa(\mu,\alpha) = -i\omega_0^{-1}\mu\Phi(\alpha) + \ldots \quad ,$$

which takes the place of (6.16), gives the period

(7.21) $$T = (1-\kappa)\frac{2\pi}{\omega_0}$$

as a function of μ and the initial value $\alpha = u(0,\mu)$. There is thus a one-parameter family, with parameter α, of periodic solutions for each--sufficiently small--value of μ; it contains the solution, described in Section 6, which has the period $T_0 = 2\pi/\omega_0$. For $\mu = 0$, of course, this family reduces to the one-parameter family

(7.22) $$u = \alpha e^{i\theta} \quad .$$

There is another type of problem in which an additional parameter occurs naturally, namely the problem of finding periodic motions of a system whose energy is constant. The differential equations are of the form

(7.23) $$u_t = f(u,\phi+\omega t,h,\mu) \quad ,$$

(7.24) $$\phi_t = g(u,\phi+\omega t,h,\mu) \quad ,$$

in which $u=\{u_1,\ldots,u_n\}$, $f = \{f_1,\ldots,f_n\}$, and h is the given constant energy. Solutions $\{u(t),\phi(t)\}$ are sought which have the period $T = 2\pi/\omega$. The right members depend on the time t only through the combination $\phi + \omega t$, which plays the role of an angular variable.

Let $\{\overset{o}{u}(t), \overset{o}{\phi}(t)\}$ be a generating solution for $\mu = 0$ and $h = \overset{o}{h}$. Then the function

$$(7.25) \qquad \{\delta u(t), \delta\phi(t)\} = \{\overset{o}{u}_t(t), \overset{o}{\phi}_t(t) + \omega\}$$

satisfies the variational equation

$$(7.26) \qquad \delta u_t = \overset{o}{f}_u \delta u + \overset{o}{f}_\phi \delta\phi \quad ,$$

$$(7.27) \qquad \delta u_\phi = \overset{o}{g}_u \delta u + \overset{o}{g}_\phi \delta\phi \quad ,$$

in which the arguments of f_u, f_ϕ, g_u, g_ϕ are $\overset{o}{u}(t)$, $\overset{o}{\phi}(t) + \omega t$, $\overset{o}{h}$, 0. The problem is thus degenerate. If, however, the energy h is allowed to vary and if an additional condition such as

$$(7.28) \qquad \phi(0) = 0$$

is imposed, the problem so modified may well become non-degenerate. Periodic solutions $\{u(t,\mu), \phi(t,\mu)\}$ then exist which involve an energy $h(\mu)$ which also depends on the parameter μ.

A natural parameter frequently enters in multiply degenerate problems. Allowing this parameter to vary, one will try to solve only s-1 bifurcation equations in order to eliminate the s-1 artificial parameters. Typical cases of this will be discussed in the subsequent section.

8. Totally Degenerate Problems of Second Order

We proceed to discuss a class of doubly degenerate problems which involve the differential equation

$$u_{tt} + \omega_o^2 u + j(u, u_t, \omega t, \mu) = 0 \quad ; \tag{8.1}$$

the problems of Duffing and van der Pol are included in this class. The function j is assumed to have the period 2π in its third argument $\theta = \omega t$; we further require that for $\mu = 0$ it reduce to a function $j_o(\theta)$ which is independent of u and u_t:

$$j(u, u_t, \theta, 0) = j_o(\theta) \quad . \tag{8.2}$$

Other properties of j will be specified later on.

In order to reduce equation (8.1) to a system of first-order equations, we introduce the function v defined by the relation

$$u_t = -\omega_o v \quad , \tag{8.3}$$

so that equation (8.1) becomes

$$v_t = \omega_o u + \omega_o^{-1} j(u, -\omega_o v, \omega t, \mu) \quad . \tag{8.4}$$

It is convenient to simplify the system (8.3), (8.4) for the pair of functions $\{u, v\}$ by formally setting

$$w = u + iv \quad , \tag{8.5}$$

enabling us to write this system as the single equation

$$w_t = i\omega_o w + i\omega_o g(w, \bar{w}, \omega t, \mu) \quad , \tag{8.6}$$

where we have set

$$g(w, \bar{w}, \theta, \mu) = \omega_o^{-2} j\left(\tfrac{1}{2}(w + \bar{w}), \frac{i\omega_o}{2}(w - \bar{w}), \theta, \mu\right) \quad . \tag{8.7}$$

By virtue of (8.2) the variational equation for $\mu = 0$ is

$$\delta w_t = i\omega_0 \delta w \qquad (8.8)$$

since it has two solutions $\delta w = e^{i\omega_0 t}$ and $\delta w = ie^{i\omega_0 t}$ which are independent in terms of real numbers, the problem is doubly degenerate.

In order to modify the problem we introduce the real-valued parameter

$$\kappa = 1 - \frac{\omega_0}{\omega} \qquad (8.9)$$

and the variable

$$\theta = \omega t \quad . \qquad (8.10)$$

The equation then assumes the form

$$w_\theta - iw = i(1-\kappa)g(w,\overline{w},\theta,\mu) - i\kappa w \quad . \qquad (8.11)$$

In addition we impose the initial condition

$$w(0) = c \quad , \qquad (8.12)$$

where c is a complex number.

Since the problem is doubly degenerate, two parameters should enter the modified problem. We can introduce two such parameters by allowing the number κ to be complex. Since eventually we will want κ real, the initial value c is to be determined in such a way that the imaginary part of κ vanishes. This last condition will then be the bifurcation equation.

The real part of κ --and hence the period T--will be left variable. Accordingly, one condition should be imposed on the initial value $c = w(0)$. This will be done in such a way that the bifurcation equation has solutions.

In terms of the function g, defined by (8.7), condition (8.2) assumes the form

$$g(w,\overline{w},\theta,C) = g_0(\theta) \quad , \qquad (8.13)$$

with

(8.14)
$$g_o(\theta) = \omega_o^{-2} j_o(\theta) \quad .$$

We require that this function $g_o(\theta)$ satisfy the condition

(8.15)
$$\int_0^{2\pi} g_o(\theta) e^{-i\theta} d\theta = 0 \quad .$$

As a consequence, equations (8.11) and (8.12) have for $\mu = 0$ the periodic solution

(8.16)
$$w_c(\theta) = c e^{i\theta} + i e^{i\theta} \int_0^\theta g_o(\tau) e^{-i\tau} d\tau \quad , \quad \kappa = 0 \quad ,$$

which we shall call the "initial solution". For $c = c_o$ this solution will be denoted by $w_o(\theta)$, $\kappa_o = 0$ and taken as the "generating" solution. For this generating solution the variational equation becomes

(8.17)
$$\delta w_\theta - i \delta w = -i g_o \delta \kappa - i w_o \delta \kappa \quad ,$$

(8.18)
$$\delta w(0) = 0 \quad ;$$

it has the solution

(8.19)
$$\delta w(\theta) = -i \delta \kappa e^{i\theta} \int_0^\theta [w_o(\tau) + g_o(\tau)] e^{-i\tau} d\tau \quad .$$

We now introduce the expression

(8.20)
$$\Gamma_o(c) = c - \frac{i}{2\pi} \int_0^{2\pi} \theta g_o(\theta) e^{-i\theta} d\theta$$

and deduce from assumption (8.15) the relation

(8.21)
$$\Gamma_o(c) = \frac{1}{2\pi} \int_0^{2\pi} [w_c(\theta) + g_o(\theta)] e^{-i\theta} d\theta \quad .$$

Then we require of c_0 that it satisfy the condition

$$\Gamma_0(c_0) \neq 0 \tag{8.22}$$

or

$$c_0 \neq \frac{i}{2\pi} \int_0^{2\pi} \theta g_0(\theta) e^{-i\theta} d\theta \quad . \tag{8.23}$$

As a consequence, the solution δw of the variational equation given by (8.19) is not periodic unless $\delta\kappa = 0$. In other words, the only periodic solution of the variational equation (8.16), (8.17) is $\delta w(\theta) \equiv 0$, $\delta\kappa = 0$.

We therefore know that the modified problem (8.11), (8.12) possesses periodic solutions

$$w = w(\theta,\mu,c,\bar{c}), \quad \kappa = \kappa(\mu,c,\bar{c}) \tag{8.24}$$

which for $\mu = 0$ reduce to the initial solution (8.16), provided that $|c - c_0|$ is sufficiently small.

In order to investigate the nature of the bifurcation equation

$$\operatorname{Im} \kappa = 0 \quad , \tag{8.25}$$

we note that the solution $\{w(\theta),\kappa\}$ of the modified problem (8.11), (8.12) satisfies the equation

$$w(\theta) = ce^{i\theta} + i(1-\kappa)e^{i\theta} \int_0^{\theta} e^{-i\tau} g(w(\tau),\overline{w(\tau)},\tau,\mu)d\tau - i\kappa e^{i\theta} \int_0^{\theta} e^{-i\tau} w(\tau) d\tau \quad . \tag{8.26}$$

Since $w(\theta)$ is periodic, we must have

$$\kappa \int_0^{2\pi} e^{-i\theta} w(\theta) d\theta = (1-\kappa) \int_0^{2\pi} e^{-i\theta} g(w(\theta),\overline{w(\theta)},\theta,\mu) d\theta \quad . \tag{8.27}$$

This latter relation will be written in the form

$$(8.28) \qquad 2\pi\kappa\,\Gamma(c,\bar{c},\mu) = 2\pi(1-\kappa)\,\Phi(c,\bar{c},\mu) \quad .$$

The quantity $\Phi(c,\bar{c},\mu)$ vanishes for $\mu = 0$ by virtue of (8.15), and because of (8.13) its derivatives with respect to c and $\bar{c}$ vanish for $\mu = 0$. It is therefore convenient to make the assumption that g is of the form

$$(8.29) \qquad g(w,\bar{w},\theta,\mu) = g_0(\theta) + \mu g_1(w,\bar{w},\theta,\mu)$$

and to introduce the quantity η by setting

$$(8.30) \qquad \kappa = \mu\eta \quad .$$

Relation (8.27) then reduces to

$$(8.31) \qquad \eta\int_0^{2\pi} e^{-i\theta}w(\theta)d\theta = (1-\mu\eta)\int_0^{2\pi} e^{-i\theta}g_1(w(\theta),\overline{w(\theta)},\theta,\mu)d\theta \quad ,$$

which we shall write as

$$(8.32) \qquad \eta\,\Gamma(c,\bar{c},\mu) = (1-\mu\eta)\,\Phi_1(c,\bar{c},\mu) \quad .$$

As may be seen from (8.21) and (8.15), the coefficient of η on the left-hand side of (8.32) reduces to $\Gamma_0(c)$ for $\mu = 0$; the right member reduces to

$$(8.33) \qquad \Phi_1(c,\bar{c}) = \Phi_1(c,\bar{c},0) = \frac{1}{2\pi}\int_0^{2\pi} e^{-i\theta}g_1(w_c(\theta),\overline{w_c(\theta)},\theta,0)d\theta \quad .$$

Setting

$$(8.34) \qquad \eta(c,\bar{c}) = \Gamma_0^{-1}(c)\Phi_1(c,\bar{c}) \quad ,$$

which we can do for $|c - c_0|$ sufficiently small in virtue of condition (8.22), we thus find that

$$(8.35) \qquad \eta \longrightarrow \eta(c_0,\bar{c}_0) \quad \text{as} \quad \mu \longrightarrow 0 \quad .$$

In order to insure that the bifurcation equation (8.25) has a solution, we try to choose the value c_0 such that the condition

(8.36) $$\operatorname{Im} \eta(c_0, \bar{c}_0) = 0 \quad ,$$

which we shall call the bifurcation condition, is satisfied. Furthermore, we try to choose a function $c = c(\lambda)$ of a real parameter λ such that

(8.37) $$c(0) = c_0$$

and

(8.38) $$\operatorname{Im} \frac{d}{d\lambda} \eta(c(\lambda), \overline{c(\lambda)}) \Big|_{\lambda=0} \neq 0 \quad .$$

Then the implicit function theorem can be applied to establish the existence for sufficiently small $|\mu|$ of a function $\lambda = \lambda(\mu)$ such that

(8.39) $$\lambda(0) = 0$$

and

(8.40) $$\operatorname{Im} K(\mu, c(\lambda(\mu)), \overline{c(\lambda(\mu))}) = 0 \quad .$$

9. Duffing's Equation

As a first special problem we consider Duffing's equation

(9.1) $$u_{tt} + \omega_0^2 u + \beta u^3 = F \cos \omega t \quad .$$

It governs the displacement u of a particle of unit mass under the influence of a nonlinear restoring force $-\omega_0^2 u - \beta u^3$ and a periodic external force $F \cos \omega t$.

We assume that the real numbers β and F are small of the same order:

(9.2) $$\beta = \mu \beta_1 \quad , \qquad F = \mu F_1 \quad .$$

Then the theory developed in Section 8 is applicable; the function j is given by

$$j(u,u_t,\theta,\mu) = \mu[\beta_1 u^3 - F_1 \cos\theta] \quad , \tag{9.3}$$

so that

$$g(w,\overline{w},\theta,\mu) = \mu\omega_0^{-2}[\tfrac{1}{8}\beta_1(w+\overline{w})^3 - F_1 \cos\theta] \quad . \tag{9.4}$$

Since $g_0(\theta) \equiv 0$, the initial solution is

$$w_0(\theta) = ce^{i\theta} \quad , \quad \kappa = 0 \quad . \tag{9.5}$$

Furthermore

$$\Gamma_0(c) = c \quad ; \tag{9.6}$$

according to (8.22), therefore, we should assume

$$\underset{0}{c} \neq 0 \quad . \tag{9.7}$$

For the expression $\Phi_1(c,\overline{c})$ given by (8.33), we find

$$\Phi_1(c,\overline{c}) = \tfrac{3}{8}\omega_0^{-2}\beta_1 c^2\overline{c} - \tfrac{1}{2}\omega_0^{-2}F_1 \quad ; \tag{9.8}$$

hence by (8.34)

$$\eta(c,\overline{c}) = \tfrac{3}{8}\omega_0^{-2}\beta_1|c|^2 - \tfrac{1}{2}\omega_0^{-2}F_1 c^{-1} \quad . \tag{9.9}$$

The bifurcation equation, which requires that η be real, can easily be solved in this case. The bifurcation condition

$$\operatorname{Im}\eta(\underset{0}{c},\underset{0}{\overline{c}}) = 0 \tag{9.10}$$

requires precisely that $\underset{0}{c}$ be real, since β_1 and F_1 are assumed to be real. We recall that we should impose one condition on the initial value c. Since $c = \underset{0}{c}$ must be real for $\mu = 0$ it is natural to prescribe the real part $a = \underset{0}{c}$ of

(9.11) $$c = a + ib ,$$

and set the parameter λ equal to the imaginary part b:

(9.12) $$\lambda = b .$$

Of course, we could just as well have prescribed the absolute value of c and set $c = |c|e^{i\lambda}$.

For $\mu = 0$, $c = a$ we now have

(9.13) $$\operatorname{Im} \frac{\partial}{\partial b} \eta(c,\bar{c})\Big|_{b=0} - \frac{1}{2}\omega_o^{-2}F_1 a^{-2} \neq 0 ,$$

so that condition (8.38) is satisfied. Therefore the implicit function theorem is applicable, and the bifurcation equation

(9.14) $$\operatorname{Im} \kappa = 0$$

has a solution $b = b(\mu)$ for sufficiently small values of μ. In fact it could easily be shown that $b(\mu)$ is identically zero in the present case.

Formula (9.9) yields the relation

(9.15) $$\kappa = \frac{3}{8}\omega_o^{-2}\beta a^2 - \frac{1}{2}\omega_o^{-2} F a^{-1} + \ldots$$

--where the terms omitted are of higher than first order in μ--and hence, in view of (8.9),

(9.16) $$\omega = \omega_o + \omega_o^{-1}[\frac{3}{8}\beta a^2 - \frac{1}{2} F a^{-1}] + \ldots .$$

From Figures 1 and 2, in which ω and F are each plotted as a function of $|a|$ for a fixed value of the other and a fixed $\beta > 0$, we infer that three periodic solutions exist for values of ω or F within certain limits. If one varies ω --or F--beyond these limits, a solution which belongs to a disappearing branch should jump over into the other branch. Such jumps are in fact observed experimentally.

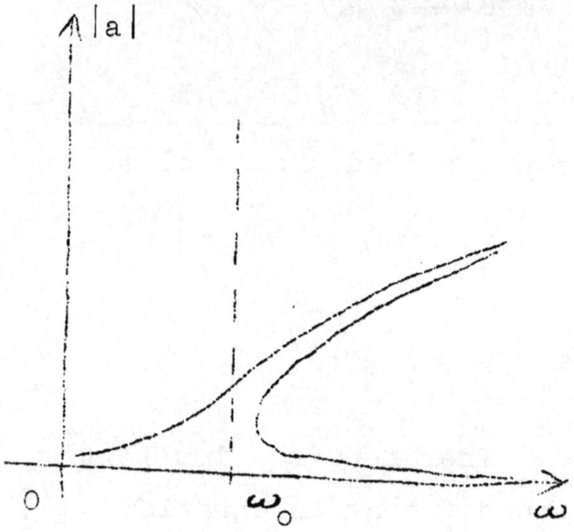

Figure 1
Frequency Response of Duffing's Vibrator

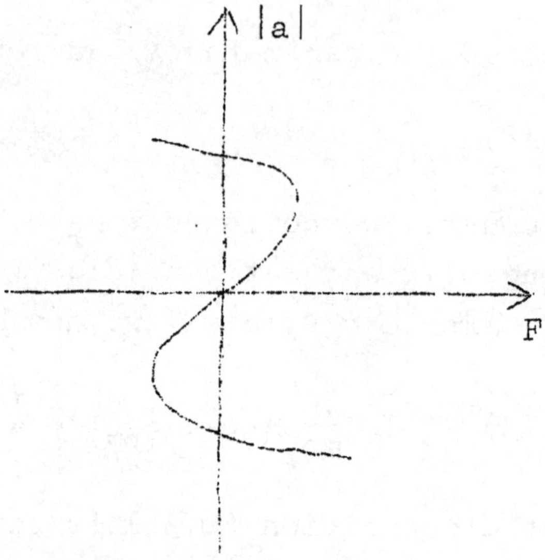

Figure 2
Force-amplitude Response of Duffing's Vibrator

If one lets β approach zero while keeping ω fixed, only one of the three solutions approaches the solution for $\beta = 0$. Thus it is seen that the phenomena just described could not have been revealed by a non-degenerate perturbation procedure.

10. Subharmonic Oscillations

Duffing's equation (9.1) has a great number of other periodic solutions which are not revealed by the procedure described. We want to discuss a certain class of these solutions which have as period an integral multiple of $2\pi/\omega$. These solutions represent the so-called "subharmonic" oscillations.

Since we wish to apply the formulas developed in Section 8, it will be necessary to retain the value

$$T = 2\pi/\omega \tag{10.1}$$

for the period of the solution. Therefore, we modify the right side of equation (9.1) and write this equation in the form

$$(10.2) \qquad u_{tt} + \omega_0^2 u + \beta u^3 = F \cos m\omega t \quad .$$

Here m is one of the integers 2,3,4,... .

We retain the first assumption of (9.2), namely

$$(10.3) \qquad \beta = \mu\beta_1 \quad ,$$

but not the second one. Instead we assume that F is independent of μ. The function g given by (8.7) becomes

$$(10.4) \qquad g(w,\bar{w},\theta,\mu) = -F\omega_0^{-2} \cos m\theta + \tfrac{1}{8}\mu\beta_1\omega_0^{-2}(w+\bar{w})^3 \quad .$$

Since in this case

$$(10.5) \qquad g_0(\theta) = -F\omega_0^{-2} \cos m\theta \quad ,$$

the initial solution $w_c(\theta)$ of the equation for $\mu = 0$ is

$$(10.6) \qquad w_c(\theta) = \Gamma_0(c)e^{i\theta} - \frac{1}{2}\frac{F\omega_0^{-2}}{m-1} e^{im\theta} + \frac{1}{2}\frac{F\omega_0^{-2}}{m+1} e^{-im\theta}$$

with

$$(10.7) \qquad \Gamma_0(c) = c + \frac{F\omega_0^{-2}}{m^2 - 1} \quad ;$$

see (8.16) and (8.20). The generating solution $w_{c_0}(\theta)$ results by setting $c = c_0$.

The quantity $\Phi_1(c,\bar{c})$ given by (8.33) is found to be

$$(10.8) \qquad \Phi_1(c,\bar{c}) = \tfrac{3}{8}\beta_1\omega_0^{-2}\Gamma_0(c)\left[|\Gamma_0(c)|^2 + 2|c - \Gamma_0(c)|^2\right]$$

if $m \neq 3$, while

$$(10.9) \qquad \Phi_1(c,\bar{c}) = \tfrac{3}{8}\beta_1\omega_0^{-2}\left\{\Gamma_0(c)\left[|\Gamma_0(c)|^2 + 2|c - \Gamma_0(c)|^2\right] + \overline{\Gamma_0(c)}^2(c - \Gamma_0(c))\right\}$$

if m = 3.

Evidently,

$$(10.10) \qquad \eta(c,\bar{c}) = \frac{3}{8}\beta_1\omega_0^{-2}\left[|\Gamma_0(c)|^2 + 2|c - \Gamma_0(c)|^2\right]$$

if $m \neq 3$. The bifurcation condition (8.36) is therefore satisfied identically in c_0. In order to solve the bifurcation equation in case $m \neq 3$ it is therefore necessary to investigate terms of higher than first order in μ.

In case $m = 3$ we have

$$(10.11) \quad \eta(c,\bar{c}) = \frac{3}{8}\beta_1\omega_0^{-2}\Big\{|\Gamma_0(c)|^2 + 2|c - \Gamma_0(c)|^2 + \Gamma_0(c)^{-1}\overline{\Gamma_0(c)}^2(c - \Gamma_0(c))\Big\} .$$

This quantity is certainly real if c is real; it may also be real for other values of c, namely those which are such that $\arg \Gamma_0(c)$ is a multiple of $\frac{\pi}{3}$. In any case, for a prescribed value of the real part a of $c = a + ib$, there is at least one solution $c_0 = a$, $b = 0$ satisfying the bifurcation condition. Since

$$(10.10) \qquad \operatorname{Im} \frac{\partial}{\partial b}\eta(c,\bar{c})\Big|_{b=0} = \frac{9}{64}F\beta_1\omega_0^{-4} \neq 0$$

if $F \neq 0$, which we assume, the bifurcation equation can be solved.

By a procedure similar to that used in the derivation of formula (9.16), we can find the approximate value of the frequency ω of vibration in terms of $|a|$; the result is plotted in Figure 3.

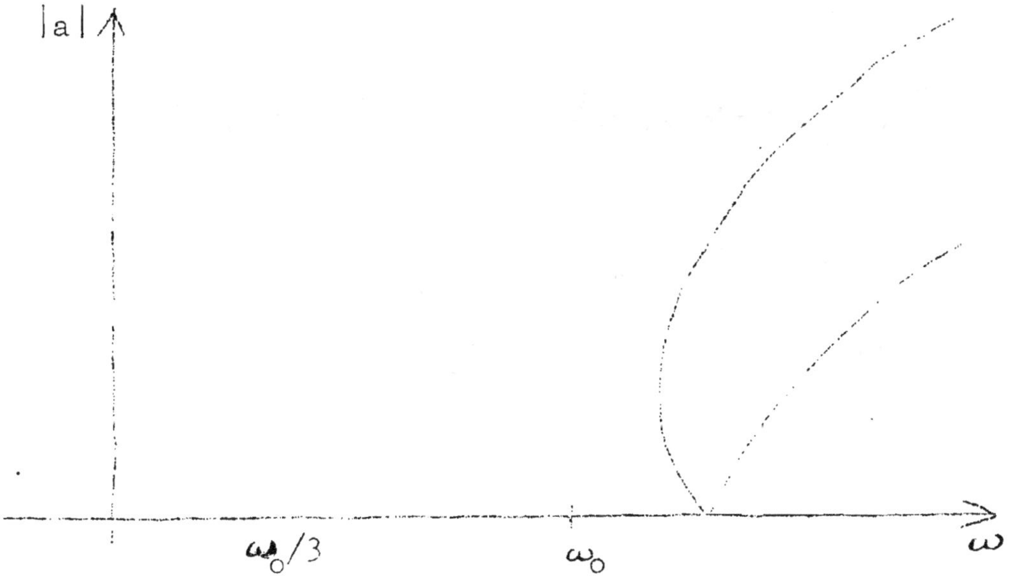

Figure 3
Subharmonic response of order 3 of Duffing's vibrator

11. Van der Pol's Equation

In van der Pol's equation

(11.1) $$u_{tt} + \omega_o^2 u = \beta u_t - \gamma u_t^3 + F \cos \omega t$$

nonlinear terms enter which represent a resistance which is negative if the velocity u_t is small and positive if it is large. We set

(11.2) $$\beta = \mu\beta_1 \;, \quad \gamma = \mu\gamma_1 \;, \quad F = \mu F_1$$

so that $g_o(\theta) \equiv 0$ and $g = \mu g_1$ with

(11.3) $$g_1(w,\bar{w},\theta) = -\frac{1}{2} i\beta_1 \omega_o^{-1}(w-\bar{w}) - \frac{1}{8} i\gamma_1 \omega_o (w-\bar{w})^3 - \omega_o^{-2} F_1 \cos \theta \quad .$$

The initial solution is

(11.4) $$w_c(\theta) = ce^{i\theta} \;, \quad \kappa = 0 \quad ;$$

further $\Gamma_0(c) = c$. From (8.33) and (11.3) we find

(11.5) $$\Phi_1(c,\bar{c}) = -\tfrac{1}{2}i\beta_1\omega_0^{-1}c + \tfrac{3}{8}i\gamma_1\omega_0 c^2\bar{c} - \tfrac{1}{2}\omega_0^{-2}F_1 ,$$

so that

(11.6) $$\eta(c,\bar{c}) = -\tfrac{1}{2}i\beta_1\omega_0^{-1} + \tfrac{3}{8}i\gamma_1\omega_0|c|^2 - \tfrac{1}{2}\omega_0^{-2}F_1 c^{-1} .$$

The bifurcation condition (8.36) becomes

(11.7) $$b_o F_1 = |c_0|^2[\beta_1\omega_0 - \tfrac{3}{4}\gamma_1\omega_0^3|c_0|^2] ,$$

where $c_0 = a_0 + ib_0$.

In the case $F_1 = 0$ of free vibrations, this condition determines the amplitude

(11.8) $$|c_0| = \omega_0^{-1}[\tfrac{4}{3}\beta_1/\gamma_1]^{1/2} = \omega_0^{-1}[\tfrac{4}{3}\beta/\gamma]^{1/2} ,$$

since $c_0 = 0$ is excluded by (8.22). The phase ϕ_0 defined by

(11.9) $$c_0 = |c_0|e^{i\phi_0}$$

can then be chosen arbitrarily.

In case $F_1 \neq 0$ we may also prescribe ϕ_0 arbitrarily. Then equation (11.7) has a solution $|c_0|$ if $F_1 \sin\phi_0$ is sufficiently small; indeed, it has two solutions if $F_1 \sin\phi_0 > 0$.

We may then in either case take $\lambda = |c|$ as parameter. Since it is easily verified that

(11.10) $$\frac{\partial}{\partial\lambda}\operatorname{Im}\eta \neq 0 \quad \text{for} \quad \lambda = |c_0|$$

if $F_1 \sin\phi_0$ is sufficiently small, the bifurcation equation has a solution for such small values of $F_1 \sin\phi_0$, and indeed two solutions if in addition $F_1 \sin\phi_o > 0$.

It should be noted that in van der Pol's case the phase of c_0 is prescribed while the amplitude is determined by solving the bifurcation equation, while in Duffing's case the situation is reversed. This fact accounts for the differences in the manifold of periodic solutions determined by the procedure described.

12. Bifurcation from a Stationary State

We say that the solution $U(t)$ of the equation

$$U_t = F(U, \mu) \tag{12.1}$$

describes a stationary state if $U(t)$ is a constant. We suppose that to each value of μ a constant solution U_μ is given, and that for a certain value of μ, say $\mu = 0$, the variational equation

$$\delta U_t = F_U(U_0, 0)\,\delta U \tag{12.2}$$

has a periodic solution with given period $2\pi/\omega_0$. Then, in general, a manifold of non-constant periodic solutions will branch off from the solution $U = U_0$. Since the coefficients in equation (12.2) are constant, a periodic solution δU is of the form

$$\delta U = a \cos \omega_0 t + b \sin \omega_0 t \quad . \tag{12.3}$$

Thus at the same time

$$\delta U = -a \sin \omega_0 t + b \cos \omega_0 t \tag{12.4}$$

is also a solution which is independent of the first, so that the degree of degeneracy of the problem is at least 2. We assume that it is exactly equal to 2.

It is convenient to introduce the quantity

$$u = U - U_\mu \tag{12.5}$$

instead of U and to set

$$(12.6) \qquad F(u + U_\mu, \mu) = uF_U(U_o, 0) + j(u, \mu) \quad .$$

Then equation (12.1) can be written in the form

$$(12.7) \qquad u_t = F_U(U_o, 0)u + j(u, \mu) \quad .$$

We note that the definition (12.6) of j implies that

$$(12.8) \qquad j(0, \mu) = 0$$

and

$$(12.9) \qquad j_u(0, 0) = 0 \quad .$$

For the sake of simplicity we assume that the column u contains only two elements,

$$(12.10) \qquad u = \{u_1, u_2\} \quad .$$

Further we assume that the matrix $F_U(U_o, 0)$ is

$$(12.11) \qquad F_U(U_o, 0) = \omega_o \begin{pmatrix} 0 & -1 \\ 1 & 0 \end{pmatrix} \quad ,$$

so that we can take

$$a = \begin{pmatrix} 1 \\ 0 \end{pmatrix} \quad , \quad b = \begin{pmatrix} 0 \\ 1 \end{pmatrix}$$

in (12.3). Setting, in addition,

$$(12.13) \qquad w = u_1 + iu_2$$

and

$$(12.14) \qquad g(w, \overline{w}, \mu) = j_1(u, \mu) + ij_2(u, \mu) \quad ,$$

we may write equation (12.7) in the form

$$(12.15) \qquad w_t = i\omega_o w + g(w, \overline{w}, \mu) \quad ,$$

which is of the type considered in Section 8.

Relations (12.8) and (12.9) attain the form

$$(12.16) \qquad g(0,0,\mu) = 0$$

and

$$(12.17) \qquad g_w(0,0,0) = g_{\overline{w}}(0,0,0) = 0 \quad .$$

In the present form the theory of Section 8 is not applicable, however, as $g(w,\overline{w},0)$ is not in general independent of w and $\overline{w}$; moreover, the generating solution in the present case is $w_0(\theta) \equiv 0$, which was excluded in Section 8. To remedy this defect, we shall introduce a new independent parameter ν and substitute νw for w in equation (12.14). Setting

$$(12.18) \qquad g(w,\overline{w},\nu,\mu) = \nu^{-1} g(\nu w,\nu\overline{w},\mu) \quad ,$$

this equation becomes

$$(12.19) \qquad w_t = i\omega_0 w + g(w,\overline{w},\nu,\mu) \quad .$$

As we shall see, the methods of Section 8 are now applicable.

It would have been possible to treat the problem independently of Section 8, using the general modification procedure described in Section 5. It is, however, preferable to introduce the stretching parameter ν. In fact, it is customary to employ such a stretching also in cases of more than two unknown quantities.

The definition (12.18) must be supplemented by the stipulation

$$(12.20) \qquad g(w,\overline{w},0,\mu) = g_w(0,0,\mu)w + g_{\overline{w}}(0,0,\mu)\overline{w} \quad ,$$

which is consistent with the assumed differentiability of $g(w,\overline{w},\mu)$ with respect to w and $\overline{w}$; combined with (12.17), this yields

$$(12.21) \qquad g(w,\overline{w},0,0) = 0 \quad ,$$

whence

(12.22) $$g_w(w,\bar{w},0,0) = g_{\bar{w}}(w,\bar{w},0,0) = 0 \quad .$$

In applying the theory of Section 8, we consider μ and ν as independent parameters. The function g_0 obtained from g by setting $\mu = \nu = 0$ is then

(12.23) $$g_0 \equiv 0$$

by virtue of (12.21). The initial solution is again

(12.24) $$w_c(\theta) = ce^{i\theta} \quad , \quad \kappa = 0 \quad .$$

Hence $\Gamma_0(c) = c$ and $c_o \neq 0$ may be prescribed arbitrarily. Consequently, periodic solutions $w(\theta) = w(\theta,\nu,\mu,c)$ and $\kappa = \kappa(\nu,\mu,c)$ exist which for $\nu = \mu = 0$ reduce to $w(\theta) = w_c(\theta)$ and $\kappa = 0$. The quantity κ satisfies the relation

(12.25) $$\frac{\kappa}{2\pi} \int_0^{2\pi} e^{-i\theta} w(\theta)d\theta = \frac{1-\kappa}{2\pi\omega_o} \int_0^{2\pi} e^{-i\theta} g(w(\theta),\overline{w(\theta)},\nu,\mu)d\theta$$

or

(12.26) $$\kappa\Gamma(c,\bar{c},\nu,\mu) = (1-\kappa)\Phi(c,\bar{c},\nu,\mu) \quad ,$$

cf. (8.27) and (8.28), and the bifurcation equation requires that the imaginary part of κ be zero. Clearly, in view of (12.21),

(12.27) $$\Gamma(c,\bar{c},0,0) = c \quad , \quad \Phi(c,\bar{c},0,0) = 0 \quad .$$

Four parameters are available, namely $c = a + ib$, ν, and μ. If we were to follow the procedure employed in the previous cases we would prescribe one component of c and then determine the other component as a function of ν and μ. This is not possible in the present case, since

(12.28) $$\Phi_c(c,\bar{c},0,0) = \Phi_{\bar{c}}(c,\bar{c},0,0) = 0 \quad ,$$

as follows from (12.22). The proper procedure here is to prescribe both components of c and to determine μ as a function of ν.

We assume that $g(w,\overline{w},\mu)$ and its derivatives g_w and $g_{\overline{w}}$ have continuous derivatives g_μ, $g_{w\mu}$, $g_{\overline{w}\mu}$ --at least for $\mu = 0$-- and further we assume that

$$(12.29) \qquad \operatorname{Re} g_{w\mu}(0,0,0) \neq 0 \quad .$$

By (12.28), (12.20), and (12.17), we have

$$(12.30) \qquad \Phi_\mu(c,\overline{c},0,0) = -i\omega_0^{-1} c g_{w\mu}(0,0,0) \quad .$$

Hence, in view of (12.26), we have

$$(12.31) \qquad \frac{\partial}{\partial \mu}(\operatorname{Im} \kappa)\Big|_{\mu=\nu=0} = -\omega_0^{-1} \operatorname{Re} g_{w\mu}(0,0,0) \neq 0 \quad .$$

Furthermore, in view of the second statement of (12.27), $\kappa = 0$ for $\mu = \nu = 0$.

The implicit function theorem can thus be applied to obtain a function $\mu = \mu(\nu)$ such that $\operatorname{Im} \kappa \equiv 0$, and the existence of periodic solutions with the period

$$(12.32) \qquad T = 2\pi[1 - \kappa(\nu,\mu(\nu), c)]\, \omega_0^{-1}$$

is established. The solution is then of the form

$$(12.33) \qquad w = w(\theta,\nu,\mu(\nu),c) \quad .$$

The function νw is then the solution of the original problem. We may also express this as follows: if $|c|$ is chosen sufficiently small the value $\nu = 1$ is included in the neighborhood in which the function $\mu(\nu)$ is defined. Then the solution of the original problem will be

$$(12.34) \qquad w(\theta,1,\mu(1),c) \quad .$$

Note that we have determined the parameter μ in terms of the amplitude c, thus reversing the procedure of our other examples.

SPECIAL TOPICS IN ANALYSIS

Part B

Asymptotic Integration of Differential Equations

1. Asymptotic Expansions

Suppose a function $f(z)$ of the complex variable z possesses a power series expansion

$$f(z) = a_0 + a_1 z + a_2 z^2 + \dots \quad . \tag{1.1}$$

Then we know that the partial sum

$$f_n(z) = a_0 + a_1 z + \dots + a_n z^n \tag{1.2}$$

approximates the function $f(z)$ in such a way that the difference $f(z) - f_n(z)$ vanishes to higher than n-th order in the neighborhood of the origin. In other words, the relation

$$\lim_{z \to 0} z^{-n}[f(z) - f_n(z)] = 0 \tag{1.3}$$

holds. This relation refers not at all to the convergence of the infinite series; in fact, it does not even imply that the series involved is infinite. A series

$$a_0 + a_1 z + \dots + a_N z^N$$

such that relation (1.3) holds for $0 \leq n \leq N$ is said to give an <u>asymptotic power series expansion</u> of order N of the function $f(z)$ near $z = 0$.

More precisely, let the function $f(z)$ be defined in a sector $\mathcal{S}_{\alpha\beta}$ of the complex z-plane with vertex at the origin. Such a sector is given by the inequalities

$$0 < |z| \leq \alpha \ , \quad |\arg z| \leq \beta \quad ,$$

where α is a positive number and $0 \leq \beta \leq \pi$; $\arg z$ is defined by the relation $z = |z| e^{i \arg z}$. Note that the "vertex" $z = 0$ is excluded. Then we say that the series

$$a_0 + a_1 z + \dots + a_N z^N \tag{1.4}$$

gives an N-th order asymptotic power series expansion of f(z) if for every $\varepsilon > 0$ and for each $n \leq N$ there exists a positive number $\delta_n(\varepsilon)$ such that

$$|f(z) - f_n(z)| \leq \varepsilon |z|^n \tag{1.5}$$

holds whenever $z \in \mathcal{S}_{\alpha\beta}$ and $|z| \leq \delta_n(\varepsilon)$, where $f_n(z)$ is defined by formula (1.2).

Although asymptotic series have been used more or less implicitly since Euler's time, the first systematic explicit theories of such series were given by Poincaré and Stieltjes in 1886.

The most familiar case of an asymptotic series is the well-known Taylor expansion. If a function f(z) possesses continuous derivatives up to order N in the neighborhood of z = 0, its finite Taylor series up to the term in z^N provides an N-th order asymptotic expansion. It would be quite easy to construct a function of this type which has no asymptotic expansion of order N+1.

Moreover, as is well known, there are functions possessing derivatives of every order for which the infinite Taylor series does not converge to the function expanded; $f(x) = e^{-x^{-2}}$ is such a function for real x. Nevertheless, each partial sum of this Taylor series gives an asymptotic expansion of the function. Furthermore, the asymptotic power series expansion -- if it exists--of a function of a complex variable in the neighborhood of a singular point--at which the function possesses no convergent Taylor series--may make possible a theoretical or numerical analysis of the function near this singularity.

Frequently, though, expansions of a type more general than power series must be used for this purpose. Various generalizations of the notion of asymptotic expansion have therefore been introduced. We mention one which is frequently used. A series

$$a_o\phi_o(z) + \dots + a_N\phi_N(z) \tag{1.6}$$

is said to give an <u>asymptotic expansion</u> of the function $f(z)$ near the point $z = z_o$ if there exists a sequence of functions $p_o(\alpha) \equiv 1$, $p_1(\alpha), \dots, p_N(\alpha)$ defined for a positive real variable α which have the following properties:

$$p_n(\alpha) > 0 \qquad \text{for } \alpha > 0 \ , \tag{1.7}$$

$$\lim_{\alpha \to 0} \frac{p_{n+1}(\alpha)}{p_n(\alpha)} = 0 \qquad \text{for } n = 0, \dots, N-1 \ , \tag{1.8}$$

$$\lim_{z \to z_o} p_n(|z-z_o|)^{-1}[f(z)-f_n(z)] = 0 \text{ for } n = 0, \dots, N \ , \tag{1.9}$$

where $f_n(z)$ is the partial sum

$$f_n(z) = a_o\phi_o(z) + \dots + a_n\phi_n(z) \ . \tag{1.10}$$

In the following pages we shall be concerned primarily with asymptotic power series. Later, however, we shall also consider more general types of asymptotic expansions. Moreover, we shall at first be concerned with analytic functions of a complex variable, while later on functions will predominate whose arguments are essentially real.

One may approach the study of asymptotic expansion in two ways: either one investigates various types of expansions of the form (1.6) or of other forms and applies the results to special functions, or one starts with various special functions and then searches for the appropriate type of expansion for them. Except for a short introductory section concerning general properties of asymptotic power series, we shall essentially confine ourselves to the second approach.

The various special functions we shall investigate will usually arise as solutions of differential equations. The variable involved in the expansion, at present denoted by z, will in general not be one of the independent variables on which the solution of the differential equation depends.

More often, we shall consider a set of differential equations depending on a parameter, and try to find an appropriate asymptotic expansion of the desired solution with respect to the parameter. This procedure is frequently the most effective way to carry out a theoretical or a numerical analysis of the solution of a differential equation.

2. Asymptotic Power Series

We make a few remarks about asymptotic power series in general.

We first note that two such series may be formally added or subtracted term-by-term to give an asymptotic power-series expansion for the sum or difference of the two originally expanded functions, since the sum or difference of two quantities which vanish to a certain order k as z approaches zero will itself vanish to at least the same order.

We next make the uniqueness statement that the coefficients $a_o, a_1, \ldots, a_n$ of an asymptotic series, if one exists, for the function f(z) are uniquely determined by that function. Since the formal difference of any two asymptotic series for the same function will be an asymptotic series for the function $g(z) \equiv 0$, it is sufficient to show that in any asymptotic series expansion $b_o + b_1 z + \ldots + b_N z^N$ for this latter function all coefficients b_n are zero. The definition (1.3) of an asymptotic series requires that the relation

$$\lim_{z \to 0} z^{-n}(b_o + \ldots + b_n z^n) = 0 \tag{2.1}$$

hold for all n from 0 to N. We first use this relation for $n = 0$ and obtain $b_o = 0$; next for $n = 1$, giving us $b_1 = 0$; and so on successively until all the b_n are shown to vanish.

On the other hand, the function f(z) is not uniquely determined by its asymptotic expansion; for, as already noted in the preceding section, there are non-vanishing functions such as $\exp\{-z^{-2}\}$ whose asymptotic series vanish identically.

Next we make a statement concerning <u>multiplication</u> of asymptotic series. Let $f(z)$ and $g(z)$ be two functions defined in the same sector $\mathcal{S}_{\alpha\beta}$ and possessing asymptotic series of order N. Then the product $h(z) = f(z)g(z)$ has an asymptotic expansion of order N which can be obtained by formal multiplication of the expansions of $f(z)$ and $g(z)$. To see this, let $h_n(z)$ be the partial sum of the terms up to order n of the formal product, $f_n(z)$ and $g_n(z)$ the corresponding partial sums in the original expansion. We need now only observe that the difference

$$h_n(z) - f_n(z)g_n(z) \tag{2.2}$$

consists of a finite sum of terms of order higher than n, and that

$$\lim_{z \to 0} z^{-n}[h(z) - f_n(z)g_n(z)] = 0 \quad , \quad n = 0,\ldots,N \quad . \tag{2.3}$$

This latter relation follows from the identity

$$h(z) - f_n(z)g_n(z) = [f(z) - f_n(z)]g_n(z) + f(z)[g(z) - g_n(z)] \tag{2.4}$$

and the fact that $g_n(z)$ --a polynomial--and $f(z)$ --asymptotic to a polynomial--are bounded in the neighborhood of $z = 0$. But by subtraction of (2.2) from (2.3) we obtain the relation

$$\lim_{z \to 0} z^{-n}[h(z) - h_n(z)] = 0 \qquad \text{for} \quad 0 \le n \le N \quad , \tag{2.5}$$

which gives the desired asymptotic relationship.

The <u>reciprocal</u> $f^{-1}(z) = 1/f(z)$ of a function $f(z)$ with an asymptotic power series expansion of order N possesses an asymptotic series of the same order, provided that this reciprocal is <u>bounded</u> in $\mathcal{S}_{\alpha\beta}$. This series can be obtained by formal division, which can be carried out since the boundedness of $f^{-1}(z)$ implies that the constant term a_o in the expansion of $f(z)$ is not zero. We denote the n-th order partial sum of the series resulting from formal division by

$g_n(z)$; as usual, $f_n(z)$ will denote the corresponding partial sum of the original series. Clearly, the product $f_n(z)g_n(z)$ differs from 1 by terms of order higher than n:

$$\lim_{z \to 0} z^{-n}[1 - f_n(z)g_n(z)] = 0 \quad . \tag{2.6}$$

By the definition of an asymptotic series and the boundedness of the polynomial $g_n(z)$,

$$\lim_{z \to 0} z^{-n}[f_n(z) - f(z)]g_n(z) = 0 \quad . \tag{2.7}$$

Adding (2.6) and (2.7) and multiplying by the bounded function $f^{-1}(z)$, we finally obtain the relation

$$\lim_{z \to 0} z^{-n}[f^{-1}(z) - g_n(z)] = 0 \quad , \tag{2.8}$$

which proves our statement.

Finally, we state that the <u>integral</u>

$$F(z) = \int_0^z f(\zeta)d\zeta \quad , \tag{2.9}$$

taken along a ray through the origin, of a function f(z) which is continuous in $\mathcal{S}_{\alpha\beta}$ and possesses an asymptotic series of order N itself possesses an asymptotic series of order N+1 obtained by formal integration. To see this we need only integrate the inequalities (1.5)

No similar general statement, however, can be made concerning the <u>differentiation</u> of asymptotic series, just as none can be made in the corresponding theory of convergent power series. All we can say is that <u>if</u> the (continuous) derivative f'(z) does possess an asymptotic power-series expansion, <u>then</u> this expansion may be obtained from that of f(z) by formal differentiation, for then by the preceding paragraph the formal indefinite integral of this expansion will coincide with the expansion of f(z) except possibly for the constant term.

In the explicit examples which we shall presently consider, asymptotic expansions will be desired in the vicinity of $z = \infty$ rather than of $z = 0$. It is obvious that the definitions and statements of this section could be adapted to $z = \infty$ as "vertex" simply by introducing z^{-1} as independent variable in place of z.

3. The Exponential Integral

It is customary--with good reason--to begin the specific study of asymptotic expansion with the function

$$E(z) = \int_z^\infty e^{-\zeta} \zeta^{-1} d\zeta \quad , \tag{3.1}$$

which is related to the "exponential integral"

$$Ei(z) = -E(-z) \quad ; \tag{3.2}$$

in this integral the upper limit ∞ is taken to mean the point at infinity on the positive real axis. Obviously, the function E(z) vanishes together with all derivatives if z approaches infinity along the real axis. Therefore the asymptotic series of E(z) in the neighborhood of $z = \infty$ must vanish identically. The function

$$F(z) = e^z E(z) = \int_z^\infty e^{z-\zeta} \zeta^{-1} d\zeta \quad , \tag{3.3}$$

however, does possess a non-vanishing asymptotic expansion near $z = \infty$.

In principle, one could determine this asymptotic series as the Taylor series, by evaluating the limits of the derivatives of F(z) with respect to z^{-1} as z approaches infinity. In evaluating these limits one would employ certain processes of integration by parts. Instead of proceeding in this way, it is much more convenient to directly integrate F(z) by parts. We find successively

$$(3.4)\qquad F(z) = z^{-1} - \int_z^\infty e^{z-\zeta}\,\zeta^{-2}d\zeta$$

$$= z^{-1} - z^{-2} + 2\int_z^\infty e^{z-\zeta}\,\zeta^{-3}d\zeta$$

$$= z^{-1} - z^{-2} + 2z^{-3} - 6\int_z^\infty e^{z-\zeta}\,\zeta^{-4}d\zeta$$

and so on. Generally, we find

$$(3.5)\qquad F(z) = F_n(z) + R_n(z) \quad ,$$

with

$$(3.6)\qquad F_n(z) = \sum_{\nu=1}^{n} (-1)^{\nu-1}(\nu-1)!\,z^{-\nu} \quad ,$$

$$(3.7)\qquad R_n(z) = (-1)^n n! \int_z^\infty e^{z-\zeta}\,\zeta^{-n-1}d\zeta \quad .$$

In fact, if one defines $R_n(z)$ and $R_{n+1}(z)$ from (3.7), one easily verifies the relation

$$(3.8)\qquad R_n(z) = (-1)^n n!\,z^{-n-1} + R_{n+1}(z) \quad ,$$

after a single integration by parts. From (3.8) relation (3.5) follows by induction, as (3.5) holds for $n = 0$ by the definition (3.3) of $F(z)$.

Let us first restrict z to the positive real axis:

$$(3.9)\qquad z = x > 0 \quad ,$$

so that $R_n(z)$ becomes a real integral

$$(3.10)\qquad R_n(x) = (-1)^n n! \int_x^\infty e^{x-\xi}\xi^{-n-1}d\xi \quad .$$

The positive quantity ξ^{-n-1} attains its maximum in the interval of integration at the left-hand endpoint $\xi = x$. Hence

$$(3.11)\qquad |R_n(x)| \leq n! x^{-n-1} \int_x^\infty e^{x-\xi} d\xi$$

$$= n! x^{-n-1} \quad ,$$

and the relation

$$(3.12)\qquad \lim_{x \to \infty} x^n R_n(x) = 0$$

holds. Hence $F_n(z)$ provides for <u>real</u> z an asymptotic power series expansion of $F(z)$ near $z = \infty$.

The function $F(z)$ can of course be defined for any value of $z \neq 0$ by choosing the path of integration in (3.3) so as to avoid the point $z = 0$. We first restrict z to the "slit plane"

$$|z| > 0 \quad , \quad |\arg z| \leq \pi \quad .$$

To obtain an estimate for the remainder $R_n(z)$, we choose as path $\mathcal{P}$ of integration the segment $|\zeta| = |z|$, $0 \leq |\arg \zeta| \leq |\arg z|$, $\operatorname{sgn} \arg \zeta = \operatorname{sgn} \arg z$ of the circle $|\zeta| = |z|$ between the points $\zeta = z$ and $\zeta = |z|$, together with the ray $|z| \leq \zeta < \infty$, $\arg \zeta = 0$ of the positive real axis. As a consequence of the assumption $|\arg z| \leq \pi$ relation

$$(3.13)\qquad \operatorname{Re} \zeta \geq \operatorname{Re} z$$

holds on the path $\mathcal{P}$, so that

$$(3.14)\qquad |e^{z-\zeta}| \leq 1$$

along this path. Furthermore, on the circular arc we have

$$(3.15)\qquad |d\zeta| = |z| \cdot d\theta \quad ,$$

where $\theta = \arg \zeta$. Hence

$$(3.16)\qquad |R_n(z)| \leq n! |z|^{-n} \int_0^{|\arg z|} d\theta + n! \int_{|z|}^\infty \xi^{-n-1} d\xi$$

$$\leq n! |z|^{-n} (\pi + n^{-1})$$

$$= (n-1)! (n\pi + 1) |z|^{-n} \quad .$$

This estimate is not yet sufficient to insure that the $F_n(z)$ form an asymptotic expansion of $F(z)$, for it only asserts that $R_n(z)$ approaches zero to order n in z^{-1}, not to order higher than n as required. We may, however, rectify this by first using relation (3.8) to express $R_n(z)$ in terms of $R_{n+1}(z)$ and then estimating $R_{n+1}(z)$ by (3.16). In this way we obtain

$$(3.17)\qquad |R_n(z)| \le n!|z|^{-n-1} + n![(n+1)\pi + 1]|z|^{-n-1}$$

$$= n!(n\pi + \pi + 2)|z|^{-n-1} \quad .$$

Thus it is seen to be indeed true that

$$(3.18)\qquad z^n R_n(z) \longrightarrow 0 \quad \text{as} \quad z \longrightarrow \infty \quad ,$$

for any position of z in the slit plane $|z| > 0$, $|\arg z| \le \pi$. Hence $F(z)$ has the asymptotic expansion

$$(3.19)\quad F(z) \sim z^{-1} - z^{-2} + 2z^{-3} - 6z^{-4} + - \dots + (-1)^{n-1}(n-1)!z^{-n} + \dots$$

in the slit z-plane.

It is clear, for two independent reasons, that this asymptotic series for $F(z)$ does not converge. First of all, its coefficient $a_n = (-1)^{n-1}(n-1)!$ violates the condition that $|a_n|^{1/n}$ be bounded, which would be necessary for convergence. But even apart from this, if the series did converge the function $F(z)$ would be regular at $z = \infty$. This is not the case, however; indeed, $F(z)$ is not even a single-valued function on a circuit surrounding $z = \infty$, since the residue of the integrand of (3.3) at its singular point $\zeta = 0$ is different from zero.

Clearly, the function $F(z)$ can be continued analytically beyond the slit $|\arg z| = \pi$, and will still be given by the integral (3.3), except that the path of integration will now partially or completely encircle the origin. We denote by $F(ze^{2\pi i})$ the value of the function F at the endpoint of a complete circuit which begins at the point z and along which arg z increases by 2π. The jump of the function F associated with such a circuit is defined as

$$[F(z)] = F(ze^{2\pi i}) - F(z) \quad . \tag{3.20}$$

From the definition (3.3) of F(z) we infer that this jump is

$$[F(z)] = -2\pi i e^z \quad . \tag{3.21}$$

Thus it is evident that F(z) is not single-valued.

Nevertheless, the asymptotic series of the multiple-valued function F(z) is single-valued. This remarkable phenomenon is typical for a large class of asymptotic expansions.

We naturally ask why no contradiction is implied by this difference in behavior. We note that the points z for which the asymptotic series for F(z) and $F(ze^{2\pi i})$ have both been established up to now are those of the negative real axis. For these points the jump $-2\pi i e^z$ approaches zero as $z = x \longrightarrow -\infty$ more strongly than any negative power of $|z|$. Thus this jump has for negative real z an asymptotic expansion which is identically zero; hence, it does not contribute to the asymptotic expansion of F(z).

We naturally ask next whether the same is true for the branches of the function F(z) which are obtained by continuation across the negative real axis. Since the continuation of the function F(z) into the slit plane

$$\pi \leq \arg z \leq 3\pi \tag{3.22}$$

is defined by

$$F(z) = F(ze^{-2\pi i}) - 2\pi i e^z \quad , \tag{3.23}$$

the expansion

$$F(z) \sim -2\pi i e^z + z^{-1} - z^{-2} + \ldots + (-1)^{n-1}(n-1)!z^{-n} + \ldots \tag{3.24}$$

is valid in the slit plane (3.22). In any sector

$$\pi \leq \arg z \leq \tau < \frac{3\pi}{2} \tag{3.25}$$

the function e^z approaches zero as $z \to \infty$ more strongly than any power of $|z|$. In this sector, therefore, the original asymptotic expansion (3.19) holds.

In the half plane

$$\frac{3\pi}{2} \leq \arg z \leq \frac{5\pi}{2} \quad , \tag{3.26}$$

however, the exponential function e^z dominates the powers as $z \to \infty$. The exponential function cannot, therefore, be omitted from the expansion (3.24). Thus we see that the <u>asymptotic expansion of the analytic continuation of the function F(z) across the ray arg z = $\frac{3\pi}{2}$ is not the analytic continuation of the asymptotic expansion of the function F(z)</u> on the initial slit plane. This occurrence is the famous "Stokes phenomenon" discovered by Stokes in 1857 in connection with the somewhat more involved Airy integral. Its proper appreciation is decisive for the understanding of a number of the most interesting problems in the theory of differential equations.

The question naturally arises whether or not the estimate of the remainder given above could be carried through when the point z lies beyond the ray $\arg z = \pi$. It is clear that this could not be possible beyond the ray $\arg z = \frac{3\pi}{2}$; it is possible, however, in the sector $\pi \leq \arg z \leq \tau < \frac{3\pi}{2}$. We shall carry out these estimates in connection with a more general class of integrals.

4. Generalized Exponential Integrals

As a generalization of the function F(z) treated in Section 3 we shall now consider the function

$$(4.1) \qquad f(z) = F^{(\gamma)}(z;p) = z^{\gamma-1}e^{z} \int_{z}^{\infty} p(\zeta)e^{-\zeta}\zeta^{-\gamma}d\zeta$$

involving a complex number

$$(4.2) \qquad \gamma = \alpha + i\beta$$

and a function p(z) which we assume defined at least for $|\arg z| \leq \frac{3\pi}{2}$. The functions z^{γ} and ζ^{γ} are meant to be the analytic continuations of the functions defined by

$$(4.3) \qquad x^{\gamma} = x^{\alpha}e^{i\beta \log x} \quad , \qquad \zeta^{\gamma} = \xi^{\alpha}e^{i\beta \log \xi}$$

on the positive real axis $\arg z = \arg \zeta = 0$, where $z = x$, $\zeta = \xi$.

Our aim is to determine an asymptotic expansion of f(z). We shall first derive an estimate for its absolute value. In doing this we shall assume that the real part of γ is greater than 1:

$$(4.4) \qquad \alpha > 1 \quad ,$$

a restriction which we shall later remove. We shall also assume that the function p(z) is bounded:

$$(4.5) \qquad |p(z)| \leq P$$

in a sector $\mathcal{S}_{R,\Theta}$ defined by

$$(4.6) \qquad |z| \geq R \quad , \quad |\arg z| \leq \Theta \quad ,$$

with $\Theta \geq \frac{3\pi}{2}$.

We first let z be on the positive real axis:

$$(4.7)\qquad z = x \geq R \quad .$$

In view of $|x^\gamma| = |x|^\alpha$, $|\xi^\gamma| = |\xi|^\alpha$ we have

$$(4.8)\qquad |f(x)| \leq Px^{\alpha-1}e^x \int_x^\infty e^{-\xi}\xi^{-\alpha}d\xi \leq Px^{-1} \quad .$$

Next we let z lie in the half-plane

$$(4.9)\qquad 0 \leq \arg z \leq \pi \quad , \quad |z| \geq R \quad .$$

As in Section 3 we select the path $\mathcal{P}$ of integration to run first along the circle $|\zeta| = |z|$ from $\zeta = z$ to $\zeta = |z|$ and then along the positive real axis from $\zeta = |z|$ to $\zeta = \infty$. In view of the fact that the estimate

$$(4.10)\qquad |z^\gamma \zeta^{-\gamma}| = |z|^\alpha |\zeta|^{-\alpha} e^{-\beta(\arg z - \arg \zeta)} \leq \left|\frac{z}{\zeta}\right|^\alpha e^{|\beta|\Theta}$$

holds on $\mathcal{P}$, we find that

$$(4.11)\qquad |f(z)| \leq c_\gamma P \quad \text{for} \quad 0 \leq \arg z \leq \pi \quad , \quad |z| \geq R \quad ,$$

with

$$(4.12)\qquad c_\gamma = [\pi + \frac{1}{\alpha-1}]e^{|\beta|\Theta} \quad .$$

Finally, we let z be in the quadrant $\pi \leq \arg z < \frac{3\pi}{2}$. We shall derive a uniform estimate only in a region

$$(4.13)\qquad \mathcal{R}_\tau : \quad \pi \leq \arg z \leq \frac{3\pi}{2} - \tau \quad , \quad x \leq -R$$

(see Figure 1) involving an arbitrary angle $\tau < \frac{\pi}{2}$. The restriction $x \leq -R$ was made so that we can choose a path $\mathcal{P}$ of integration along which

$$(4.14)\qquad \operatorname{Re} \zeta \geq \operatorname{Re} z \quad .$$

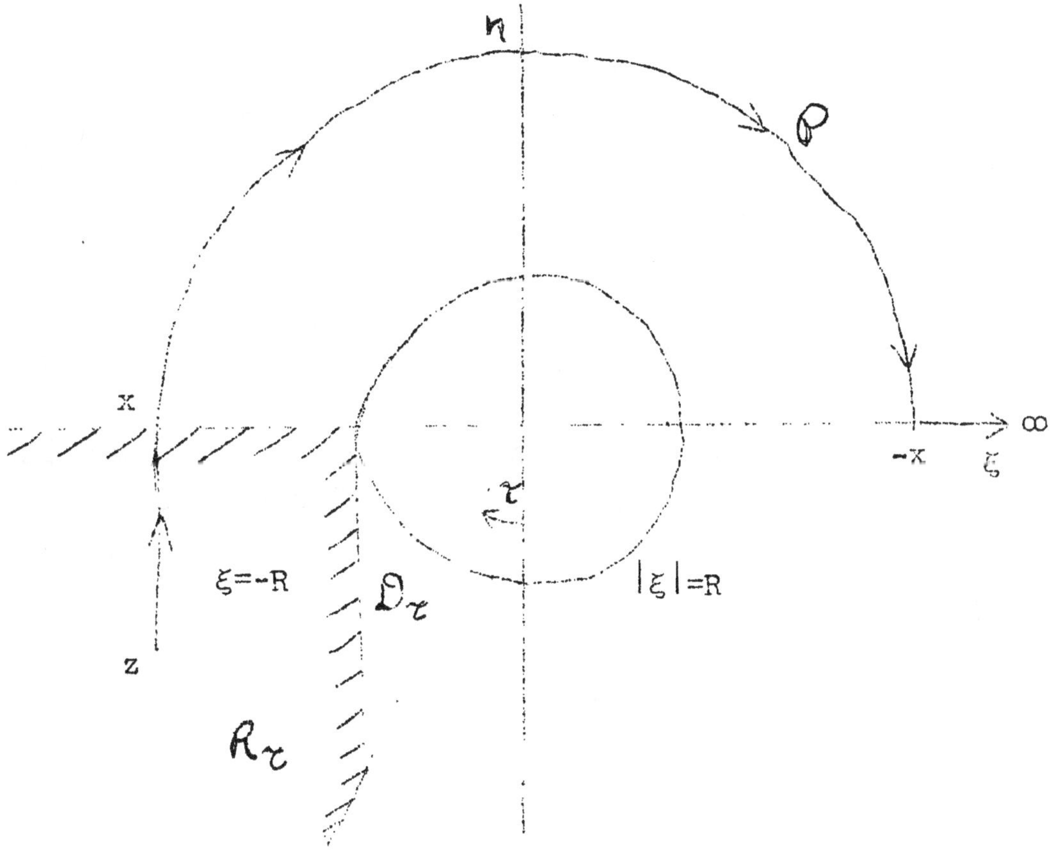

Figure 1

Estimation of the Generalized Exponential Integral in the Third Quadrant

We choose this path as consisting of three sections, as shown in the figure. It begins with the straight segment $\xi = x$, $y \leq \eta \leq 0$ from $\zeta = z$ to $\zeta = x$, then the semicircle $|\zeta| = -x$, $0 \leq \arg \zeta \leq \pi$ from $\zeta = x$ to $\zeta = -x$, and ends with the ray $\zeta = \xi \geq -x$ on the real axis from $\zeta = -x$ to $\zeta = \infty$. As condition (4.14) is indeed satisfied on this path, we have

(4.15) $$|e^{z-\zeta}| \leq 1 \quad \text{on } \mathcal{P},$$

so that by estimate (4.10) we obtain

(4.16) $$|f(z)| \leq P|z|^{\alpha-1}\{|x|^{-\alpha}|y| + |x|^{-\alpha+1}(\pi + \tfrac{1}{\alpha-1})\}e^{|\beta|\Theta} \quad .$$

By virtue of the restriction $\arg z \leq \frac{3\pi}{2} - \tau$, we have

(4.17) $$|z|/|x| \le [\sin \tau]^{-1} \quad .$$

Therefore the inequality

(4.18) $$|f(z)| \le C_\alpha P \quad ,$$

with

(4.19) $$C_\alpha = C_\alpha(\tau) = [1+\pi+\frac{1}{\alpha-1}][\sin \tau]^{-\alpha} e^{|\beta|\Theta} \quad ,$$

holds for z in $\mathcal{R}_\tau$. This formula will be useful in estimating the remainder terms in the asymptotic expansion of f(z); note that it also holds for z in the slit plane $|\arg z| \le \pi$, since the c_γ of (4.11) is smaller than $C_\alpha e^{|\beta|\Theta}$.

Relations (4.11) and (4.18) state that f(z) is bounded in certain regions of the plane. Clearly these estimates remain unchanged if we replace z by $\bar{z}$, ζ by $\bar{\zeta}$, and they therefore hold in the symmetrical regions in which arg z is negative. Furthermore, f(z) is a continuous function in the bounded region

(4.20) $$\mathcal{D}_\tau : \quad \pi \le \arg z \le \frac{3\pi}{2} - \tau \quad , \quad |z| \ge R \quad , \quad x \ge -R \quad ,$$

hence must be bounded there. Combining all these results, we have shown that the function f(z) is bounded in every sector $\mathcal{S}_{R,\frac{3\pi}{2}-\tau}$.

To derive an asymptotic expansion for f(z), we first specialize the function p(z) to be identically equal to 1. The resulting function $f(z) = F^{(\gamma)}(z;1)$ will be denoted by $F^{(\gamma)}(z)$:

(4.21) $$F^{(\gamma)}(z) = z^{\gamma-1} e^z \int_z^\infty e^{-\zeta} \zeta^{-\gamma} d\zeta \quad .$$

The asymptotic expansion of this function will be given by a formula of the type

(4.22) $$F^{(\gamma)}(z) = F_n^{(\gamma)}(z) + R_n^{(\gamma)}(z) \quad ,$$

in which $F_n^{(\gamma)}(z)$ is the finite sum

$$(4.23)\qquad F_n^{(\gamma)}(z) = z^{-1} - \gamma z^{-2} + \gamma(\gamma+1)z^{-3} - + \dots + (-1)^{n-1}\gamma(\gamma+1)\dots(\gamma+n-2)z^{-n} \quad ,$$

while the remainder $R_n^{(\gamma)}z$ can be simply expressed as

$$(4.24)\qquad R_n^{(\gamma)}(z) = (-1)^n\gamma(\gamma+1)\dots(\gamma+n-1)z^{-n}F^{(\gamma+n)}(z) \quad .$$

As in Section 3 one readily verifies by integration by parts that the definitions (4.23) and (4.24) imply the relation

$$(4.25)\qquad R_n^{(\gamma)}(z) = (-1)^n\gamma(\gamma+1)\dots(\gamma+n-1)z^{-n-1} + R_{n+1}^{(\gamma)}(z) \quad ,$$

from which formula (4.22) follows by induction.

From formula (4.18) employed for $p \equiv 1$ and for $\gamma + n$ instead of γ we obtain the estimate

$$(4.26)\qquad |R_n^{(\gamma)}(z)| \leq |\gamma(\gamma+1)\dots(\gamma+n-1)||z|^{-n}C_{\alpha+n} \quad .$$

Combining this (for n+1 instead of n) with the relation (4.25) gives us the better estimate

$$(4.27)\qquad |R_n^{(\gamma)}(z)| \leq D_n^{(\gamma)}|z|^{-n-1} \quad ,$$

where

$$(4.28)\qquad D_n^{(\gamma)} = |\gamma(\gamma+1)\dots(\gamma+n-1)|[1 + (\gamma+n)C_{\alpha+n+1}] \quad .$$

This estimate is valid in the entire sector $\mathcal{S}_{R,\frac{3\pi}{2}-\tau}$ with the exception of the bounded region $\mathcal{D}_\tau$, which can have no effect on any asymptotic expansion, as it does not extend outside the circle $|z| = R[\sin\tau]^{-1}$. As a consequence, the power series expansion (4.23) is an asymptotic expansion of $F^{(\gamma)}(z)$ in the sector $\mathcal{S}_{R,\frac{3\pi}{2}-\tau}$ for any positive $\tau < \frac{\pi}{2}$ and any $R > 0$.

It should be noted that the integration by parts involved in (4.25) can be performed even if condition (4.4) on α fails to hold, so that (4.22) is also true for $\alpha \leq 1$. In this case, however, the estimate (4.27) of the remainder term holds only for $\alpha + (n+1) > 1$, i.e. for $n > -\alpha$. Thus formula (4.23) gives an asymptotic expansion of $F^{(\gamma)}(z)$ in the precise sense of definition (1.6) only if sufficiently many of the initial terms are grouped as one term. This is, of course, no essential restriction.

As in the special case $\gamma = 1$ treated in Section 3, the asymptotic expansion of the function $F^{(\gamma)}(z)$ is single-valued while the function itself is not. The jump of this function is easily determined. We assume $\alpha < 1$. Then the path of integration may be passed through the origin, since the integral taken around a circle of radius r centered at the origin is bounded in absolute value by $2\pi r^{1-\alpha}$ and can thus be ignored for small enough r. Specifically, we take a path $\mathcal{P}$ leading in a straight line from $\zeta = z$ to $\zeta = 0$, then along the real axis to $\zeta = \infty$.

On the first section the integrand depends on whether $\zeta^{-\gamma}$ is determined by continuation from the positive real axis via the upper or via the lower half-plane; the ratio of the two integrands so obtained is equal to $e^{-2\pi i\gamma}$. The value of the factor $z^{\gamma-1}$ in front of the integral also depends on the direction of its definition, and the ratio of the two possible values is $e^{+2\pi i\gamma}$. Evidently, the factors cancel, and consequently the contributions to the two integrals $F^{(\gamma)}(z)$ and $F^{(\gamma)}(ze^{2\pi i})$ from the first part of the path $\mathcal{P}$ are the same.

On the second section of $\mathcal{P}$, along the positive real axis, the integrands are the same, but the factors $z^{\gamma-1}$ are not. Since, using the notation of (3.20),

$$(4.29) \qquad [z^{\gamma-1}] = (e^{2\pi i\gamma} - 1)z^{\gamma-1} \quad ,$$

we find that

$$(4.30) \qquad [F^{(\gamma)}(z)] = (e^{2\pi i\gamma} - 1)z^{\gamma-1}e^{z} \int_0^\infty e^{-\xi}\xi^{-\gamma}d\xi \quad .$$

Clearly, the function $z^{\gamma-1}e^{z}$ approaches zero if $z \longrightarrow \infty$ in the left half-plane $x \leq 0$. It is thus clear that the two functions $F^{(\gamma)}(z)$ and $F^{(\gamma)}(ze^{2\pi i})$ have the same asymptotic expansions when z is in any subsector $-\frac{3\pi}{2} + \tau \leq \arg z \leq -\frac{\pi}{2} - \tau$ of the left half-plane.

Formula (4.30) at the same time exhibits the fact that, unless γ is zero or a negative integer, the functions $F^{(\gamma)}(z)$ and $F^{(\gamma)}(ze^{2\pi i})$ do not have the same asymptotic expansion on the right half-plane. Thus Stokes' phenomenon is again exhibited: the analytic continuation of the asymptotic expansion is not the asymptotic expansion of the analytic continuation.

Note that formula (4.30) was determined under the assumption $\alpha < 1$. In case $\alpha \geq 1$ a number of integrations by parts must be performed before the path of integration may be drawn into the origin. The result will be formally the same if the integral

$$(4.31) \qquad \int_0^\infty e^{-\xi}\xi^{-\gamma}d\xi \quad ,$$

which actually does not exist for $\alpha \geq 1$, is redefined as representing the result of formally integrating by parts as many times as is necessary to raise the exponent of ξ to a number greater than -1 and dropping all boundary terms thus introduced.

We now consider the general function $f(z) = F^{(\gamma)}(z;p)$ given by (4.1). We suppose that the function $p(z)$ possesses an asymptotic expansion near $z = \infty$:

$$(4.32) \qquad p(z) = \sum_{\nu=0}^{n} p_\nu z^{-\nu} + z^{-n}\rho_n(z), \qquad n = 0,1,\ldots,N \quad ,$$

with

(4.33) $$\rho_n(z) \longrightarrow 0 \quad \text{as} \quad z \longrightarrow \infty \quad \text{in } \mathcal{S}_{R,\Theta} .$$

We may write

(4.34) $$f(z) = \sum_{\nu=0}^{n} p_\nu z^{-\nu} F^{(\gamma+\nu)}(z) + z^{-n} f_n(z) ,$$

with

(4.35) $$f_n(z) = z^{\gamma+n-1} e^{z} \int_z^\infty \rho_n(\zeta)\zeta^{-\gamma-n} e^{-\zeta} d\zeta .$$

We apply estimate (4.18) to this function, taking $\gamma+n$ in place of γ and a variable r instead of R. We obtain

(4.36) $$|f_n(z)| \leq C_{a+n} P_n(r) \quad \text{for} \quad |z| \geq r , \quad |\arg z| \leq \frac{3\pi}{2} - \tau ,$$

where $P_n(r)$ denotes the least upper bound of the function $\rho_n(z)$ for z in $\mathcal{S}_{r,\Theta}$. Now assumption (4.33) implies that $P_n(r)$ approaches 0 as $r \longrightarrow \infty$. Thus $f_n(z) \longrightarrow 0$ as $z \longrightarrow \infty$, and formula (4.34) gives the asymptotic expansion of the function $f(z)$. Again it is seen that this expansion is valid for $|\arg z| \leq \frac{3\pi}{2} - \tau$, and again Stokes' phenomenon will occur--in general.

The most important of the functions $F^{(\gamma)}(z)$, except for the function $F^{(1)}(z) = F(z)$ treated in Section 3, is the function

(4.37) $$F^{(1/2)}(z) = z^{-1/2} e^{z} \int_z^\infty e^{-\zeta}\zeta^{-1/2} d\zeta .$$

This function is closely related to the error integral

(4.38) $$\operatorname{erf} w = \frac{2}{\sqrt{\pi}} \int_0^w e^{-\omega^2} d\omega .$$

Setting $z = w^2$, $\zeta = \omega^2$ and observing that

$$(4.39) \qquad \frac{1}{\sqrt{\pi}} \int_0^\infty e^{-\zeta} \zeta^{-1/2} d\zeta = \frac{2}{\sqrt{\pi}} \int_0^\infty e^{-\omega^2} d\omega = 1 \quad ,$$

we get

$$(4.40) \qquad \operatorname{erf} w = 1 - \pi^{-1/2} w\, e^{-w^2} F^{(1/2)}(w^2) \quad .$$

From the asymptotic expansion of the function $F^{(1/2)}(z)$ we therefore can derive the asymptotic expansion of the function erf w near $w = \infty$. This expansion is valid for

$$(4.41) \qquad |\arg w| \leq \frac{3\pi}{4} - \tau \;, \quad |w| \geq R$$

with arbitrary positive τ and R. It is not strictly a power series expansion, but is rather of the form

$$(4.42) \qquad \operatorname{erf} w \sim 1 - \pi^{-1/2} e^{-w^2} \left\{ w^{-1} - \frac{1}{2} w^{-3} + \ldots \right\} \quad .$$

A further application of the asymptotic expansion of the function $F^{(1/2)}(z)$ is obtained by restricting z to the positive imaginary axis, i.e. by setting $z = iy$, $y > 0$. We have

$$(4.43) \qquad F^{(1/2)}(iy) = (iy)^{-1/2} e^{iy} \int_{iy}^{\infty} e^{-\zeta} \zeta^{-1/2} d\zeta$$

$$= (iy)^{-1/2} e^{iy} \left(\sqrt{\pi} - \int_0^{iy} e^{-\zeta} \zeta^{-1/2} d\zeta \right)$$

$$= (1-i)\sqrt{\frac{\pi}{2}}\, y^{-1/2} e^{iy} - y^{-1/2} e^{iy} \int_0^y e^{-i\eta} \eta^{-1/2} d\eta .$$

Splitting into real and imaginary parts, we have

$$(4.44) \qquad -y^{1/2} e^{-iy} F^{(1/2)}(iy) = \left[-\sqrt{\frac{\pi}{2}} + \int_0^y \cos\eta \frac{d\eta}{\sqrt{\eta}} \right]$$

$$- i \left[-\sqrt{\frac{\pi}{2}} + \int_0^y \sin\eta \frac{d\eta}{\sqrt{\eta}} \right] \quad .$$

But from the asymptotic expansion (4.22) with $\gamma = \frac{1}{2}$ and n = 1 there follows

$$(4.45)\qquad -y^{1/2}e^{-iy}F^{(1/2)}(iy) = iy^{-1/2}e^{-iy} + y^{-1/2}r(y) \quad ,$$

where $r(y) \to 0$ as $y \to \infty$, so that the left-hand side of equation (4.44) has limit zero as $y \to \infty$. Thus from the right-hand side we get the important integral-evaluation formulas

$$(4.46)\qquad \int_0^\infty \cos\eta \frac{d\eta}{\sqrt{\eta}} = \int_0^\infty \sin\eta \frac{d\eta}{\sqrt{\eta}} = \sqrt{\frac{\pi}{2}} \quad .$$

The integrals occurring in the right member of equation (4.44) are, except for a constant factor, the Fresnel integrals, which have been used by Poisson and Cauchy in problems of water waves and by Fresnel in problems of optics. These Fresnel integrals are defined as

$$(4.47)\qquad C(y) = \frac{1}{\sqrt{2\pi}}\int_0^y \cos\eta \frac{d\eta}{\sqrt{\eta}} \quad ,$$

and

$$(4.48)\qquad S(y) = \frac{1}{\sqrt{2\pi}}\int_0^y \sin\eta \frac{d\eta}{\sqrt{\eta}} \quad ,$$

so that by (4.44)

$$(4.49)\qquad C(y) - iS(y) = \frac{1-i}{2} - \frac{1}{\sqrt{2\pi}} y^{1/2}e^{-iy}F^{(1/2)}(iy) \quad .$$

This formula allows one to derive the asymptotic expansions of C(y) and S(y) from that of $F^{1/2}(z)$.

5. Laplace Integrals at Infinity

It is sometimes convenient to express the function $F^{(\gamma)}(z)$ given by (4.21) as an integral with definite limits. Setting

$$\zeta = z + \hat{\zeta} \tag{5.1}$$

we have

$$F^{(\gamma)}(z) = z^{-1} \int_0^\infty e^{-\hat{\zeta}}(1 + z^{-1}\hat{\zeta})^{-\gamma} d\hat{\zeta} \quad . \tag{5.2}$$

The asymptotic expansion near $z = \infty$ can then simply be obtained by expanding the function $(1 + z^{-1}\hat{\zeta})^{-\gamma}$ in descending powers of z and integrating term by term. Note that one may just as well say that this function is expanded in ascending powers of $\hat{\zeta}$.

Still another method of expressing $F^{(\gamma)}(z)$ is often desirable. Setting

$$\zeta = z + \hat{\zeta} = z(1 + w) \quad , \tag{5.3}$$

we have

$$F^{(\gamma)}(z) = \int_0^\infty e^{-zw}(1 + w)^{-\gamma} dw \quad . \tag{5.4}$$

We note that the asymptotic expansion of $F^{(\gamma)}(z)$ is now obtained by expanding the function $(1 + w)^{-\gamma}$ in ascending powers of w. Thus the behavior of this latter function near $w = 0$ determines the behavior of the integral $F^{(\gamma)}(z)$ near $z = \infty$. This kind of relationship is typical of functions arising from a class of integral transformations which we shall proceed to study quite generally.

Let us consider a function g(z) defined as an integral

$$g(z) = \int_0^\infty e^{-zw}\psi(w) dw \tag{5.5}$$

in terms of another function $\psi(w)$ defined at least for $\operatorname{Re} w \geq 0$ and satisfying certain other conditions to be formulated below. The transformation of the function $\psi(w)$ into the function $g(z)$ is called the Laplace transformation and $g(z)$ is said to be the Laplace transform of $\psi(w)$. Integrals of the type (5.5) are usually referred to as "Laplace integrals".

Suppose that $\psi(w)$ is defined for $w = u$ real, and that ψ is absolutely integrable:

$$(5.6) \qquad \int_0^\infty |\psi(u)| du = C < \infty \quad .$$

Then $g(z)$ is defined in the half-plane $\operatorname{Re} z \geq 0$ by

$$(5.7) \qquad g(z) = \int_0^\infty e^{-zu}\psi(u) du \quad .$$

Furthermore, $g(z)$ is analytic in the open half-plane $\operatorname{Re} z > 0$, and its derivative is given by differentiation under the integral sign:

$$(5.8) \qquad g'(z) = -\int_0^\infty ue^{-zu}\psi(u) du \quad ;$$

the latter integral exists, as for a fixed $z = x + iy$ with $x > 0$ the quantity ue^{-zu} is bounded in u.

According to the remarks made above, we expect that the asymptotic expansion of the function $g(z)$ near $z = \infty$ can be obtained from the expansion of $\psi(w)$ about the point $w = 0$; in fact, only an asymptotic expansion of $\psi(w)$ is needed.

First we assert that, under mild conditions on $\psi(w)$, the function $g(z)$ approaches zero as z tends to infinity.

Theorem 5.1: Let the function $\psi(u)$ be defined in $0 < u < \infty$ and absolutely integrable there (i.e. condition (5.6) holds), and let the function $g(z)$ be defined by (5.7) in the half-plane $\operatorname{Re} z = x \geq 0$. Then

(5.9) $$g(z) \Longrightarrow 0 \quad \text{as } z \longrightarrow \infty \quad \text{and} \quad x \geq 0 \quad ;$$

the double arrow for convergence is used here to remind us that we are speaking of convergence in the complex plane, which must be <u>uniform</u> with respect to arg z.

This theorem is a generalization of the Riemann-Lebesgue theorem on Fourier transforms, to which it reduces when $z = iy$ is purely imaginary. The requirement that $|\psi(u)|$ be integrable near $u = 0$,

(5.10) $$\int_0^1 |\psi(u)|\,du < \infty \quad ,$$

is the important part of condition (5.6); the requirement

(5.11) $$\int_1^\infty |\psi(u)|\,du < \infty$$

of integrability up to $u = \infty$ can be relaxed considerably. It can, for example, be replaced by the weaker condition that

(5.11a) $$\int_1^\infty e^{-\sigma u}\,|\psi(u)|\,du < \infty$$

for an appropriate positive σ. The statements made in the following then hold whenever the restriction $x > 0$ is replaced by the stronger restriction $x > \sigma$. We shall not, however, carry out this modification.

In order to prove Theorem 5.1, we must find for any $\varepsilon > 0$ numbers $x_\varepsilon > 0$ and $y_\varepsilon > 0$ such that

(5.12) $$|g(z)| \leq \varepsilon \quad \text{for} \quad x \geq x_\varepsilon \quad ,$$

(5.13) $$|g(z)| \leq \varepsilon \quad \text{for} \quad |y| \geq y_\varepsilon \quad \text{if} \quad 0 \leq x \leq x_\varepsilon \quad .$$

To establish (5.12) we observe that

$$(5.14)\qquad |e^{-zu}| \leq e^{-ax}$$

for $x \geq 0$ and $u \geq a > 0$, whence

$$(5.15)\qquad |g(z)| \leq \int_0^a |\psi(u)|du + e^{-ax}\int_a^\infty |\psi(u)|du$$

$$\leq \int_0^a |\psi(u)|du + Ce^{-ax} \quad .$$

Now one need only choose $a = a_\varepsilon$ so small that

$$(5.16)\qquad \int_0^{a_\varepsilon} |\psi(u)|du \leq \frac{\varepsilon}{2} \quad ,$$

and then x_ε so large that

$$(5.17)\qquad Ce^{-a_\varepsilon x_\varepsilon} \leq \frac{\varepsilon}{2} \quad .$$

In order to prove statement (5.13) we introduce the function $\tilde{\psi}(u)$ defined by

$$(5.18)\qquad \tilde{\psi}(u) = \begin{cases} \psi(u) & \text{for } u > 0 \\ 0 & \text{for } u \leq 0 \end{cases} \quad ,$$

set

$$(5.19)\qquad \chi(u,x) = \tilde{\psi}(u)e^{-ux} \quad ,$$

and write

$$(5.20)\qquad g(z) = \int_{-\infty}^{\infty} \chi(u,x)e^{-iuy}du \quad .$$

Then we need only make use of the fact that the Riemann-Lebesgue theorem holds uniformly in x for $0 \leq x \leq x_\varepsilon$.

To show that this is so, we observe that g(z) can be written in the form

$$(5.21)\qquad g(z) = -\int_{-\infty}^{\infty} \chi(u,x)e^{-iuy+i\pi}du$$

$$= -\int_{-\infty}^{\infty} \chi(u+\frac{\pi}{y},x)e^{-iuy}du \quad ,$$

whence

$$(5.22)\qquad 2g(z) = \int_{-\infty}^{\infty} [\chi(u,x) - \chi(u+\frac{\pi}{y},x)]e^{-iuy}du \quad ,$$

and

$$(5.23)\qquad |g(z)| \leq \frac{1}{2}\int_{-\infty}^{\infty} |\chi(u,x) - \chi(u+\frac{\pi}{y},x)|du \quad .$$

By virtue of the absolute integrability of $\tilde{\psi}(u)$ a $\delta_\varepsilon > 0$ exists such that

$$(5.24)\qquad \int_{-\infty}^{\infty} |\tilde{\psi}(u+\delta) - \tilde{\psi}(u)|du \leq \varepsilon \quad \text{for} \quad |\delta| \leq \delta_\varepsilon$$

holds. A short derivation of this well-known fact will be given below. As a consequence of it we have

$$(5.25)\qquad \int_{-\infty}^{\infty} |\chi(u+\delta,x) - \chi(u,x)|du \leq \varepsilon + Cx_\varepsilon|\delta|$$

for $|\delta| \leq \delta_\varepsilon$, $0 \leq x \leq x_\varepsilon$. Statement (5.13) then follows if y_ε is chosen so large that

$$(5.26)\qquad \pi/y_\varepsilon \leq \min\,(\delta_\varepsilon, \varepsilon/Cx_\varepsilon) \quad .$$

The validity of statement (5.24) for continuous functions $\tilde{\psi}_c(u)$ which vanish outside some interval $|u| < u_0$ is an immediate consequence of the uniformity of this continuity.

Now, every integrable function $\tilde{\psi}(u)$ can be approximated by a continuous function $\tilde{\psi}_c(u)$ such that

$$(5.24a) \qquad \int |\tilde{\psi}(u) - \tilde{\psi}_c(u)| du \leq \varepsilon/3$$

holds. Hence, also

$$(5.24b) \qquad \int |\tilde{\psi}(u+\delta) - \tilde{\psi}_c(u+\delta)| du \leq \varepsilon/3$$

and we only need choose δ_ε such that (5.24) holds for $\tilde{\psi}_c(u)$ with $\varepsilon/3$ instead of ε.

In the following we shall need a corollary of Theorem 5.1.

<u>Corollary:</u> Assume that, for certain $a \geq 0$ and $\sigma \geq 0$, condition

$$(5.27) \qquad \psi(u) \equiv 0 \quad \text{for} \quad u \leq a$$

and condition (5.11a) hold. Then

$$(5.28) \qquad g(z)e^{az} \Rightarrow 0 \quad \text{as} \quad z \rightarrow \infty \quad \text{with} \quad x \geq \sigma \quad .$$

This statement follows immediately from Theorem 5.1 by using it with $u - a$, $z - \sigma$, $\psi(u)e^{-u\sigma}$, $g(z)e^{az}$ in place of u, z, $\psi(u)$, $g(z)$ respectively. For, we may write

$$(5.29) \qquad g(z)e^{az} = e^{a\sigma} \int_0^\infty e^{-(u-a)(z-\sigma)} \psi(u)e^{-u\sigma} d(u-a) \quad .$$

Note that condition (5.27) on the behavior of $\psi(u)$ near $u = 0$ is stronger than condition (5.10) if $a > 0$, while condition (5.11a) on the behavior of $\psi(u)$ at ∞ is weaker than condition (5.11) if $\sigma > 0$.

The following lemma shows that the function $g(z)$ vanishes more strongly than $z^{-\gamma-1}$ at ∞ if the function $\psi(u)$ vanishes more strongly than u^γ at the origin. Here $\gamma = \alpha + i\beta$ is any number satisfying the condition

$$(5.30) \qquad \alpha > -1 \quad .$$

Lemma 5.1: Suppose the function $\psi(u)$ satisfies condition

(5.31) $$u^{-\gamma}\psi(u) \longrightarrow 0 \quad \text{as} \quad u \longrightarrow 0 \quad ,$$

in addition to condition (5.6). Then for the function $g(z)$ defined by (5.7) the relation

(5.32) $$z^{\gamma+1}g(z) \Longrightarrow 0 \quad \text{as} \quad z \longrightarrow \infty$$

holds in every sector

$$\mathcal{S}_\tau : \qquad |\arg z| \leq \frac{\pi}{2} - \tau , \quad \tau > 0 \quad .$$

Proof: For an arbitrary $a > 0$ we set

(5.33) $$g(z) = k_a(z) + g_a(z) \quad ,$$

with

(5.34) $$k_a(z) = \int_0^a e^{-uz}\psi(u)du \quad ,$$

$$g_a(z) = \int_a^\infty e^{-uz}\psi(u)du \quad .$$

To every $\varepsilon_1 > 0$ we may choose an $a = a(\varepsilon_1) > 0$ such that

(5.35) $$|u^{-\alpha}\psi(u)| = |u^{-\gamma}\psi(u)| \leq \varepsilon_1$$

if $0 < u \leq a$. Hence

(5.36) $$|k_a(z)| \leq \varepsilon_1 \int_0^a e^{-ux}u^\alpha du$$

$$\leq \varepsilon_1 \int_0^\infty e^{-ux}u^\alpha du = \varepsilon_1 \alpha! x^{-\alpha-1} \quad .$$

The symbol $\alpha!$ is here defined in terms of the Eulerian gamma function:

(5.37) $$\alpha! = \Gamma(\alpha+1) = \int_0^\infty e^{-s}s^\alpha ds$$

and possesses the property

(5.38) $$\alpha!(\alpha+1) = (\alpha+1)!$$

characteristic of ordinary factorials. Clearly, setting

(5.39) $$\theta_\gamma = [\cos \tau]^{-\alpha-1}e^{\beta\pi/2} \quad ,$$

we have

(5.40) $$x^{-\alpha-1} \leq \theta_\gamma |z^{-\gamma-1}|$$

for z in $\mathcal{S}_\tau$, so that

(5.41) $$|z^{\gamma+1}||k_a(z)| \leq \varepsilon_1 \alpha! \theta_\gamma = \varepsilon_2 \quad .$$

According to the corollary to Theorem 5.1 there is an $x_\varepsilon > 0$ such that

(5.42) $$|g_a(z)| \leq \varepsilon e^{-ax} \quad \text{for} \quad x \geq x_\varepsilon \quad ,$$

whence

(5.43) $$|z^{\gamma+1}||g_a(z)| \leq \varepsilon\theta_\gamma x^{\alpha+1}e^{-ax}$$

$$\leq \varepsilon\theta_\gamma \left(\frac{\alpha+1}{a}\right)^{\alpha+1}e^{-\alpha-1} = \varepsilon_3 \quad .$$

Thus we have

(5.44) $$|z^{\gamma+1}g(z)| \leq \varepsilon_2 + \varepsilon_3 \quad \text{for} \quad x \geq x_\varepsilon \quad .$$

To a given $\varepsilon_0 > 0$ we set $\varepsilon_2 = \varepsilon_0/2$, $\varepsilon_1 = \varepsilon_2/\alpha!\theta_\gamma$, fix $a = a(\varepsilon_1)$, choose ε so small that $\varepsilon_3 \leq \varepsilon_0/2$, and finally determine x_ε by the corollary of Theorem 5.1. Then for $x \geq x_\varepsilon$, thus surely for z in $\mathcal{S}_\tau$ and satisfying

(5.45) $$|z| \geq [\cos \tau]^{-1}x_\varepsilon$$

we have

(5.46) $$|z^{\gamma+1} g(z)| \leq \varepsilon_0 \quad ,$$

as desired.

Corollary: Lemma 5.1 holds without restriction even if condition (5.6) on $\delta(u)$ is replaced by the weaker conditions (5.10), (5.11a).

We use the lemma to prove

Theorem 5.2: Assume that the function $\psi(u)$ possesses near $u = 0$ an asymptotic expansion of the form

(5.47) $$\psi(u) = \sum_{n=0}^{N} c_n u^{\gamma_n} + \rho_N(u)$$

in which the $\gamma_n = \alpha_n + i\beta_n$ are numbers satisfying the condition

(5.48) $$-1 < \alpha_0 < \alpha_1 < \dots < \alpha_N$$

while the function $\rho_N(u)$ satisfies the conditions

(5.49) $$u^{-\gamma_N} \rho_N(u) \longrightarrow 0 \quad \text{as} \quad u = 0 \quad ,$$

(5.50) $$\int_{-\infty}^{\infty} |\rho_N(u)|\, du < \infty \quad .$$

Then the function

(5.51) $$g(z) = \int_0^{\infty} e^{-zu} \psi(u)\, du \quad ,$$

defined for $\operatorname{Re} z = x \geq 0$, has the asymptotic expansion

(5.52) $$g(z) = \sum_{n=0}^{N} \gamma_n! \, z^{-\gamma_n - 1} + r_N(z) \quad ,$$

with

(5.53) $$z^{\gamma_N + 1} r_N(z) \longrightarrow 0 \quad \text{as} \quad z \longrightarrow \infty \quad ,$$

in the sector $|\arg z| \leq \frac{\pi}{2} - \tau$, $\tau > 0$.

This statement--except for minor modifications in the formulation--is referred to as Watson's Lemma in the literature; apparently it was first formulated and proved by Watson in 1918.

To prove the theorem we substitute (5.47) into (5.51), first using the identity

$$\int_0^\infty e^{-zu} u^{\gamma_n} du = \gamma_n! z^{-\gamma_n - 1} , \tag{5.54}$$

and then applying Lemma 5.1 with the remainder $\rho_N(u)$ as kernel instead of $\psi(u)$.

The asymptotic expansion (5.47) is of the more general type described earlier, cf. (1.6). The question naturally arises whether or not this expansion is unique, i.e. whether or not the coefficients c_n are uniquely determined by the function $\psi(u)$. Because of assumption (5.48), the expansion is unique; this can be shown by the same kind of reasoning as was used to prove the uniqueness of the asymptotic power series expansion.

As an example in which Theorem 5.2 can be applied we consider the Hankel functions of order zero:

$$H^{(\varepsilon)}(z) = -\frac{2\varepsilon i}{\pi} \int_{-\varepsilon i}^{\infty} e^{-zt}[1+t^2]^{-1/2} dt \quad ; \quad \varepsilon = \pm 1 , \tag{5.55}$$

where the path of integration can be taken as the horizontal ray

$$\operatorname{Im} t = -\varepsilon \quad , \quad 0 \le \operatorname{Re} t < \infty , \tag{5.56}$$

and the square root $[1+t^2]^{-1/2}$ is so chosen as to be asymptotic to t^{-1} for large values of Re t. Our $H^{(-1)}$ is the function denoted in the literature by $H^{(2)}$. To bring the lower limit into the point 0 we set

$$t + \varepsilon i = w , \tag{5.57}$$

obtaining

$$(5.58)\quad H^{(\varepsilon)}(z) = \frac{2}{\pi} e^{\varepsilon i(z-\frac{\pi}{4})} \int_0^\infty e^{-zw}(2w+\varepsilon iw^2)^{-1/2}dw \quad .$$

Since the function $\psi^{(\varepsilon)}(w) = (2w+\varepsilon iw^2)^{-1/2}$ has the binomial expansion

$$(5.59)\quad \psi^{(\varepsilon)}(w) = 2^{-1/2}w^{-1/2} - 2^{-5/2}\varepsilon iw^{1/2} - 3\cdot 2^{-11/2}w^{3/2} + \ldots$$

near $w = 0$, the function $H^{(\varepsilon)}(z)$ has near $z = \infty$ the asymptotic expansion

$$(5.60)\quad H^{(\varepsilon)}(z) \sim \sqrt{\frac{2}{\pi z}}\, e^{\varepsilon i(z-\frac{\pi}{4})}[1 - \tfrac{1}{8}\varepsilon iz^{-1} - \tfrac{9}{128}z^{-2} + \ldots] \quad ,$$

valid in every sector $|\arg z| \leq \frac{\pi}{2} - \tau$. We obtain this expansion directly from Theorem 5.2 with $\gamma_n = n - \frac{1}{2}$, recalling that

$$(5.61)\quad (-\tfrac{1}{2})! = \Gamma(\tfrac{1}{2}) = \int_0^\infty e^{-s}s^{-1/2}ds = 2\int_0^\infty e^{-t^2}dt = \sqrt{\pi} \quad .$$

The statement of Theorem 5.2 refers only to the asymptotic behavior of $g(z)$ in the sector $|\arg z| \leq \frac{\pi}{2} - \tau$. For later applications it is important to know the asymptotic behavior of $g(z)$ in the whole half-plane $|\arg z| \leq \frac{\pi}{2}$. This behavior can be determined if one has more information about the remainder $\rho_N(u)$ than supplied by condition (5.49). We restrict ourselves to giving such a condition in the case $N = 0$.

<u>Theorem 5.3</u>: Assume that the function $\psi(u)$ possesses an asymptotic expansion near $u = 0$ of the form

$$(5.62)\qquad \psi(u) = c_0 u^{\gamma_0} + \rho_0(u)$$

in which $\gamma_0 = \alpha_0 + i\beta_0$ with

$$(5.63)\qquad -1 < \alpha_0 < 0 \quad .$$

Further assume that the function $\rho_o(u)$ possesses for $0 < u \leq a$ a continuous derivative $\rho_o'(u)$ which is absolutely integrable:

$$(5.64) \qquad \int_0^a |\rho_o'(u)|du < \infty \quad ,$$

and that

$$(5.65) \qquad \rho_o(u) \longrightarrow \quad \text{as} \quad u \longrightarrow 0 \quad .$$

Then the function $k_a(z)$ defined by (5.34) is of the form

$$(5.66) \qquad k_a(z) = c_o\gamma_o!z^{-\gamma_o-1} - \psi(a)z^{-1}e^{-az} + m_1(z)$$

with

$$(5.67) \qquad zm_1(z) \Longrightarrow 0 \quad \text{as} \quad z \longrightarrow \infty \ , \quad x \geq 0 \quad .$$

For the proof we need only verify by partial integration the identity

$$(5.68) \qquad k_a(z) = c_o \int_0^\infty e^{-uz}u^{\gamma_o}du$$

$$- c_oz^{-1}e^{-az}a^{\gamma_o} - c_o\gamma_oz^{-1}\int_a^\infty e^{-uz}u^{\gamma_o-1}du$$

$$- \rho_c(a)z^{-1}e^{-az} + z^{-1}\int_0^a e^{-uz}\rho_o'(u)du \quad ,$$

and apply Theorem 5.1 to estimate the integrals $\int_a^\infty e^{-uz}u^{\gamma_o-1}du$ and $\int_0^a e^{-uz}\rho_o'(u)du$ for large $|z|$.

If the function $\psi(u)$ of the real argument u results from an analytic function $\psi(w)$ of a complex variable w defined in a sector

$$(5.69) \qquad \mathcal{S}_-^+ : \quad -\Theta_- \leq \arg w \leq \Theta_+ \quad ,$$

the function $g(z)$ can be continued analytically beyond the lines $\arg z = \pm \frac{\pi}{2}$, provided the function $\psi(w)$ is absolutely integrable:

$$(5.70) \qquad \int_0^\infty |\psi(w)dw| < \infty$$

on each ray $\arg w =$ const. in the sector $\mathcal{S}_-^+$, and provided that for some real constant b

$$(5.71) \qquad |\psi(w)| \leq e^{b|w|}$$

holds for all w in this sector. To show this it is convenient to introduce the new variables

$$(5.72) \qquad \tilde{z} = ze^{-i\theta} \quad , \quad \tilde{w} = we^{i\theta}$$

with the aid of an angle θ which will be appropriately restricted later. Expressing z and w in the expression (5.5) for $g(z)$ in terms of $\tilde{z}$ and $\tilde{w}$, we have

$$(5.73) \quad g(\tilde{z}e^{i\theta}) = e^{-i\theta} \int_0^\infty e^{-\tilde{z}\tilde{w}}\psi(\tilde{w}e^{-i\theta})d\tilde{w} \quad ,$$

the integration being extended on the ray on which $\tilde{w}e^{-i\theta}$ is real. Since $\psi(w)$ is defined in $\mathcal{S}_-^+$, the function $\psi(\tilde{w}e^{-i\theta})$ is defined in the sector

$$(5.74) \qquad \mathcal{S}_-^+(\theta): \qquad -\Theta_- + \theta \leq \arg \tilde{w} \leq \Theta_+ + \theta \quad .$$

We want to restrict the angle θ so that this sector contains the ray $\arg \tilde{w} = 0$ (or $\tilde{w} = \tilde{u} \geq 0$). To this end we require

$$(5.75) \qquad -\Theta_+ \leq \theta \leq \Theta_- \quad .$$

In view of condition (5.71) we may deform the path of integration in (5.73) into the positive real axis $\tilde{w} = \tilde{u}$. Having done so we may apply our previous results to the function $g(\tilde{z}e^{i\theta})$ instead of $g(z)$. In particular, we know that the function $g(\tilde{z}e^{i\theta})$ is defined when $\tilde{z}$ is in the half plane

$$(5.76) \qquad -\frac{\pi}{2} \leq \arg \tilde{z} \leq \frac{\pi}{2} \quad .$$

By virtue of definition (5.72) this is equivalent to the half plane

$$-\frac{\pi}{2} + \theta \leq \arg z \leq \frac{\pi}{2} + \theta \quad .$$

Since θ may be any angle satisfying the function $g(z)$ is defined in the sector

$$(5.77) \qquad -\frac{\pi}{2} - \Theta_+ \leq \arg z \leq \frac{\pi}{2} + \Theta_- \quad .$$

The function $g(z)$ can therefore be continued analytically.

Applying Theorem 5.2 to the function $g(\tilde{z}e^{i\theta})$, we see that the asymptotic expansion of the function $g(z)$ can be continued into the sector

$$(5.78) \qquad -\frac{\pi}{2} - \Theta_+ + \tau \leq \arg z \leq \frac{\pi}{2} + \Theta_- - \tau \quad .$$

However, a Stokes phenomenon may be expected if the function $g(z)$ is continued beyond the sector (5.77).

We apply these remarks to the Hankel functions $H^{(\varepsilon)}(z)$. Since the function $(2w + \varepsilon i w^2)^{-1/2}$ is regular in the sector

$$(5.79a) \qquad -\frac{3\pi}{2} < \arg w < \frac{\pi}{2} \quad \text{for} \quad \varepsilon = 1 \quad ,$$

$$(5.79b) \qquad -\frac{\pi}{2} < \arg w < \frac{3\pi}{2} \quad \text{for} \quad \varepsilon = -1 \quad ,$$

the asymptotic expansion of the Hankel function, given by (5.60), is valid in the sectors

$$(5.80a)\qquad -\pi+\tau \le \arg z \le 2\pi-\tau \quad \text{for} \quad \varepsilon = 1 \quad ,$$

$$(5.80b)\qquad -2\pi+\tau \le \arg z \le \pi-\tau \quad \text{for} \quad \varepsilon = -1 \quad .$$

From formula (5.60) one observes that both Hankel functions die out exponentially in the "middle" half planes

$$(5.81)\qquad \left|\arg z - \varepsilon\frac{\pi}{2}\right| < \frac{\pi}{2} \quad ,$$

while they increase exponentially in the "outer" sectors

$$(5.82)\qquad \frac{\pi}{2} < \left|\arg z - \varepsilon\frac{\pi}{2}\right| < \frac{3\pi}{2} \quad .$$

Thus the asymptotic "behavior" of the function $g(z)$ "jumps" at the lines $\arg z = 0$ and $\arg z = \varepsilon\pi$, while the asymptotic <u>expansion</u> does not have a jump until one crosses the lines $\arg z = \varepsilon\frac{\pi}{2} \pm \frac{3\pi}{2}$. These remarkable facts will be seen later on to be typical for the most significant features of the asymptotic behavior of the solution of differential equations.

Finally, we indicate how to obtain the continuation of the asymptotic expansion beyond the "Stokes" lines. All that is necessary is to express the jump of $g(z)$ when z makes a full circuit. We assume that the function $\psi(w)$ is regular in the exterior of the circle $|w| = R$. Clearly, we then have

$$(5.83)\qquad g(ze^{2\pi i}) - g(z) = -\oint_{|w|=R} e^{-zw}\psi(w)\,dw \quad .$$

Accordingly, the asymptotic expansion of $g(ze^{2\pi i})$ differs from that of $g(z)$ by the expansion of the jump

$$(5.84)\qquad [g(z)] = -\oint_{|w|=R} e^{-zw}\psi(w)\,dw \quad .$$

To obtain the latter expansion one deforms the path $|w| = R$ into a path on which the minimum of $u = \text{Re } w$ is as large (algebraically) as possible. Let u_0 be the largest value of u such that $\psi(w)$ is regular for $u < u_0$. Then it may be expected, at least for real z, that the asymptotic behavior of the jump $[g(z)]$ is essentially described by the function $e^{-u_0 z}$. Since $u_0 < 0$, under the circumstances considered, the jump should show an exponential increase, while the function $g(z)$ itself behaves like a power of z. Thus the presence of an actual Stokes phenomenon is indicated.

6. Laplace Integrals at the Origin

Since the asymptotic expansion near $z = \infty$ of the Laplace transform of the function $\psi(u)$ depends on the asymptotic expansion of $\psi(u)$ near $u = 0$, we expect that the behavior of the transform near $z = 0$ depends on the behavior of $\psi(u)$ at infinity.

In order to find out whether or not this is so we first consider the function

$$(6.1) \qquad F(z) = F^{(1)}(z) = \int_0^\infty e^{-zu}(1+u)^{-1}du \quad .$$

This function evidently is not ddfined for $z = 0$, as the integral diverges there. In order to investigate the behavior of $F(z)$ near this singular point $z = 0$ we first integrate by parts:

$$(6.2) \qquad F(z) = z \int_0^\infty e^{-zu} \log (1+u)du \quad ;$$

the boundary terms vanish if, as we assume, the real part x of z is positive. Next we write $F(z)$ in the form

$$(6.3) \qquad F(z) = Q(z) + R_0(z) \quad ,$$

with

(6.4) $$Q(z) = -z \int_{-1}^{0} e^{-zu} \log(1+u)du \quad ,$$

(6.5) $$R_o(z) = z \int_{-1}^{\infty} e^{-zu} \log(1+u)du \quad .$$

The reason for this split is that the function $R_o(z)$ can be evaluated explicitly, while the function $Q(z)$ is regular at $z = 0$. The latter fact is obvious, since $\log(1+u)$ is absolutely integrable up to $u = -1$. In order to evaluate $R_o(z)$ explicitly, we introduce the variable $\xi = z(1+u)$, and find

(6.6) $$R_o(z) = -[C + \log z]e^{z} \quad ,$$

where C is "Euler's constant", defined by

(6.7) $$C = -\int_{0}^{\infty} e^{-\xi} \log \xi \, d\xi$$

and with a numerical value of approximately 0.577. Consequently, the behavior of $F(z)$ at $z = 0$ is given by the formula

(6.8) $$F(z) = -e^{z} \log z + Q_o(z) \quad ,$$

in which

(6.9) $$Q_o(z) = -Ce^{z} + Q(z)$$

is a function regular at $z = 0$. By expanding $Q_o(z)$ and e^z in ascending powers of z, we obtain an expansion of $F(z)$ in terms of the functions

$$\log z,\ 1,\ z \log z,\ z,\ z^2 \log z,\ z^2, \ldots,$$

which begins as follows:

(6.10) $$F(z) = -\log z - C - z \log z + (1-c)z + \ldots \quad .$$

The expansion of $F(z) + \log z$ is uniform in every sector with vertex at $z = 0$ and $\beta < \frac{\pi}{2}$, but it is not a power series expansion. Still we may consider such expansions as generalized asymptotic expansions.

Let us now consider the general Laplace integral

$$(6.11) \qquad g(z) = \int_0^\infty e^{-zu}\psi(u)du$$

and assume that the function $\psi(u)$ is absolutely integrable in every finite interval:

$$(6.12) \qquad \int_0^a |\psi(u)|du < \infty \quad ,$$

while at $u = \infty$, $\psi(u)$ possesses an asymptotic expansion

$$(6.13) \qquad \psi(u) = \sum_{n=0}^{N} c_n u^{-\gamma_n} + \rho_N(u) \quad ,$$

valid for $u > R$, with

$$(6.14) \qquad u^{\gamma_N}\rho_N(u) \to 0 \quad \text{as} \quad u \to \infty \quad .$$

Since the function

$$(6.15) \qquad k_R(z) = \int_0^R e^{-zu}\psi(u)du$$

is regular at $z = 0$ in virtue of condition (6.12), it is sufficient to consider the function

$$(6.16) \qquad g_R(z) = \int_R^\infty e^{-zu}\psi(u)du \quad .$$

We first consider a typical term of $g_R(z)$ obtained by substituting into (6.16) the expansion (6.13) of $\psi(u)$, namely the term

$$(6.17)\qquad g_R^{(\gamma)}(z) = \int_R^\infty e^{-zu}u^{-\gamma}du \quad .$$

To evaluate $g_R^{(\gamma)}(z)$, we first suppose that the real part of γ is less than 1:

$$(6.18)\qquad \alpha = \mathrm{Re}\ \gamma < 1 \quad .$$

The corresponding function

$$(6.19)\qquad g^{(\gamma)}(z) = \int_0^\infty e^{-zu}u^{-\gamma}du$$

can then be evaluated explicitly:

$$(6.20)\qquad g^{(\gamma)}(z) = (-\gamma)!z^{\gamma-1} \quad ,$$

while the finite portion

$$(6.21)\qquad k_R^{(\gamma)}(z) = \int_0^R e^{-zu}u^{-\gamma}du$$

is regular at $z = 0$. Thus we obtain the expansion of $g_R^{(\gamma)}(z)$ near $z = 0$ by writing

$$(6.22)\qquad g_R^{(\gamma)}(z) = (-\gamma)!z^{\gamma-1} - k_R^{(\gamma)}(z)$$

and expanding $k_R^{(\gamma)}(z)$ in powers of z.

In case $\gamma = 1$, we integrate by parts, obtaining

$$(6.23)\qquad g_R^{(1)}(z) = z\int_R^\infty e^{-zu}\log(u/R)du$$

$$= -[C + \log Rz] - z\int_0^R e^{-zu}\log(u/R)du \quad .$$

Since the latter integral is regular at $z = 0$ the behavior of $g_R^{(1)}(z)$ is established.

If $\gamma \neq 1$ and $1 \leq \alpha < 2$ we can also integrate by parts and proceed as above, obtaining

$$(6.24) \qquad g_R^{(\gamma)}(z) = \frac{R^{-\gamma+1}}{\gamma-1} e^{-zR} + \frac{z}{\gamma-1} g_R^{(\gamma-1)}(z)$$

$$= -(-\gamma)! z^{\gamma-1} - \frac{1}{\gamma-1} z k_R^{(\gamma-1)}(z) + \frac{R^{-\gamma+1}}{\gamma-1} e^{-zR} ,$$

having used formula (6.22) for $\gamma-1$ instead of γ. Since the last two terms in expression (6.24) are regular at $z = 0$, the behavior of $g_R^{(\gamma)}(z)$ near $z = 0$ is determined for this case also.

In case $m \leq \alpha < m+1$ the function $g_R^{(\gamma)}(z)$ can be reduced to cases already treated by m-1 integrations by parts; the boundary terms introduced will in every case be regular at $z = 0$.

We want to make use of these results in the determination of the behavior of the function $g(z)$ given by (6.11) in terms of a function $\psi(u)$ satisfying the conditions (6.12), (6.13). The behavior of the contributions from the first $N+1$ terms on the right hand side of (6.13) are already completely determined. In order to determine the behavior of the contribution due to the remainder $\rho_N(u)$ we set

$$(6.25) \qquad \hat{g}(z) = \int_R^{\infty} e^{-zu} \rho_N(u)\,du$$

and determine a non-negative integer κ such that

$$(6.26) \qquad \int_R^{\infty} u^{\kappa} \rho_N(u)\,du < \infty \quad .$$

As seen from (6.14) any integer $\kappa < \gamma_N - 1$ satisfies this condition. It is then clear that the function $\hat{g}(z)$ possesses derivatives with respect to z up to the order κ which are continuous at $z = 0$. The finite Taylor series of order κ of the function $\hat{g}(z)$ then gives the behavior of this function near $z = 0$.

This result is not quite satisfactory, since the remainder term in the latter series may be of a lower order than the highest term of the contribution from the first N+1 terms on the right hand side of (6.13). This defect could be remedied after imposing appropriate additional conditions. However, we do not attempt to do so.

We now consider the special case in which the function $\psi(u)$ results from an analytic function $\psi(w)$ which is defined for $|w| \geq R_0$ and regular at infinity. From the preceding considerations it is clear that the Laplace transform g(z) given by (6.11) possesses an expansion in terms of $\log z, 1, z \log z, z, z^2 \log z, \ldots$. We want to show that it is possible to write the function g(z) in the form

(6.27) $$g(z) = g_0(z) \log z + g_1(z)$$

with analytic functions $g_0(z)$ and $g_1(z)$ which are regular at $z = 0$.

To this end we write g(z) in the form

(6.28) $$g(z) = g_R(z) + k_R(z)$$

with $g_R(z)$ and $k_R(z)$ given by (6.15) and (6.16) for some $R > R_0$. Since $k_R(z)$ is regular at $z = 0$ we need pay attention only to the function $g_R(z)$.

Using Cauchy's integral representation

(6.29) $$\psi(w) = \frac{1}{2\pi i} \oint_{|\zeta|=R_0} (w - \zeta)^{-1} \psi(\zeta) d\zeta \quad ,$$

valid for $|w| > R_0$, we may write

$$(6.30) \qquad g_R(z) = \frac{1}{2\pi i} \int_R^\infty \oint_{|\zeta|=R_0} e^{-zw}(w-\zeta)^{-1}\psi(\zeta)d\zeta dw$$

$$= \frac{1}{2\pi i} \oint_{|\zeta|=R_0} \left\{ \int_R^\infty e^{-zw}(w-\zeta)^{-1}dw \right\} \psi(\zeta)d\zeta \quad ;$$

the interchange of order of integration is justified by the rapidity of convergence of the exponential factor, since we have assumed Re $z > 0$. The function in the braces happens to be equal to $e^{-z\zeta}g^{(1)}_{R-\zeta}(z)$; cf. (6.17). Its behavior near $z = 0$ will, however, be independently derived. We find

$$(6.31) \qquad \int_R^\infty e^{-zw}(w-\zeta)^{-1}dw$$

$$= z \int_R^\infty e^{-zw} \log (w-\zeta)dw - e^{-zR} \log (R-\zeta)$$

$$= -z \int_\zeta^R e^{-zw} \log (w-\zeta)dw - e^{-zR} \log (R-\zeta)$$

$$- e^{-z\zeta}[C + \log z] \quad .$$

Insertion into (6.30) indeed yields the representation (6.27) with

$$(6.32) \qquad g_o(z) = - \frac{1}{2\pi i} \oint_{|\zeta|=R_0} e^{-z\zeta}\psi(\zeta)d\zeta$$

and

$$(6.33) \qquad g_1(z) = - \frac{1}{2\pi i} \oint_{|\zeta|=R_0} \left\{ e^{-zR} \log (R-\zeta) + Ce^{-z\zeta} \right.$$

$$\left. + z \int_\zeta^R e^{-zw} \log (w-\zeta)dw \right\} \psi(\zeta)d\zeta \quad .$$

Clearly, the functions $g_0(z)$ and $g_1(z)$ are regular at $z = 0$.

As an application of this result we may consider the Hankel functions (5.58). The relevant function

$$(6.34)\qquad \psi(w) = \psi^{(\varepsilon)}(w) = (2w + \varepsilon i w^2)^{-1/2}$$

is regular for $|w| \geq R_0 > 1$, as by definition it is $e^{-\varepsilon i \frac{\pi}{4}} w^{-1}$ near $w = \infty$. Thus the corresponding function $g_0(z)$ is given by

$$(6.35)\qquad g_0(z) = g_0^{(\varepsilon)}(z) = -\frac{1}{2\pi i} \oint_{|\zeta|=R_0} e^{-z\zeta}(2\zeta + \varepsilon i \zeta^2)^{-1/2} d\zeta$$

$$= \frac{\varepsilon}{2\pi} e^{-\varepsilon i (z - \frac{\pi}{4})} \oint_{|t|=2} e^{-zt}(1+t^2)^{-1/2} dt$$

$$= \varepsilon i e^{-\varepsilon i (z - \frac{\pi}{4})} J_0(z) \quad ,$$

where $J_0(z)$ is the Bessel function of order zero. Consequently, the function

$$(6.36)\qquad H^{(\varepsilon)}(z) - \frac{2\varepsilon i}{\pi} J_0(z) \log z$$

is regular at $z = 0$. This formula gives the well-known description of the behavior of the Hankel functions near $z = 0$.

The decomposition (6.27) of the Laplace transform $g(z)$ is valid, not only for a small neighborhood of $z = 0$, but also for z in any circle about the origin in which resulting functions $g_0(z)$ and $g_1(z)$ given by (6.32) and (6.33) remain analytic. This follows immediately from the method of proof used. In the case of the Hankel functions, in particular, the corresponding Bessel function $J_0(z)$ is analytic for all z, so that (6.36) can even be used to study the behavior of the Hankel functions at infinity and to determine their jumps and Stokes phenomenon from properties of the much better known function $J_0(z)$. We shall not carry this out in detail here.

7. Bromwich Integrals

Closely related to the Laplace integrals are the integrals

$$(7.1)\qquad \psi(t) = \frac{1}{2\pi i}\int_{\uparrow} e^{zt} g(z)\,dz$$

in which g(z) is an analytic function defined in the right half plane $x > 0$ and the symbol $\uparrow$ indicates any path

$$x = x_0 > 0 \quad , \quad -\infty < y < \infty \quad .$$

Such a path in connection with the integral (7.1) is frequently referred to as a Bromwich path, and therefore we find it convenient to refer to this integral as the Bromwich integral.

On the function g(z) we impose the conditions

$$(7.2)\qquad \int_{-\infty}^{\infty} |g(x+iy)|\,dy < \infty \quad \text{for} \quad x > 0 \quad ,$$

$$(7.3)\qquad \int_{-\infty}^{\infty} |g(x+iy)|\,dy \longrightarrow 0 \quad \text{as} \quad x \longrightarrow 0 \quad ,$$

and

$$(7.4)\qquad g(x+iy) \Rightarrow 0 \text{ uniformly as } |y| \longrightarrow \infty ,$$

$$0 < x_1 \leq x \leq x_2 < \infty \quad .$$

Clearly, the integral (7.1) is then defined for $t \geq 0$ and continuous in t, as follows from (7.2); because of (7.4), its value is independent of the position $x = x_0$ of the path. Thus we may immediately estimate $\psi(0)$ by moving the path as far to the right as we please. We find from (7.3) that the integral expression (7.1) for $\psi(0)$ approaches zero as $x_0 \longrightarrow \infty$; since $\psi(0)$ is independent of x_0, we have

$$(7.5)\qquad \psi(0) = 0 \quad .$$

The Bromwich integral is in a sense the inverse of the of the Laplace integral. Their precise relationship is apparent from

Theorem 7.1: For $\xi = \operatorname{Re} \zeta > 0$ and $\psi(t)$ as given by (7.1),

$$(7.6) \qquad \int_0^\infty e^{-\zeta t}\psi(t)dt = g(\zeta)$$

holds.

To prove this theorem, we take any positive $x < \xi$ and compute

$$(7.7) \qquad \int_0^{t_0} e^{-\zeta t}\psi(t)dt = \frac{1}{2\pi i}\int_0^{t_0} e^{-\zeta t}\left[\int_\uparrow e^{zt}g(z)dz\right]dt$$

$$= \frac{1}{2\pi i}\int_\uparrow\left[\int_0^{t_0} e^{(z-\zeta)t}dt\right]g(z)dz$$

$$= \frac{1}{2\pi i}\int_\uparrow (z-\zeta)^{-1}\left[e^{(z-\zeta)t_0} - 1\right]g(z)dz \quad ,$$

where the interchange of order of integration is justified by condition (7.4) on $g(z)$ and by the fact that in the region of integration $|e^{(z-\zeta)t}| \leq 1$. For the same reasons we can let t_0 approach infinity under the integral sign, obtaining

$$(7.8) \qquad \int_0^\infty e^{-\zeta t}\psi(t)dt = -\frac{1}{2\pi i}\int_\uparrow (z-\zeta)^{-1}g(z)dz \quad .$$

Because of conditions (7.3) and (7.4), this latter integral is equal to the residue of its integrand at the point $z = \zeta$, namely to $g(\zeta)$. This proves Theorem 7.1.

Our main interest lies in the investigation of the behavior of $\psi(t)$ as $t \to \infty$. We easily derive the statement

(7.9) $$e^{-\xi t}\psi(t) \longrightarrow 0 \quad \text{as} \quad t \longrightarrow \infty \quad \text{for any} \quad \xi = 0 \quad ,$$

by taking as path of integration $x = x_0$ with $0 < x_0 < \xi$. In order to obtain more refined information we must push the path of integration as much as possible to the left, i.e. towards $x = -\infty$. To what extent this can be done depends on the nature of the function $g(z)$.

If the function $g(z)$ permits an analytic continuation into the half plane $x = \text{Re } z > \tilde{x}$, and properties (7.2), (7.4) hold there, relation (7.9) also holds for any $\xi > \tilde{x}$. Thus, if $\tilde{x} < 0$, the function $\psi(t)$ is seen to die out exponentially as $t \longrightarrow \infty$.

To obtain more specific information assume that the function $g(z)$ branches at a point $z_0 = x_0 + iy_0$ with $x_0 \leq 0$ and is otherwise defined in a half plane $x \geq x_1$ with $x_1 < x_0$. In this case, $g(z)$ is defined even for $y = y_0$, $x \geq x_1$, but may assume different values according as y approaches y_0 from $y > y_0$ or $y < y_0$. We even allow $g(z)$ to be infinite at $z = z_0$, provided that $|g(z)|$ is integrable on any straight path through $z = z_0$.

In order to investigate the behavior of $\psi(t)$ as $t \longrightarrow \infty$, we deform the path $x > 0$, $-\infty < y < \infty$ into the path

(7.10) $$\mathcal{P} = \mathcal{P}_1^- + \mathcal{P}_0^- - \mathcal{P}_0^+ + \mathcal{P}_1^+$$

consisting of the lines

(7.11a) $$\mathcal{P}_1^-: \quad x = x_1 \quad , \qquad -\infty < y \leq y_0 - 0 \quad ,$$

(7.11b) $$\mathcal{P}_0^-: \quad y = y_0 - 0 \quad , \qquad x_1 \leq x \leq x_0 \quad ,$$

(7.11c) $$\mathcal{P}_0^+: \quad y = y_0 + 0 \quad , \qquad x_1 \leq x \leq x_0 \quad ,$$

(7.11d) $$\mathcal{P}_1^+: \quad x = x_1 \quad , \qquad y_0 + 0 \leq y < \infty \quad .$$

The symbols $y_o \pm 0$ indicate that the value y_o is to be approached from the regions $y > y_o$ and $y < y_o$ respectively. We set

$$(7.12) \qquad \mathcal{P}_1 = \mathcal{P}_1^- + \mathcal{P}_1^+$$

and introduce the jump

$$(7.13) \qquad [g(z)] = g(z + i0) - g(z - i0)$$

for z on $\mathcal{P}_o^-$ or $\mathcal{P}_o^+$. Then we may write

$$(7.14) \qquad \psi(t) = \psi_o(t) + \psi_1(t) \quad ,$$

with

$$(7.15) \qquad \psi_o(t) = -\frac{1}{2\pi i} \int_{\mathcal{P}_o^-} e^{zt}[g(z)]dz$$

and

$$(7.16) \qquad \psi_1(t) = \frac{1}{2\pi i} \int_{\mathcal{P}_1} e^{zt} g(z)dz$$

It is clear that $\psi_1(t)$ dies out more strongly than $e^{x_o t}$; indeed,

$$(7.17) \qquad e^{-\xi t}\psi_1(t) \longrightarrow 0 \quad \text{as} \quad t \longrightarrow \infty \quad \text{for any} \quad \xi > x_1 \quad .$$

The asymptotic behavior of $\psi(t)$ is therefore given by that of the contribution $\psi_o(t)$. Setting

$$(7.18) \qquad z = z_o - u \quad ,$$

the function $\psi_o(t)$ may be written in the form

$$(7.19) \qquad \psi_o(t) = -\frac{1}{2\pi i} e^{z_o t} \int_0^{x_o - x_1} e^{-ut}[g(z_o - u)]du \quad .$$

Thus the function $e^{-z_o t}\psi_o(t)$ is seen to be a Laplace integral--provided that the function $[g(z_o-u)]$ is continued to be zero for $u > x_o-x_1$. The results about the asymptotic behavior of Laplace integrals, derived in Section 5, therefore yield, under the circumstances assumed, the asymptotic behavior of the Bromwich integral.

Let in particular $g(z)$ have the asymptotic expansion

$$(7.20) \qquad g(z) \sim \sum_\nu c_\nu (z-z_o)^{\delta_\nu - 1}$$

near the branch point $z = z_o$, valid in the slit plane $|\arg (z-z_o)| \leq \pi$. Since

$$(7.21) \qquad z_o - u + 0i = z_o + ue^{\pi i} , \qquad z_o - u - 0i = z_o + ue^{-\pi i} ,$$

we see that the function $[g(z_o-u)]$ has near $u = 0$ the asymptotic expansion

$$(7.22) \qquad [g(z_o-u)] \sim \sum_\nu c_\nu \left[-e^{\delta_\nu \pi i} + e^{-\delta_\nu \pi i}\right] u^{\delta_\nu - 1}$$

$$= -2i \sum_\nu c_\nu (\sin \delta_\nu \pi) u^{\delta_\nu - 1} .$$

From Watson's lemma, formula (5.52), with $\gamma_\nu = \delta_\nu - 1$, we thus deduce the asymptotic expansion

$$(7.23) \qquad \psi(t) \sim \frac{1}{\pi} e^{z_o t} \sum_\nu c_\nu (\delta_\nu - 1)! (\sin \delta_\nu \pi) t^{-\delta_\nu}$$

or

$$(7.24) \qquad \psi(t) \sim e^{z_o t} \sum_\nu c_\nu \delta_\nu ! \, \frac{\sin \delta_\nu \pi}{\delta_\nu \pi} \, t^{-\delta_\nu}$$

for $\psi(t)$ near $t = \infty$.

Attention should be called to a slightly different method of deriving the last formula. Instead of pulling the path of integration into the slit one may leave part of the path as a loop around the point z_0 and then apply expansion (7.20). The condition of integrability of $[g(z-z_0)]$ along the slit could then be dispensed with. We have not employed this variant because we wanted to make use of Watson's lemma derived before.

Formula (7.23) was derived under rather restrictive conditions on the type of singularity of the function g(z). Considerable work has been done in studying the asymptotic behavior of the Bromwich integral under much weaker conditions[1].

A few remarks may be added about the relationship between the expansion just described and the asymptotic expansion introduced by Heaviside in connection with his Operational Calculus.

The operators of this calculus act on functions which are defined for $t \geq 0$ and may be considered to be identically zero for $t < 0$. The basic operator is the operator "p" which transforms continuously differentiable functions f(t) which vanish at t = 0 into their derivatives,

$$pf(t) = \frac{d}{dt} f(t) \qquad \text{if} \quad f(0) = 0 \quad . \tag{7.25}$$

The inverse p^{-1} of p then transforms a function g(t) into

$$p^{-1}g(t) = \int_0^t g(\tau)d\tau \quad .$$

Polynomials in p^{-1} are then easily defined and applicable on any integrable function g(t), in particular on the "unit" function defined by

$$1(t) = \begin{cases} 1 & \text{for} \quad t \geq 0 \\ 0 & \text{for} \quad t < 0 \end{cases} \quad . \tag{7.26}$$

---

[1] For the work of Haar in this direction, see H. A. Antosiewicz, Ph. Davis, F. Oberhettinger, "Selected Topics in the Theory of Asymptotic Expansions", The American University, National Bureau of Standards Report 2392, U.S. Department of Commerce.

We note that this function can be represented for $t \neq 0$ as the Bromwich integral

$$(7.27) \qquad 1(t) = \frac{1}{2\pi i} \int_{\uparrow} e^{zt} \frac{dz}{z} ,$$

although the function $g(z) = z^{-1}$ does not satisfy the condition (7.2).

If $P_o(z)$ is a polynomial in z^{-1} which is regular for $x > 0$, the function $g(z) = \frac{P_o(z) - P_o(\infty)}{z}$ satisfies the conditions (7.2) to (7.4) and therefore the function

$$(7.28) \quad h(t) = \frac{1}{2\pi i} \int_{\uparrow} e^{zt} P_o(z) \frac{dz}{z}$$

$$= \frac{1}{2\pi i} \int_{\uparrow} e^{zt} \frac{P_o(z) - P_o(\infty)}{z} dz + P_o(\infty) 1(t)$$

is defined. Let $P(z)$ be another such polynomial; then one easily verifies the relation

$$(7.29) \qquad P(p)h(t) = \frac{1}{2\pi i} \int_{\uparrow} e^{zt} P(z)P_o(z)\frac{dz}{z} .$$

This fact motivates us to define quite generally the operator $G(p)$ by the relation

$$(7.30) \qquad G(p)h(t) = \frac{1}{2\pi i} \int_{\uparrow} e^{zt} G(z)P_o(z)\frac{dz}{z} ,$$

provided the function $G(z)$ is such that the function

$$(7.31) \qquad g(z) = z^{-1}[G(z) - G(\infty)]$$

satisfies the conditions imposed above. In this fashion the operator $G(p)$ is defined only for a special class of functions $h(t)$. It is not difficult to free oneself from this restriction, but this will not be done here.

Heaviside's asymptotic expansion mentioned above is an attempt to expand the function

(7.32) $$\psi(t) = G(p)1(t) \quad ;$$

it is obtained by employing the expansion

(7.33) $$G(z) = \sum_{\nu} c_{\nu} z^{\delta_{\nu}}$$

formally. It reads

(7.34) $$\psi(t) \sim \sum_{\nu} c_{\nu} \left(\frac{d}{dt}\right)^{\delta_{\nu}} 1(t) \quad ,$$

where the terms on the right are defined by

(7.35) $$\left(\frac{d}{dt}\right)^{\delta} 1(t) = \frac{t^{-\delta}}{(-\delta)!} \quad .$$

For negative integers δ the latter definition is consistent with the definition of p^{-1} given above. For positive integers δ one should set

(7.36) $$\frac{1}{(-\delta)!} = 0 \quad .$$

In view of the well-known identity

(7.37) $$\delta!(-\delta)! = \frac{\delta\pi}{\sin \delta\pi} \quad ,$$

Heaviside's expansion agrees with expansion (7.24) derived above provided $z_0 = 0$. Actually, Heaviside uses his expansion only in cases where the function $\frac{G(z)}{z}$ has a single branch point at $z = z_0 = 0$ and satisfies there the conditions imposed above. Apparently, however, he never explicitly states this restrictive condition. To be sure, there are important cases in which this condition is not satisfied; e.g., when

(7.38) $$G(z) = \frac{z}{\sqrt{1 + z^2}} \quad .$$

Here the function $\frac{G(z)}{z}$ has two branch points on the imaginary axis at $z = \pm i \neq 0$.

8. Methods of Stationary Exponents

A great many problems of asymptotic expansion can be reduced to the investigation of integrals of the form

$$(8.1) \qquad \phi(t) = \int_{s_1}^{s_2} e^{tw(s)} q(s) ds \quad .$$

Clearly, the Laplace integral may be regarded as a special integral of this type: we need only set $w(s) = s$, $s_1 = 0$, $s_2 = \infty$.

Integrals of the form

$$(8.2) \qquad \phi(t) = \int_{s_1}^{s_2} e^{tu(s)} q(s) ds$$

with real valued functions $w(s) = u(s)$ were considered by Laplace. He observed that the asymptotic character of $\phi(t)$ depends only on the behavior of the integrand in the neighborhood of the value of s for which $u(s)$ assumes its maximum. Let us assume that this maximum is attained at a single point s_0 in the interior of the interval $s_1 < s < s_2$; let us further assume that the function $u(s)$ possesses a continuous second derivative, so that

$$(8.3) \qquad u(s) = u(s_0) - c(s - s_0)^2 + r(s)(s - s_0)^2$$

with an appropriate constant

$$(8.4) \qquad c = -\tfrac{1}{2} u''(s_0) \quad ,$$

assumed to be actually positive, and a function $r(s)$ for which $r(0) = 0$. Also we assume that $q(s)$ is continuous.

The statement then is that asymptotically the function $\phi(t)$ is given as

$$(8.5) \qquad \phi(t) \sim q(s_0) e^{tu(s_0)} \int_{-\infty}^{\infty} e^{-ct(s-s_0)^2} ds \quad ,$$

i.e., by

$$(8.6)\qquad \phi(t) \sim \sqrt{\frac{\pi}{ct}}\, q(s_o)e^{tu(s_o)} \quad .$$

Here the constant c is given by (8.4). We shall refer to this result as the "Laplace formula". It can easily be deduced from the results of Section 5 concerning the Laplace integral, and specifically from Watson's Lemma (5.52).

First of all, since s_o is assumed to be the only maximum point of u(s), we can find for any number $a > 0$ a sufficiently small number $\varepsilon = \varepsilon(a) > 0$ such that the maximum value of the function u(s) outside of the interval $|s - s_o| < a$ is less than $u(s_o) - \varepsilon$:

$$(8.7)\qquad u(s) \leq u(s_o) - \varepsilon \quad \text{for} \quad |s - s_o| \geq a \quad .$$

We then set

$$(8.8)\qquad \phi(t) = \phi_a^+(t) + \phi_a^-(t) + \chi_a(t)$$

with

$$(8.9)\qquad \phi_a^{\pm}(t) = \pm \int_{s_o}^{s_o \pm a} e^{tu(s)} q(s)ds \quad ,$$

$$(8.10)\qquad \chi_a(t) = \left[\int_{s_1}^{s_o - a} + \int_{s_o + a}^{s_2}\right] e^{tu(s)} q(s)ds \quad .$$

Clearly,

$$(8.11)\qquad |\chi_a(t)| \leq e^{-\varepsilon t}\, e^{tu(s_o)} \int_{s_1}^{s_2} |q(s)|ds \quad ,$$

so that $e^{-tu(s_o)}\chi_a(t)$ approaches zero exponentially as $t \to \infty$. In order to prove relation (8.6) it is therefore sufficient to prove the same relation with $\phi_a^+(t) + \phi_a^-(t)$ in place of $\phi(t)$.

We may assume the value of a to be taken so small that u(s) is monotone for $s_o - a \leq s \leq s_o$ and for $s_o \leq s \leq s_o + a$. In these intervals we then may invert the function u(s); i.e., we may introduce

(8.12) $$\sigma = u(s_o) - u(s)$$

as independent variable in place of s, and consider s as given by two functions $s^{\pm}(\sigma)$ defined in the intervals $0 \leq \sigma \leq \sigma^{\pm} = u(s_o) - u(s_o \pm a)$ respectively. Accordingly, we have

(8.13) $$\phi_a^{\pm}(t) = \pm e^{tu(s_o)} \int_0^{\sigma^{\pm}} e^{-t\sigma} q(s^{\pm}(\sigma)) \frac{d\sigma}{-u'(s^{\pm}(\sigma))} .$$

Defining the integrand as identically zero beyond $\sigma^{\pm}$, we see that the function $e^{-tu(s_o)} \phi_a^{\pm}(t)$ is a Laplace integral.

From the assumption (8.3) we infer that the functions $s^{\pm}(\sigma)$ possess expansions of the form

(8.14) $$s^{\pm}(\sigma) \sim s_o \pm \sqrt{\frac{\sigma}{c}} + \ldots .$$

Hence the derivative

(8.15) $$u'(s) = -2c(s - s_o) + \ldots$$

possesses an expansion of the form

(8.16) $$u'(s^{\pm}(\sigma)) \sim \mp 2\sqrt{c\sigma} + \ldots .$$

Further, we have

(8.17) $$q(s^{\pm}(\sigma)) = q(s_o) + \ldots .$$

From Watson's Lemma, Theorem 5.2, we can therefore deduce that the functions $\phi_a^{\pm}(t)$ possess the asymptotic expansions

(8.18) $$\phi_a^{\pm}(t) \sim \frac{1}{2}\sqrt{\frac{\pi}{ct}}\, q(s_o) e^{tu(s_o)} ,$$

whence the Laplace formula (8.6) follows.

The argument given makes it clear that one could determine the complete asymptotic expansion of the function $\phi(t)$ by reduction to the asymptotic expansion of the Laplace integral.

A somewhat different procedure is more convenient for this purpose. In terms of the original variables s one writes the exponent u(s) in the form (8.3), expands $\exp\{t\, r(s)(s-s_0)^2\}$ in a power series,

$$e^{t\cdot r(s)(s-s_0)^2} = 1 + t\, r(s)(s-s_0)^2 + \dots \tag{8.19}$$

and applies Watson's Lemma to each term. Since in the resulting series the leading terms of the asymptotic expansions of the individual terms of (8.19) are successively of higher order --as could be proved--the series of asymptotic expansions leads to the desired asymptotic expansion of the function $\phi(t)$.

Among the many applications of the formula (8.6) we mention the asymptotic description of the gamma function, or what is equivalent, of the factorial

$$n! = \int_0^\infty e^{-\alpha}\alpha^n d\alpha \tag{8.20}$$

$$= \int_0^\infty e^{-\alpha + n \log \alpha} d\alpha \quad .$$

The variable t in the Laplace formula (8.6) is here replaced by the parameter n. Since the function $\log \alpha$ does not assume a maximum at a finite value of α this formula is not applicable directly. Therefore, we set

$$\alpha = ns \quad ; \tag{8.21}$$

then the function

$$n!n^{-(n+1)} = \int_0^\infty e^{n[\log s - s]} ds \tag{8.22}$$

is of the form (8.2). The function log s-s assumes a single maximum at s = 1 and is of the form

$$\log s - s = -1 - \tfrac{1}{2}(s-1)^2 + \dots \quad . \tag{8.23}$$

Hence the Laplace formula (8.6) yields "Stirling's formula"

$$n! \sim n^n e^{-n} \sqrt{2\pi n} \tag{8.24}$$

as the asymptotic description of the factorial.

As a second example we consider the integral

$$\int_a^b p^n(x)dx \quad , \tag{8.25}$$

in which $p(x)$ is a non-negative function which assumes a single maximum at $x = x_0$ in the interior of the interval $a < x_0 < b$ and has a continuous second derivative which is negative at $x = x_0$. Writing the integral in the form

$$\int_a^b e^{n \log p(x)} dx \tag{8.26}$$

and applying the Laplace formula, we obtain the interesting result

$$\int_a^b p^n(x)dx \sim p^n(x_0) \sqrt{\frac{2\pi p(x_0)}{-np''(x_o)}} \quad . \tag{8.27}$$

Since $c^{1/n} \longrightarrow 1$ for any positive number c, and even $n^{1/n} \longrightarrow 1$, as $n \longrightarrow \infty$, relation (8.27) leads to the formula

$$\lim_{n \to \infty} \left[\int_a^b p^n(x)dx \right]^{1/n} = p(x_o) \quad , \tag{8.27a}$$

which, incidentally, holds under weaker conditions.

A counterpart to Laplace's formula is Kelvin's formula of "stationary phase". It refers to integrals

$$\phi(t) = \int_a^b e^{itv(s)} q(s)ds \tag{8.28}$$

of the type (8.1) in which the function $w(s) = iv(s)$ is purely imaginary. The "phase" is the imaginary part $tv(s)$ of the exponent.

We assume that the function $v(s)$ possesses a continuous derivative which vanishes at exactly one point, $s = s_0$, in the interval $a < s < b$. Further, we assume that $v(s)$ possesses a continuous second derivative which does not vanish at $s = s_0$, so that

(8.29) $$v(s) = v(s_0) - d(s-s_0)^2 + r(s)(s-s_0)^2 \quad ,$$

(8.30) $$d = -\frac{1}{2}v''(s_0) \quad ,$$

with $d = 0$ and $r(0) = 0$. Also we assume $q(s)$ to have a continuous derivative.

We write $\phi(t)$ in the form

(8.31) $$\phi(t) = \phi^+(t) + \phi^-(t) \quad ,$$

with

(8.32) $$\phi^+(t) = \int_{s_0}^{b} e^{itv(s)}q(s)ds \quad ,$$

(8.33) $$\phi^-(t) = \int_{a}^{s_0} e^{itv(s)}q(s)ds \quad .$$

In each of these integrals we may introduce $\sigma = v(s_0) - v(s)$ as a new independent variable, since by assumption $v'(s) \neq 0$ for $s \neq s_0$. The original variable $s = s^{\pm}(\sigma)$ again becomes a function of σ. We then set up formulas corresponding to (8.15), (8.16), and (8.17). Finally, we apply Theorem 5.3, a corollary to Watson's Lemma, which we can do since $q'(s)$ was assumed continuous, and thus infer the validity of the asymptotic expansion to one term of $\phi^{\pm}(t)$. Thus we obtain

(8.34) $$\phi^{\pm}(t) \sim \frac{1}{2}\sqrt{\frac{\pi}{idt}}\, q(s_o) e^{itv(s_o)} ,$$

whence Kelvin's formula

(8.35) $$\phi(t) \sim \sqrt{\frac{\pi}{idt}}\, q(s_o) e^{itv(s_o)} , \quad d = -\frac{1}{2} v''(s_o) ,$$

results; by $\sqrt{i}$ is meant $e^{i\pi/4}$.

We shall not give here applications of this formula; we intend to do so later on.

In case the exponent $tw(s)$ is neither purely real nor purely imaginary, it is not possible to apply the methods employed to derive Laplace's and Kelvin's formulas. The reason is that--in general--the real and imaginary parts of the derivative $w'(s)$ do not vanish simultaneously in the interval $a \leq s \leq b$. If the real part--but not the imaginary part--vanishes at a point s_o, the oscillatory character of $\exp\{it[v(s) - v(s_o)]\}$ reduces the order of the term given by Laplace's formula; if the imaginary part--but not the real part--vanishes at $s = s_o$, the exponential character of $\exp\{t[u(s) - u(s_o)]\}$ modifies the order of the term given by Kelvin's formula. Under certain conditions, which will be satisfied in general, this difficulty can be overcome in a striking manner by the "saddle point" method due to Debye.

We consider w and q as analytic functions of a complex variable z defined in a simply connected region $\mathcal{R}$ and, accordingly, consider the integral

(8.36) $$\phi(t) = \int_{z_1}^{z_2} e^{tw(z)} q(z)dz$$

in which z_1 and z_2 are complex numbers in $\mathcal{R}$. Clearly, this integral can be majorized as follows:

(8.37) $$|\phi(t)| \leq \int_{z_1}^{z_2} e^{tu(z)} |q(z)dz| ,$$

where, as before, we have set $w(z) = u(z) + iv(z)$. Since the right member here is of the form (8.2), we may use the Laplace formula (8.6) to obtain the estimate

$$|\phi(t)| \leq \frac{C}{\sqrt{t}} e^{tu(z_0)} , \tag{8.38}$$

in which C is an appropriate constant and z_0 is the point at which the real part $u(z)$ assumes its maximum on the path $\mathcal{P}$ connecting z_1 with z_2; we assume that there is only one such point.

The actual asymptotic behavior of tho function $\phi(t)$, however, is not necessarily given by the right member of (8.38); in general, $\sqrt{t}e^{-tu(z_0)}\phi(t)$ will approach zero as t tends to ∞. Indeed, since the functions $w(z)$ and $q(z)$ are analytic, the path $\mathcal{P}$ may be deformed into other paths $\mathcal{P}'$ connecting the points z_1 and z_2 within the region $\mathcal{R}$. The maximum $u(z_0')$ of the real part $u(z)$ on such a deformed path is in general different from the maximum $u(z_0)$ on the original path; it may be less than $u(z_0)$. In that case the formula

$$|\phi(t)| \leq \frac{C'}{\sqrt{t}} e^{tu(z_0')} \tag{8.39}$$

gives a better estimate of the asymptotic behavior of $\phi(t)$ than formula (8.38). Naturally, then, one will try to deform the path $\mathcal{P}$ in such a way that the maximum of $u(z)$ on it becomes as small as possible.

It could happen that the path $\mathcal{P}$ can be deformed until the real part $u(z)$ on it assumes its maximum at one of the end points, say at $z = z_1$. Then the path could be even further deformed so as to make the imaginary part $v(z)$ constant on it in a neighborhood of z_1. The major contribution to $\phi(t)$ would therefore depend only on this neighborhood and hence be given, except for a constant factor $e^{itv(z_1)}$, by an integral of the form (8.2). Accordingly, the asymptotic behavior of $\phi(t)$ could be derived from Laplace's formula (8.6).

We shall discuss in more detail the case in which no deformation of the path $\mathcal{P}$ exists for which the maximum of u(z) on the deformed path is assumed at an end point. We shall show that under certain conditions the maximum of the real part u(z) takes on its least value for a path which leads through a point z_0 at which the derivative w'(z) vanishes:

$$w'(z_o) = 0 \quad . \tag{8.40}$$

We must discuss the behavior of the real part u(z) as a function of z in the neighborhood of such a point. For simplicity we assume that the second derivative w"(z) does not vanish there:

$$w''(z_o) \neq 0 \quad . \tag{8.41}$$

In that case, as is known from the theory of analytic functions, the surface u = u(z) has a "saddle point" or "col" at the point $z = z_0$. Any sufficiently small neighborhood of z_0 will be divided into four regions by two curves which intersect perpendicularly at z_0 and along which $u(z) = u(z_0)$. In two of these regions, which will lie opposite each other, u(z) will be greater than $u(z_0)$, while in the other two $u(z) < u(z_0)$. Within each of the four regions there is a curve, issuing from z_0 and bisecting there the angle between the two curves of constant u, on which the imaginary part v(z) is constant: $v(z) = v(z_0)$. Along these latter curves the real part u(z) has a steeper ascent or descent than on all other curves issuing from z_0. Such curves are therefore said to be of "steepest" ascent or descent.

We now make the assumption that the points z_1 and z_2 lie in the two disconnected regions in which $u(z) < u(z_0)$, and furthermore that the path $\mathcal{P}$ can be so deformed that it passes through the col $z = z_0$ and otherwise remains in the regions where $u(z) < u(z_0)$. Then $\mathcal{P}$ can be further deformed so as to run in the neighborhood of z_0 along the two curves of steepest descent.

In this case, clearly, only that portion of the path in the neighborhood of the point $z = z_0$ will contribute to the asymptotic behavior of the integral $\phi(t)$; for, outside this neighborhood we have $u(z) \leq u(z_0) - \varepsilon$ for some $\varepsilon > 0$, so that the contribution to $\phi(t)$ from outside the neighborhood is bounded by $Ke^{tu(z_0)}e^{-\varepsilon t}$ for a suitable constant K, and is hence exponentially less than the contribution from inside the neighborhood, which will be shown to be of the order of $e^{tu(z_0)}$.

Let $\hat{z}_1$ and $\hat{z}_2$ be points on the two curves of steepest descent in the neighborhood of $z = z_0$. Then the asymptotic behavior of the integral $\phi(t)$ is the same as that of

$$(8.42) \qquad \hat{\phi}(t) = \int_{\hat{z}_1}^{\hat{z}_2} e^{tw(z)} q(z)dz \quad .$$

The path of integration here is to run along the two curves of steepest descent. Since $v(z) = v(z_0)$ on these curves we may write

$$(8.43) \qquad \hat{\phi}(t) = e^{itv(z_0)} \int_{\hat{z}_1}^{\hat{z}_2} e^{tu(z)} q(z)dz \quad .$$

We may describe the path parametrically in the form $z = z(s)$, $\hat{s}_1 \leq s \leq \hat{s}_2$, and let s_0 be the parameter-value corresponding to z_0: $z(s_0) = z_0$. By insertion of $z = z(s)$ the right member of (8.43) becomes an integral of the form (8.2), namely

$$(8.44) \qquad \hat{\phi}(t) = e^{itv(z_0)} \int_{\hat{s}_1}^{\hat{s}_2} e^{tu(z(s))} q(z(s))\dot{z}(s)ds \quad ,$$

with $\dot{z}(s) = dz/ds$. Its asymptotic behavior is thus given by the Laplace formula (8.6).

The constant

$$(8.45) \qquad c = -\frac{1}{2}\frac{d^2u}{ds^2}\bigg|_{s=s_o} \quad ,$$

cf. (8.4), which occurs in this formula is easily evaluated. Using the abbreviations $\dot{z} = dz/ds$ and $\ddot{z} = d^2z/ds^2$, as well as the standard notation $w' = dw/dz$, $w'' = d^2w/dz^2$, we have

$$(8.46) \qquad \frac{du}{ds} = \frac{dw}{ds} = w'\dot{z} \quad ,$$

$$(8.47) \qquad \frac{d^2u}{ds^2} = \frac{d^2w}{ds^2} = w''\dot{z}^2 + w'\ddot{z} \quad ,$$

whence

$$(8.48) \qquad c = -\frac{1}{2}\, w''(z_o)\dot{z}^2(s_o) \quad ,$$

since $w'(z_o) = 0$. Laplace's formula thus yields the asymptotic behavior of $\hat{\phi}(t)$, or, equivalently, of $\phi(t)$:

$$(8.49) \qquad \phi(t) \sim e^{tw(z_o)} \sqrt{\frac{2\pi}{-tw''(z_o)\dot{z}^2(s_o)}}\, q(z_o)\dot{z}(s_o) \quad .$$

This formula would have a more elegant appearance if the factors $\dot{z}(s_o)$ in the numerator and denominator were cancelled. But then it would be necessary to give an additional rule to determine which sign is to be chosen for the square root. In the form (8.49), the quantity $-w''(z_o)\dot{z}^2(s_o)$ occurring under the radical is always real and positive, as it is the negative of the second derivative of the real quantity u with respect to the real parameter s evaluated at a maximum point of u. Thus if we were to cancel $\dot{z}(s_o)$ and write formula (8.49) in the form

$$(8.50) \qquad \phi(t) \sim \sqrt{\frac{2\pi}{-tw''(z_o)}}\, q(z_o)e^{tw(z_o)} \quad ,$$

corresponding formally to Laplace's formula (8.6) and Kelvin's formula (8.35), we would have to specify that $\sqrt{-w''(z_0)}$ is to be so chosen that it becomes real positive upon multiplication by $\dot{z}(s_0)$. The additional rule therefore is

$$(8.51) \qquad \arg \sqrt{-w''(z_0)} = -\arg \dot{z}(s_0) \quad .$$

In other words, the square root in formula (8.50) should be taken in the direction in which the path of integration passes through the saddle point.

Formula (8.49), or equivalently formula (8.50) with the stipulation (8.51), will be referred to as "Debye's formula". The right member of it will be called the "leading asymptotic term" of $\phi(t)$. It is to be noted that no separation into real and imaginary parts occurs in this formula, although such a separation was made in its derivation. Actually, one could avoid this separation even in the derivation of the formula. It will be recalled that in Section 5 the asymptotic expansion of the Laplace integral was proved to hold if the independent variable--of the resulting function, not of the integrand--ranges over any sector in the right half-plane. Using similar arguments one could derive formula (8.49) by employing any path through the col which leads from one of the regions in which $u(z) < u(z_0)$ to the other region; it is not necessary to insist that near the col the path run along the curves of steepest descent. This freedom in the choice of the path is particularly useful in the derivation of higher order terms in the expansion. This method of deriving this expansion is then called the "saddle point method", while the more restricted procedure previously described is called the "method of steepest descent".

A path through a col along which the real part $u(z)$ first ascends and then descends near the col will be called "admissible". Debye's formula (8.49) then remains valid if the root $\sqrt{-tw''(z_o)\dot{z}^2(s_o)}$ is so determined that its real part is positive.

It should also be noted that this formula, derived for real positive t, holds even if t is complex, provided its phase is kept constant when $|t| \to \infty$. To see this one need only let $|t|$ and $|t|^{-1}tw(z)$ take the place of t and $w(z)$ in the previous arguments.

For a detailed analysis and effective modifications of the methods presented in this section, see:

Perron, O., Über die näherungsweise Berechnung von Funktionen grosser Zahlen. Sitzungsberichte der Kgl. Bayerischen Akademie der Wissenschaften. Math. Phys. Klasse, München, 1917, May 5, pp. 191-219.

van der Waerden, B. L., On the method of saddle points. Applied Scientific Research, vol. B2, The Mathematical Centre, Amsterdam, 1951, pp. 33-45.

9. The Airy Integrals

As an example of the application of the saddle point method we shall investigate the asymptotic behavior of the Airy integral

$$(9.1) \qquad Ai(z) = \frac{1}{2\pi i}\int_{\mathcal{L}} e^{tz - \frac{1}{3}t^3}\, dt \quad ,$$

in which the path $\mathcal{L}$ runs from infinity to infinity in a manner to be prescribed presently. We first observe that for each value of z the integrand vanishes exponentially if t tends to infinity within any of the three sectors

$$(9.2) \qquad |\arg t| < \frac{\pi}{6} \quad ,$$

$$(9.3) \qquad \frac{\pi}{2} < \pm \arg t < \frac{5\pi}{6} \quad .$$

We then choose rays $\mathcal{J}_0$, $\mathcal{J}_\pm$ within these three sectors; specifically, we take

$$(9.4) \qquad \mathcal{J}_0: \quad \arg t = 0 \quad ,$$

$$(9.5) \qquad \mathcal{J}_\pm: \quad \arg t = \pm \frac{2\pi}{3} \quad ,$$

with $|t|$ running from zero to infinity (see Figure 2). Finally, we introduce the paths

$$(9.6) \qquad \mathcal{L}_0 = \mathcal{J}_+ - \mathcal{J}_- \quad ,$$

$$(9.7) \qquad \mathcal{L}_\pm = \mathcal{J}_0 - \mathcal{J}_\pm \quad .$$

The Airy integrals corresponding to these three paths $\mathcal{L}_0$, $\mathcal{L}_\pm$ will be denoted by $Ai_0(z)$ and $Ai_\pm(z)$ respectively. The identity

$$(9.8) \qquad Ai_0(z) = Ai_-(z) - Ai_+(z)$$

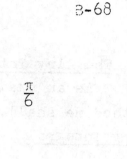

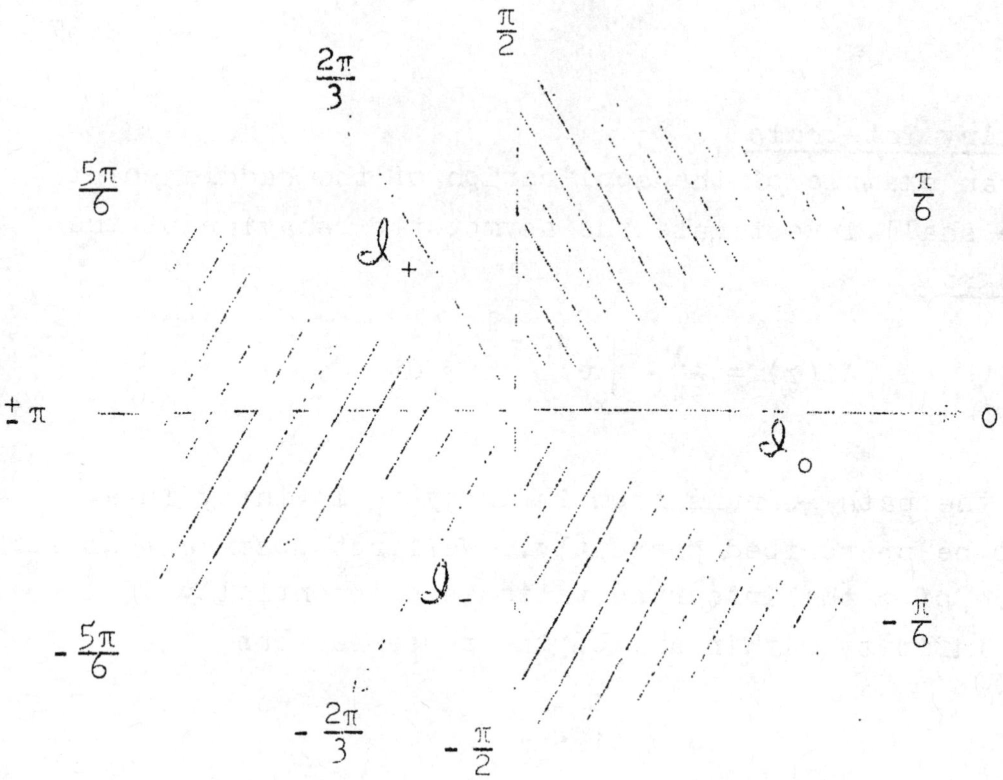

Figure 2

Paths of Integration for Airy Integrals

holds, as the corresponding identity holds for the three paths $\mathcal{L}_0$, $\mathcal{L}_\pm$.

It is clear that these functions Ai(z) are defined and regular for every value of z. That is, they are entire functions. Of course, this implies that they are single valued.

For later purposes it is important to note that the Airy functions w(z) = Ai(z) satisfy the differential equation

$$w''(z) - zw(z) = 0 \quad . \tag{9.9}$$

In fact, because of the exponential decay of the integrand, we may differentiate twice under the integral sign, obtaining

$$2\pi i\, w''(z) = \int_{\mathcal{L}} t^2 e^{zt} e^{-\frac{1}{3}t^3}\, dt = - \int_{\mathcal{L}} e^{zt} \frac{d}{dt} e^{-\frac{1}{3}t^3}\, dt$$

$$= \int_{\mathcal{L}} e^{-\frac{1}{3}t^3} \frac{d}{dt} e^{zt} dt = z \int_{\mathcal{L}} e^{-\frac{1}{3}t^3} e^{zt} dt = 2\pi i z w(z) \; .$$

Furthermore it is worthwhile to note that the function Ai(z) can be expressed in the form

$$\text{(9.10)} \qquad Ai(z) = z^{1/2}\, Z_{1/3}(\tfrac{2}{3} i\, z^{3/2})$$

in terms of an appropriate solution $Z_{1/3}(r)$ of the Bessel differential equation

$$\text{(9.11)} \qquad Z''_{1/3}(r) + r^{-1} Z'_{1/3}(r) + (1 - (3r)^{-2}) Z_{1/3}(r) = 0$$

of order 1/3. Note that the reduction of the Airy integral to the better-known Bessel functions, given by formula (9.10), is not quite satisfactory, since this formula expresses the entire function Ai(z) in terms of a function $Z_{1/3}(r)$ which has a branch singularity at $r = 0$.

The asymptotic behavior of the Airy integrals cannot be determined directly by employing the method of stationary exponents with $w(t) = t$ and $q(t) = e^{-\frac{1}{3}t^3}$, since the real part of zt approaches infinity at one or the other end of the path, no matter what the value of z is. Nevertheless, it is possible to employ the saddle point method after making an appropriate transformation of the variable t, namely the transformation

$$\text{(9.12)} \qquad t = z^{1/2} \tau \; .$$

Setting

$$\text{(9.13)} \qquad z^{3/2} = \rho$$

we have

$$(9.14)\qquad Ai(z) = \frac{z^{1/2}}{2\pi i}\int_{\mathcal{L}'(z)} e^{\rho(\tau - \frac{1}{3}\tau^3)}\,d\tau$$

where the path $\mathcal{L}'(z)$ is characterized by the condition that $z^{1/2}\tau$ runs along the path $\mathcal{L}$. The derivative of the new exponent evidenly vanishes at the points $\tau = \pm 1$. All that is needed to determine the asymptotic behavior of Ai(z) is to decide how to deform the path $\mathcal{L}'(z)$ so that it passes in an admissible way through one of these saddle points, i.e. in such a way that the real part of the exponent first ascends and then descends near this point.

Let us first assume that z lies in the sector $\mathcal{S}_0$, defined by

$$(9.15)\qquad |\arg z| < \frac{\pi}{3} \quad .$$

Then the path $\mathcal{L}'(z)$ may be deformed into the path $\mathcal{L} = \mathcal{L}'(1)$ without changing the value of Ai(z). Since in this case

$$(9.16)\qquad \operatorname{Re}\rho > 0 \quad ,$$

the path $\mathcal{L}_0$ through the col $\tau = 1$ is admissible, while through the other col $\tau = -1$ the path Re $\tau = -1$, in the imaginary direction, is admissible.

Certainly, the path $\mathcal{L}_0$ can be deformed so as to pass through the col $\tau = -1$ in the direction of the path Re $\tau = -1$. Accordingly, we may apply Debye's formula to obtain the asymptotic behavior of $Ai_0(z)$. Since the second derivative of $\tau - \frac{1}{3}\tau^3$ has the value 2 at $\tau = -1$ and $\dot{z}(s_0) = i$ on the deformed path, formula (8.49) yields

$$(9.17)\qquad Ai_0(z) \sim \frac{z^{1/2}}{2\pi i}\sqrt{\frac{2\pi}{2\rho}}\, i e^{-\frac{2}{3}\rho} \quad ,$$

or

$$(9.18)\qquad Ai_0(z) \sim \frac{1}{2\sqrt{\pi}}\, z^{-\frac{1}{4}} e^{-\frac{2}{3}z^{3/2}} \quad \text{for } |\arg z| < \frac{\pi}{3} \quad .$$

Next we consider the paths $\mathcal{L}_{\pm} = \mathcal{l}_0 - \mathcal{l}_{\pm}$. We deform $\mathcal{l}_{\pm}$ into a path which runs along the negative real axis from $\tau = 0$ to $\tau = -1$ and then first in the positive or negative imaginary direction into a region in which Re $(\tau - \frac{1}{3}\tau^3) < -\frac{2}{3}$. It is then clear that Re $\rho(\tau - \frac{1}{3}\tau^3)$ increases along the path $-\mathcal{l}_{\pm}$ up to the col at $\tau = -1$ and then continues to increase. Consequently, only the col at $\tau = +1$ contributes to the asymptotic behavior of $Ai_{\pm}(z)$, for only at this latter col is the absolute maximum of Re $\rho(\tau - \frac{1}{3}\tau^3)$ on the path $\mathcal{L}_{\pm}$ assumed. Thus from Debye' formula we obtain

$$(9.19) \qquad Ai_{\pm}(z) \sim \frac{1}{2i\sqrt{\pi}} z^{-\frac{1}{4}} e^{\frac{2}{3}z^{3/2}} \qquad \text{for } |\arg z| < \frac{\pi}{3} .$$

Note that formulas (9.18), (9.19) are consistent with the identity (9.8), since $e^{-\frac{2}{3}z^{3/2}}$ vanishes exponentially as $z \longrightarrow \infty$ with $|\arg z| < \frac{\pi}{3}$, and thus represents a term of considerably higher order than $e^{\frac{2}{3}z^{3/2}}$, which becomes infinite.

The asymptotic behavior of the Airy functions when the variable z lies outside of the sector $|\arg z| < \frac{\pi}{3}$ can be deduced from identities which connect the values of the Airy functions in different sectors with each other.

We first assume that z lies in the sector $\mathcal{S}_{+}$, defined by

$$(9.20) \qquad \frac{\pi}{3} < \arg z < \pi .$$

The paths $\mathcal{L}'(z)$ for such values of z may be deformed into the paths $\mathcal{L}'(e^{2i\pi/3})$, since condition (9.20) insures that $z^{3/2}\tau^3$ has a positive real part for $\tau = e^{-i\pi/3}$.

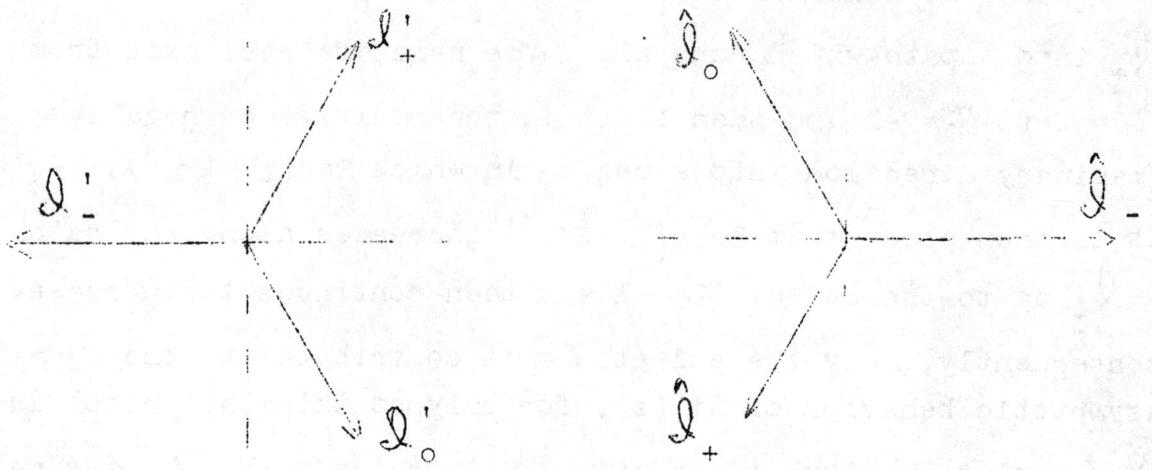

Figure 3

Paths $\mathcal{I}'(e^{2i\pi/3})$ and reflected paths $\hat{\mathcal{I}}(e^{2i\pi/3})$ for the asymptotic evaluation of the Airy integrals in $\mathcal{S}_+$.

The three paths $\mathcal{I}'(e^{2i\pi/3})$, as shown in Figure 3, can be obtained by reflection at the origin from the three paths $\mathcal{I}'(1) = \mathcal{I}$ in a permuted order. Denoting the reflected paths by $\hat{\mathcal{I}}(e^{2i\pi/3})$ we have specifically

(9.21a) $$\hat{\mathcal{I}}_o(e^{2i\pi/3}) = \mathcal{I}_+ ,$$

(9.21b) $$\hat{\mathcal{I}}_+(e^{2i\pi/3}) = \mathcal{I}_- ,$$

(9.21c) $$\hat{\mathcal{I}}_-(e^{2i\pi/3}) = \mathcal{I}_o .$$

Consequently, the reflected Airy paths $\hat{\mathcal{L}}(e^{2i\pi/3})$ become

(9.22a) $$\hat{\mathcal{L}}_o(e^{2i\pi/3}) = -\mathcal{L}_- ,$$

(9.22b) $$\hat{\mathcal{L}}_+(e^{2i\pi/3}) = \mathcal{L}_o ,$$

(9.22c) $$\hat{\mathcal{L}}_-(e^{2i\pi/3}) = -\mathcal{L}_+ .$$

The variable $\hat{\tau} = -\tau$, which we now introduce instead of τ, therefore runs over the latter paths when τ runs over the corresponding paths $\mathcal{L}'(e^{2i\pi/3})$. We also introduce instead of z the variable

$$\hat{z} = z e^{-2i\pi/3} \tag{9.23}$$

which lies in the sector $\mathcal{S}_0$ if z lies in the sector $\mathcal{S}_+$. Clearly,

$$\hat{z}^{3/2} = -z^{3/2} \tag{9.24}$$

and, consequently,

$$z^{3/2}[\tau - \tfrac{1}{3}\tau^3] = \hat{z}^{3/2}[\hat{\tau} - \tfrac{1}{3}\hat{\tau}^3] \quad . \tag{9.25}$$

Observing further that $z^{1/2} = e^{i\pi/3}\hat{z}^{1/2}$, we find

$$Ai_0(z) = e^{i\pi/3} Ai_-(\hat{z}) \quad , \tag{9.26a}$$

$$Ai_+(z) = -e^{i\pi/3} Ai_0(\hat{z}) \quad , \tag{9.26b}$$

$$Ai_-(z) = e^{i\pi/3} Ai_+(\hat{z}) \quad . \tag{9.26c}$$

These identities were derived under the condition (9.20). Nevertheless they hold without this restriction, since both sides in (9.26) are entire functions of z.

Combining formulas (9.26) with (9.18), (9.19) we obtain the asymptotic expressions

$$Ai_0(z) \sim \frac{1}{2\sqrt{\pi}} z^{-1/4} e^{-\frac{2}{3}z^{3/2}} \quad , \tag{9.27a}$$

$$Ai_+(z) \sim \frac{1}{2i\sqrt{\pi}} z^{-1/4} e^{\frac{2}{3}z^{3/2}} \quad , \tag{9.27b}$$

$$Ai_-(z) \sim \frac{1}{2\sqrt{\pi}} z^{-1/4} e^{-\frac{2}{3}z^{3/2}} \quad , \tag{9.27c}$$

which are valid if z lies in the sector $\mathcal{S}_+$, cf. (9.20).

Similarly, or by inverting formulas (9.26) so as to express $Ai(\hat{z})$ for $\hat{z}$ in $\mathcal{S}_-$ in terms of Ai(z) for z in $\mathcal{S}_o$, we may derive the asymptotic expressions

(9.28a) $$Ai_o(z) \sim \frac{1}{2\sqrt{\pi}} z^{-1/4} e^{-\frac{2}{3}z^{3/2}} ,$$

(9.28b) $$Ai_+(z) \sim -\frac{1}{2\sqrt{\pi}} z^{-1/4} e^{-\frac{2}{3}z^{3/2}} ,$$

(9.28c) $$Ai_-(z) \sim \frac{1}{2i\sqrt{\pi}} z^{-1/4} e^{\frac{2}{3}z^{3/2}} ,$$

valid when z lies in the sector $\mathcal{S}_-$, defined by

(9.29) $$-\pi < \arg z < -\frac{\pi}{3} .$$

These formulas show that the Stokes phenomenon appears for the functions $Ai_\pm(z)$ when z crosses the rays $\arg z = \mp \frac{\pi}{3}$ respectively. These functions, however, have the same leading asymptotic terms on both sides of the rays $\arg z = \pm \frac{\pi}{3}$ respectively. The function $Ai_o(z)$ has the same leading asymptotic term in all three sectors.

Naturally, one expects that the functions $Ai_o(z)$ and $Ai_-(z)$, whose leading asymptotic terms do not jump crossing the ray $\arg z = -\frac{\pi}{3}$, have the same leading asymptotic term on this ray itself as on both sides of it. This is in fact the case. To show this, one need only verify that the paths $\mathcal{L}'_o(z)$ and $\mathcal{L}'_-(z)$ may be deformed so as to pass in an admissible direction through the saddle points $\tau = -1$ and $\tau = +1$ respectively whenever z lies on the ray $\arg z = -\frac{\pi}{3}$ as well as in either of the two neighboring sectors $\mathcal{S}_o$, $\mathcal{S}_-$. It is then a direct consequence of Debye's formula that the leading asymptotic terms of $Ai_o(z)$ and $Ai_-(z)$ are the same on the ray as in these sectors.

From relations (9.28) one concludes further that the leading asymptotic terms of the functions $Ai_{\pm}(z)$ do not change when z crosses the negative real axis. This statement may seem to contradict formulas (9.27) and (9.28). It is to be noted, however, that the fractional powers of z occurring in these formulas are to be determined by analytic continuation from the ray arg $z = 0$ without crossing the ray arg $z = \pm \pi$. To verify the continuity of the leading asymptotic terms of $Ai_{\pm}(z)$ across the ray arg $z = \pi$, it is therefore sufficient to verify that the expressions for these terms given by (9.27) go over into those given by (9.28) if z is replaced by $e^{2\pi i}z$.

A similar consideration shows that the leading asymptotic term of $Ai_{0}(z)$ actually does jump when z crosses the ray arg $z = \pi$, even though this term is given in (9.27) and (9.28) by the same expression.

In any case we see that for each of the three Airy functions Ai(z) there is a slit plane in which the <u>leading asymptotic term is given by a single analytic function</u>. The slit is evidently the ray arg $z = \pi$ for $Ai_{0}(z)$ and arg $z = \mp \frac{\pi}{3}$ for $Ai_{\pm}(z)$.

The asymptotic behavior of these functions is different in different parts of the slit plane. For example, the function $Ai_{0}(z)$ dies out exponentially in the sector $|\arg z| < \frac{\pi}{3}$, while it increases exponentially in the sectors $|\arg z \mp \frac{2\pi}{3}| < \frac{\pi}{3}$.

The leading asymptotic term for any of these functions on the slit associated with it can easily be determined from the leading asymptotic terms of the other two functions by virtue of the identity (9.8). We give only the term for $Ai_{0}(z)$; the terms for $Ai_{\pm}(z)$ on arg $z = \mp \frac{\pi}{3}$ could be obtained similarly. From (9.27), we find

$$(9.30) \qquad Ai_o(z) \sim \frac{1}{2\sqrt{\pi}} z^{-1/4}\left[e^{-\frac{2}{3}z^{3/2}} + ie^{\frac{2}{3}z^{3/2}}\right]$$

for arg $z = \pi$, or, writing $z = -x = xe^{i\pi}$ on this ray,

$$(9.31) \qquad Ai_o(z) \sim \frac{1}{\sqrt{\pi}} x^{-1/4} \cos\left(\frac{2}{3}x^{3/2} - \frac{\pi}{4}\right) \quad .$$

Thus, except for the damping factor $x^{-1/4}$, the function $Ai_o(z)$ behaves asymptotically in an oscillatory way. This damped oscillatory behavior on the slit contrasts with an exponential increase on both sides of it; indeed, one or the other of the two terms in formula (9.30) becomes exponentially predominant as soon as z leaves the slit, as $z^{3/2}$ then has either a positive or negative real part, but as long as z remains on the slit $z^{3/2}$ is purely imaginary and $Ai_o(z)$ will oscillate. The transition from the exponential decline of the Airy function for $z = x > 0$ to its oscillatory behavior for $z = -x < 0$ will prove to be typical for solutions of differential equations of the form

$$(9.32) \qquad w''(z) - q(z)w(z) = 0 \quad ,$$

cf. (9.9), in which $q(z)$ changes sign at $z = 0$.

10. Asymptotic Expansion of Solutions of Differential Equations of Second Order

We come now to the most important application of asymptotic expansions, namely to the expansion of solutions of differential equations. We first consider the general second order linear ordinary differential equation

$$u_{tt} + p(t)u_t + q(t)u = 0 \quad , \tag{10.1}$$

in which the coefficients p(t), q(t) are functions of the real variable t possessing asymptotic expansions

$$p(t) \sim p_0 + p_1 t^{-1} + p_2 t^{-2} + \ldots \quad , \tag{10.2}$$

$$q(t) \sim q_0 + q_1 t^{-1} + q_2 t^{-2} + \ldots \tag{10.3}$$

near $t = \infty$.

Suppose that a solution $u = u(t)$ of equation (10.1) exists which itself possesses an asymptotic expansion

$$u(t) \sim u_0 + u_1 t^{-1} + u_2 t^{-2} + \ldots \quad , \tag{10.4}$$

with $u_0 \neq 0$ near $t = \infty$, and whose first two derivatives u_t, u_{tt} also possess asymptotic expansions near $t = \infty$. According to the results of Section 2, these latter expansions can be obtained by formal differentiation from the expansion (10.4) of u(t). By substituting these three expansions, together with (10.2) and (10.3), into equation (10.1) and comparing coefficients, there follow immediately the relations

$$q_o = 0 \ , \quad q_1 = 0 \quad , \tag{10.5}$$

$$q_2 = u_0^{-1} u_1 p_o \quad ; \tag{10.6}$$

from the second of these relations follows the condition

$$p_0 \neq 0 \ \text{ unless } \ q_2 = 0 \quad . \tag{10.7}$$

Conditions (10.5), (10.7) on the functions $p(t)$, $q(t)$ may be regarded as necessary conditions for the existence of an asymptotic power series expansion of the solution. These conditions are not satisfied for many commonly encountered differential equations; the Bessel equation

$$(10.8) \qquad u_{tt} + t^{-1}u_t + (1 - n^2t^{-2})u = 0 \quad ,$$

with $q_o = 1$, $p_o = 0$, $q_2 = -n^2$, is a notable example. We shall see later, however, that it is almost always possible to insure that they are satisfied after an appropriate transformation of variables. A differential equation for which condition (10.5) is satisfied, and, in addition, $p_o \neq 0$, is said to be regular at $t = \infty$; if $p_o = 0$ and $q_o = q_1 = q_2 = 0$, the equation is said to have a regular singularity at infinity.

In case the differential equation (10.1) is regular, the substitution mentioned in the preceding paragraph will serve to determine uniquely the asymptotic expansion (10.4), if it exists, once the initial coefficient u_o is given. Indeed, after substituting (10.4) into (10.1), one need only set the coefficient of the power t^{-r-1} equal to zero to obtain the formula

$$(10.9) \quad rp_o u_r = r(r-1)u_{r-1} - \sum_{j=1}^{r} [(r-j)p_j - q_{j+1}]u_{r-j} \quad ,$$

which, since p_o was assumed to be different from zero, can be used to express each coefficient u_r, $r \geq 1$, in terms of the preceding coefficients $u_o, u_1, \ldots, u_{r-1}$. Formula (10.9), incidentally, shows that our original assumption $u_o \neq 0$ was reasonable, as $u_o = 0$ would imply that all coefficients u_r are zero and, therefore, that the expansion (10.4) is a trivial one.

Up to now we have assumed the existence of an asymptotically expansible solution of equation (10.1), and have derived the form of the expansion. A deeper question is whether or not such solutions exist at all. Such questions were first asked and answered by Poincaré in 1886; for the case of a regular differential equation in a real variable t the answer is affirmative if $p_0 < 0$, and is given by the

Theorem: Let p(t), q(t) be two functions of the positive real variable t which near $t = \infty$ possess the asymptotic expansions (10.2), (10.3) respectively, and let $q_0 = q_1 = 0$, $p_0 < 0$. Then there exists for some $t_0 > 0$ a solution u(t) of the differential equation (10.1) which is defined for $t \geq t_0$ and which possesses an asymptotic power series expansion having any given real number u_0 as constant term.

We remark that a similar theorem holds even for $p_0 > 0$ provided p(t) and q(t) can be continued as analytic functions of the complex variable t into a domain $|t| > t_0$, $\tau_- < \arg t < \tau_+$, where the angles τ_- and τ_+ satisfy either the condition $\tau_+ > \frac{\pi}{2}$, $\tau_- < 0$ or the condition $\tau_- < -\frac{\pi}{2}$, $\tau_+ > 0$. We shall not prove this statement here; it is a special case of the general result derived in the subsequent sections.

In proving the theorem as stated we follow Bieberbach (cf. Theorie der Differentialgleichungen); see also the Friedrichs lecture notes on Advanced Ordinary Differential Equations. We shall actually construct the function u(t) in the form of a convergent series

$$(10.10) \qquad u(t) = \sum_{r=0}^{\infty} u^{(r)}(t) \quad ;$$

this series will not itself be a power series, but each of its terms will possess an asymptotic power series expansion, and these expansions will combine to form an expansion of the sum u(t). The functions $u^{(r)}(t)$ will be defined recursively from the differential equation (10.1), which we write for this purpose in a form suggested by the recursion formula (10.9), namely in the form

$$(10.11) \qquad u_{tt} - \lambda u_t = -\tilde{p}(t)u_t - q(t)u \quad ,$$

where we have set

$$\lambda = -p_o > 0 \quad , \tag{10.12}$$

$$\tilde{p}(t) = p(t) - p_o \quad . \tag{10.13}$$

We shall take for $u^{(r+1)}(t)$ a solution $w = w(t)$, vanishing at infinity, of the equation

$$w_{tt} - \lambda w_t = -\tilde{p}u_t^{(r)} - qu^{(r)} \quad ; \tag{10.14}$$

the formal sum $u = \sum_{r=0}^{\infty} u^{(r)}$ will then satisfy the differential equation (10.11), provided $u^{(o)}(t)$ is chosen as a function w for which the left hand side of (10.14) vanishes.

To present such a proof rigorously, it is necessary to investigate both the existence of the successive $u^{(r+1)}$ and the convergence of the formal series (10.10). To this end we first define certain norms on the space of functions possessing asymptotic expansions near infinity. Let t_o be a fixed positive number, and v(t) an asymptotically expansible function defined for all $t \geq t_o$. Then we set

$$\|v\|_k^o = \underset{t \geq t_o}{\text{l.u.b.}} \; |t^k v(t)| \quad , \qquad k = 0,1,2,\ldots; \tag{10.15}$$

if v(t) possesses an asymptotically expansible derivative $v_t(t)$ we further set

$$\|v\|_r = \max\{\|v\|_r^o, \|v_t\|_{r+1}^o\} \tag{10.16}$$

$$= \underset{t \geq t_o}{\text{l.u.b.}} \; \{|t^r v(t)|, |t^{r+1} v_t(t)|\}, \; r = 0,1,2,\ldots \; .$$

Let V_k^o denote the space of all functions v(t) for which $\|v\|_k^o$ is finite, and similarly let V_r stand for the space of functions v with $\|v\|_r < \infty$. Clearly, V_k^o consists of those functions possessing asymptotic expansions beginning with a term of order k or higher, while V_r consists of those functions which are in V_r^o and, in addition, have derivatives possessing asymptotic expansions beginning with a term of order at least r+1.

We next define certain integral operators on these spaces V. Specially, we define operators A and B, acting on functions $v(t)$ of V_k^o with $k \geq 2$, as follows:

$$(10.17) \qquad Av(t) = \int_t^\infty e^{\lambda(t-\tau)} v(\tau)\,d\tau \quad ,$$

$$(10.18) \qquad Bv(t) = -\int_t^\infty Av(\tau)\,d\tau \quad .$$

We wish to estimate the norms of $Bv(t)$ in terms of those of $v(t)$. Clearly, the function $Bv(t)$ possesses an asymptotic expansion provided only that the defining integrals converge, for we have seen in Section 2 that the asymptotic expansion for $v(t)$ may be integrated term by term. Thus the norms of $Bv(t)$ exist. Furthermore, the exponent $\lambda(t-\tau)$ in the definition of A is negative in the range of integration, so that we have

$$(10.19) \qquad |Av(t)| \leq \int_t^\infty e^{\lambda(t-\tau)} |v(\tau)|\,d\tau$$

$$\leq \|v\|_k^o \int_t^\infty e^{\lambda(t-\tau)} \tau^{-k}\,d\tau$$

$$\leq \lambda^{-1} t^{-k} \|v\|_k^o \quad .$$

From (10.18), then, we find that

$$(10.20) \qquad |Bv(t)| \leq \lambda^{-1} \|v\|_k^o \int_t^\infty \tau^{-k}\,d\tau$$

$$= \frac{\lambda^{-1}}{k-1} \|v\|_k^o \, t^{-k+1} \quad .$$

Relations (10.19), (10.20) may be written

$$(10.21) \qquad \|Av\|_k^o \leq \lambda^{-1} \|v\|_k^o \quad ,$$

(10.22) $$\|Bv\|^{o}_{k-1} \leq \frac{\lambda^{-1}}{k-1} \|v\|^{o}_{k} \leq \lambda^{-1} \|v\|^{o}_{k} \quad ,$$

since we assumed $k \geq 2$. But from definition (10.18)

(10.23) $$Av(t) = \frac{d}{dt} Bv(t) \quad ;$$

these two relations may therefore be written in condensed form as

(10.24) $$\|Bv\|_{k-1} \leq \lambda^{-1} \|v\|^{o}_{k} \quad ;$$

cf. (10.16). Thus $Bv(t)$ is in V_{k-1} whenever $v(t)$ is in V^{o}_{k} for any $k \geq 2$; in particular, $Bv(t)$ is well-defined and the integral (10.18) converges for any such $v(t)$.

We are now ready to define the functions $u^{(r)}$. Set

(10.25) $$u^{(o)}(t) \equiv u_{o} \quad .$$

Clearly

(10.26) $$\|u^{(o)}\|_{o} = |u_{o}| < \infty \quad ,$$

and furthermore $u^{(o)}(t)$ has as asymptotic expansion the single term u_{o} and satisfies the equation

(10.27) $$u^{(o)}_{tt} - \lambda u^{(o)}_{t} = 0 \quad ,$$

cf. (10.14). We define

(10.28) $$u^{(r+1)}(t) = B[\check{p}(t)u^{(r)}_{t}(t) + q(t)u^{(r)}(t)]$$

for $r \geq 1$, and claim that the $u^{(r)}$ are well defined and satisfy the relation

(10.29) $$\|u^{(r)}\|_{r} < \infty \quad .$$

The proof is by induction: the function $u^{(o)}$ is certainly well defined, and we have already proved (10.29) for $r = 0$.

Now suppose $u^{(r)}(t)$ has been well defined and satisfies (10.29) for some given $r \geq 0$. By the definition (10.13) of $\breve{p}(t)$ and the assumption $q_o = q_1 = 0$, the quantity

(10.30) $$c = \|\tilde{p}\|_1^o + \|q\|_2^o$$

is finite. Thus

(10.31) $$\|\tilde{p}u_t^{(r)} + qu^{(r)}\|_{r+2}^o \leq \|\tilde{p}\|_1^o \|u_t^{(r)}\|_{r+1}^o + \|q\|_2^o \|u^{(r)}\|_r^o$$

$$\leq c\,\|u^{(r)}\|_r < \omega \quad ;$$

thus $u^{(r+1)}$ is well defined--as the function upon which B operates in the right hand side of (10.28) lies in the space V_{r+2}^o --and from relation (10.24) with $k = r+2$ there follows

(10.32) $$\|u^{(r+1)}\|_{r+1} \leq \lambda^{-1}c\,\|u^{(r)}\|_r \quad .$$

Hence relation (10.29) holds for r+1 and the induction is complete.

The functions $u^{(r)}$ which we have defined are solutions to our recursion equation (10.14), as for any v in V_k^o, $k \geq 2$, the identity

(10.33) $$(Bv)_{tt} - \lambda(Bv)_t = -v$$

may be verified by direct calculation. Moreover $u^{(r)}$ vanishes at infinity for $r \geq 1$, as follows immediately from the definition (10.18) of the operator B.

Relation (10.32) is in itself not sufficient to insure the convergence of the series (10.10), as it is necessary for this purpose to estimate all the $u^{(r)}$ with the same norm. By a slight modification, however, we can achieve this result. From (10.30) we obtain

(10.34) $$\|\tilde{p}u_t^{(r)} + qu^{(r)}\|_2^o \leq c\,\|u^{(r)}\|_o \quad ;$$

applying relation (10.24) with $k = 2$ then yields the relation

$$\|u^{(r+1)}\|_1 \leq \lambda^{-1} C \|u^{(r)}\|_0 \quad . \tag{10.35}$$

But from the definition (10.16) of the norm $\|v\|_r$ it follows quite generally that

$$\|v\|_s \leq \frac{1}{t_0} \|v\|_{s+1} \quad ; \tag{10.36}$$

taking $v = u^{(r+1)}$, $s = 0$ and substituting (10.35) we finally obtain the desired relation

$$\|u^{(r+1)}\|_0 \leq \frac{C}{t_0 \lambda} \|u^{(r)}\|_0 \quad . \tag{10.37}$$

Hence if t_0 is chosen large enough, in particular if

$$t_0 > \lambda^{-1} C \quad , \tag{10.38}$$

the series (10.10), and in addition the series obtained from (10.10) by formal differentiation, will converge uniformly for $t \geq t_0$, as may be seen by comparison with the geometric series with common ratio $C/t_0\lambda$. Let $u(t)$ be the sum of the series (10.10); we know that $u(t)$ possesses a derivative u_t given by the series

$$u_t(t) = \sum_{r=0}^{\infty} u_t^{(r)}(t) \quad , \tag{10.39}$$

since the latter series converges uniformly.

The uniform convergence of both of these series implies that

$$\|u\|_0 < \infty \quad ; \tag{10.40}$$

hence the operator B may be applied to the expression $\tilde{p}u_t + qu$, and indeed in a termwise manner, so that after a straight-forward computation the relation

$$B[\tilde{p}u_t + qu] = u - u^{(o)} \tag{10.41}$$

is obtained. In view of relations (10.33) and (10.27), it follows from (10.41) that the function $u(t)$ satisfies the differential equation (10.11), hence equivalently the original differential equation (10.1).

There remains to be shown only that $u(t)$ actually possesses an asymptotic expansion in powers of t^{-1}. This asymptotic expansion, we state, will be the formal sum of the asymptotic expansions which are known to exist for the $u^{(r)}(t)$. Since by (10.29) $u^{(\rho)}(t)$ is in the space V_ρ, hence certainly in V_ρ^0, the functions $u^{(\rho)}$ with $\rho > r$ do not contribute to the r-th order term of this formal sum, so that in the definition of this sum each term can be calculated in a finite number of steps and no questions of convergence can arise. To show that this formal sum is an actual asymptotic expansion for $u(t)$, we must investigate the order of vanishing as $t \longrightarrow \infty$ of the "tail"

(10.42) $$\sum_{\rho=r+1}^{\infty} u^{(\rho)}(t) = u(t) - u^{[r]}(t) \quad ,$$

with

(10.43) $$u^{[r]}(t) = \sum_{\rho=0}^{r} u^{(\rho)}(t) \qquad \text{for } r \geq 0 \quad ,$$

$$u^{[-1]}(t) = 0 \quad .$$

Because of relations (10.41) and (10.28), we may operate on this tail as follows:

(10.44) $$B[\tilde{p}(u - u^{[r]})_t + q(u - u^{[r]})] = u - u^{[r+1]} \quad ,$$

and from (10.30) and (10.24) with $k = r+3$ we obtain

(10.45) $$\|u - u^{[r+1]}\|_{r+2} \leq \lambda^{-1} c \|u - u^{[r]}\|_{r+1} \quad .$$

We know from (10.40) that

(10.46) $$\|u - u^{[-1]}\|_0 = \|u\|_0 < \infty \quad ;$$

hence, by induction,

$$\|u - u^{[r]}\|_{r+1} < \infty \quad \text{for all } r . \tag{10.47}$$

Thus the tail (10.42) approaches zero to order r+1 as $t \to \infty$, and the asymptotic expansion of u(t) corresponds up to terms of order r with the known asymptotic expansion of $u^{[r]}(t)$. The solution u(t) possesses, therefore, an asymptotic power series expansion of order r for every r, or, in short, an infinite asymptotic expansion in powers of t^{-1}, as desired. This completes the proof of the theorem formulated above.

If the differential equation (10.1) fails to be regular because q_0 or q_1 is different from zero, the introduction of the new dependent variable

$$w(t) = e^{-i\mu t} t^{-\nu} u(t) \tag{10.48}$$

will usually lead, for a suitable choice of the parameters μ and ν, to a regular differential equation for the function w. For example, the Bessel equation (10.8) with n = 0 is reduced to the regular differential equation

$$w_{tt} \pm 2iw_t + \frac{1}{4} t^{-2} w = 0 \tag{10.49}$$

by the substitution (10.48) with $\mu = \pm 1$, $\nu = -\frac{1}{2}$.

The proof of the theorem becomes more difficult if the variable t is allowed to take on complex values, as then the two possible cases $p_0 \gtrless 0$ occur simultaneously in perpendicular directions, and a different method of proof, which applies at once to both cases, must be employed. Such a method will be developed in the following sections.

11. Systems of Differential Equations of First Order. Formal Expansions.

The earlier theory of asymptotic expansion of solutions of differential equations was concerned with one equation of any order. In the course of time it has become apparent that systems of first order can be treated in a more transparent way than one equation of higher than first order. Accordingly, we shall develop the general theory for such systems.

There is no restriction in doing this since any solution $u(z)$ of an n-th order linear equation

$$a_0(z)D_z^n u(z) + \dots + a_{n-1}(z)D_z u(z) + a_n(z)u(z) = 0 \quad , \tag{11.1}$$

in which $D_z^\nu = d^\nu/dz^\nu$, is the first component $u = u_1$ of the solution $(u_1(z),\dots,u_n(z))$ of the first order system

$$(11.2)\quad \begin{cases} D_z u_1 = u_2 \ , \\ D_z u_2 = u_3 \ , \\ \cdots\cdots \\ D_z u_{n-1} = u_n \ , \\ a_0(z)D_z u_n = -a_1(z)u_n - a_2(z)u_{n-1} - \dots - a_n(z)u_1 \ . \end{cases}$$

We shall investigate systems of equations of the form

$$(11.3)\quad \begin{aligned} D_z u_1 &= z^k \sum_{\nu=1}^{n} a_{1\nu}u_\nu \ , \\ &\cdots\cdots\cdots \\ D_z u_n &= z^k \sum_{\nu=1}^{n} a_{n\nu}u_\nu \ , \end{aligned}$$

for a system of n analytic functions $u_1(z),\dots,u_n(z)$ of z. The coefficients $a_{\mu\nu} = a_{\mu\nu}(z)$ are also assumed to be analytic functions, and k is any non-negative integer. The number k+1 is usually called the <u>rank</u> of the system.

It is convenient to introduce the "column"

(11.4) $$u = u(z) = \{u_\nu\} = \{u_1, \ldots, u_n\}$$

and the matrix

(11.5) $$A = A(z) = \{a_{\mu\nu}\} = \begin{pmatrix} a_{11}, \ldots, a_{1n} \\ \cdot \quad \cdot \quad \cdot \quad \cdot \quad \cdot \quad \cdot \\ a_{n1}, \ldots, a_{nn} \end{pmatrix}$$

and to write the system (11.3) as one equation

(11.6) $$D_z u = z^k A(z) u \quad .$$

In fact, we shall determine a fundamental system of n linearly independent solutions $u^{(1)}, \ldots, u^{(n)}$ of (11.6) and combine them into a matrix

(11.7) $$U = U(z) = \begin{pmatrix} U_1^{(1)} & \ldots & U_1^{(n)} \\ \cdot & \cdot \quad \cdot & \cdot \\ U_n^{(1)} & \ldots & U_n^{(n)} \end{pmatrix}$$

which satisfies the equation

(11.8) $$D_z U = z^k A(z) U \quad .$$

Every special solution u of (11.6) can then be expressed as a linear combination

(11.9) $$u = c_1 u^{(1)} + \ldots + c_n u^{(n)}$$

of the solutions of the fundamental system and can hence be written in the form

(11.10) $$u = Uc \quad ,$$

where c is the column $c = \{c_1, \ldots, c_n\}$.

Our problem is to determine asymptotic expansions of the solutions near $z = \infty$. Of course, the nature of these expansions depends on the nature of the matrix $A(z)$, i.e. of the coefficients $a_{\mu\nu}(z)$, near $z = \infty$. We assume that the function $A(z)$ admits a power series expansion

(11.11) $$A(z) \sim \sum_{\kappa=0}^{\infty} z^{-\kappa} A^{(\kappa)}$$

in which the matrices $A^{(\kappa)}$ are constant, and that the derivative of $A(z)$ admits the expansion

(11.12) $$D_z A(z) \sim -\sum_{\kappa=1}^{\infty} \kappa z^{-\kappa-1} A^{(\kappa)} \quad .$$

This expansion need not be required to be convergent; it is sufficient to assume that it is asymptotic in a sector $\mathcal{S}_0$ given by

(11.13) $$\Theta_- \leq \arg z \leq \Theta_+ \; , \quad |z| \geq R_0 \quad .$$

Two problems are to be solved: First, formal series expansions are to be found which, upon insertion into equation (11.8), satisfy it formally; secondly, a proper solution of this equation is to be determined which has this formal series as asymptotic expansion.

Formal solutions of single equations of higher order, e.g. (11.1), were derived very early, from 1877 on, by Thomé and others. It was Poincaré who in 1886 showed that each of these formal solutions is the asymptotic expansion of a proper solution.

In his work, Poincaré first assumed that the coefficients of the equation were polynomials; he then determined the solutions of the equation with the aid of the Laplace transformation. Later on the general problem was solved by reducing it to the case of polynomial coefficients and by several other methods.

In most approaches a formal solution is first found and a proper solution belonging to it is constructed afterwards. However, the approach used in Section 10 for a single equation of second order could be used just as well for the general problem. We recall that in this approach a proper solution is first obtained as a convergent series and then each term of this series is expanded asymptotically.

The method which will be presented here—due to W. Wasow [A]—is of the first variety. It is related to certain methods developed by Turittin and others for the "parameter problem", which will be described in a later section, but it is more concise and direct than any of these methods.

To begin with, we note that it is far from obvious what kind of asymptotic expansion the solution $U(z)$ possesses. Of course, we should not expect that it is simply a power series expansion. The following considerations aim primarily at finding the proper type of expansion formally.

We first observe that if the matrix $A(z)$ were a diagonal matrix

$$(11.14) \qquad A(z) = \begin{pmatrix} a_1(z) & 0 & \cdots & 0 \\ 0 & a_2(z) & \cdots & 0 \\ \cdot & \cdot & \cdot & \cdot \\ 0 & 0 & \cdots & a_n(z) \end{pmatrix} = (a_\nu(z))$$

the solution $U(z)$ would be given by

$$(11.15)\quad W(z) = \begin{pmatrix} \int_{e_0}^{z} \tilde{z}^k \alpha_1(\tilde{z})d\tilde{z} & 0 & \cdots & 0 \\ 0 & \int_{e_0}^{z} \tilde{z}^k \alpha_2(\tilde{z})d\tilde{z} & \cdots & 0 \\ \cdots & \cdots & \cdots & \cdots \\ 0 & 0 & & \int_{e_0}^{z} \tilde{z}^k \alpha_n(\tilde{z})d\tilde{z} \end{pmatrix}$$

$$= \left(\int_{e_0}^{z} \tilde{z}^k \alpha_\nu(\tilde{z})d\tilde{z} \right) .$$

The asymptotic behavior of the various solutions could then be determined. It is, therefore, natural to ask whether or not one can transform the given differential equation (11.8) into one with a diagonal matrix $A(z)$.

To do this we follow Wasow in employing a scheme developed by Turittin [B] for the "parameter problem". We first employ a transformation so chosen that the leading term $A^{(0)}$ of $A(z)$ becomes diagonal. The elements in the diagonal of the new matrix $A^{(0)}$ are then the eigenvalues $\alpha_1,\dots,\alpha_n$ of the original matrix $A^{(0)}$. We impose the essential restriction that <u>the eigenvalues $\alpha_1,\dots,\alpha_n$ of the matrix $A^{(0)}$ are simple</u>. We know that then $A^{(0)}$ can be diagonalized; i.e., a non-singular matrix P_0 exists such that the matrix

$$(11.16)\qquad P_0 A^{(0)} P_0^{-1} = \begin{pmatrix} \alpha_1 & 0 & \cdots & 0 \\ 0 & \alpha_2 & \cdots & 0 \\ \cdots & \cdots & \cdots & \cdots \\ 0 & 0 & \cdots & \alpha_n \end{pmatrix} = (\alpha_\nu)$$

is diagonal. Although the condition that the eigenvalues are simple is more restrictive than is necessary to insure the possibility of diagonalization of $A^{(0)}$, it is necessary for the diagonalization of $A(z)$ to be described. The modifications needed in the case in which these eigenvalues are not simple are very complicated; later on, we shall briefly indicate the the intricacies involved.

With the aid of the matrix P_0 we may introduce the column

$$U_1(z) = P_0 U(z) \tag{11.17}$$

as new unknown function instead of $U(z)$. This function is evidently a fundamental solution of the differential equation

$$D_z U_1 = z^k A_1(z) U_1 \quad , \tag{11.18}$$

with

$$A_1(z) = P_0 A(z) P_0^{-1} \quad . \tag{11.19}$$

The matrix $A_1(z)$ possesses the expansion

$$A_1(z) = \sum_{\kappa=0}^{\infty} z^{-\kappa} A_1^{(\kappa)} \quad , \tag{11.20}$$

with

$$A_1^{(\kappa)} = P_0 A^{(\kappa)} P_0^{-1} \quad . \tag{11.21}$$

Clearly, the matrix $A_1^{(0)}$ is exactly the diagonal matrix

$$A_1^{(0)} = \begin{pmatrix} a_1 & 0 & \cdots & 0 \\ 0 & a_2 & \cdots & 0 \\ \cdot & \cdot & \cdots & \cdot \\ 0 & 0 & \cdots & a_n \end{pmatrix} = (a_\nu) \quad . \tag{11.22}$$

Next, we try to diagonalize the matrix $A_1^{(1)}$ without disturbing the matrix $A_1^{(0)}$, and so on. To show that this can be done we prove the

<u>Lemma</u>: Suppose the matrix $B(z)$ possesses the asymptotic expansion

(11.23) $$B(z) = \sum_{\kappa=0}^{\infty} z^{-\kappa} B^{(\kappa)}$$

in the sector $\mathcal{S}_0$, and suppose the matrix $B^{(0)} = A_1^{(0)}$ is diagonal with distinct eigenvalues $\alpha_1, \ldots, \alpha_n$. Then there exists for each $r \geq 1$ a constant matrix Q_r such that:

1) the matrix

(11.24) $$P_r = 1 + z^{-r} Q_r$$

is non-singular in an appropriate sector

(11.25) $$\mathcal{S}_r : \ \Theta_- \leq \arg z \leq \Theta_+ \ , \quad |z| \geq R_r \ ,$$

with $R_r \geq R_0$;

2) the matrix

(11.26) $$\tilde{B}(z) = P_r B(z) P_r^{-1}$$

possesses an asymptotic expansion

(11.27) $$\tilde{B}(z) = \sum_{\kappa=0}^{\infty} z^{-\kappa} \tilde{B}^{(\kappa)}$$

valid in $\mathcal{S}_r$;

3) the first r matrices of the expansion are unchanged in the passage from B to $\tilde{B}$:

(11.28) $$\tilde{B}^{(\kappa)} = B^{(\kappa)} \quad \text{for } \kappa = 0, \ldots, r-1 \ ;$$

and

4) the matrix $\tilde{B}^{(r)}$ is diagonal.

In order to prove this lemma, we note that to every matrix P_r of the form (11.24) there is a number R_r such that P_r possesses a bounded inverse for $|z| \geq R_r$. Hence P_r^{-1} possesses a <u>convergent</u> expansion with respect to powers of z^{-r} for $|z| \geq R_r$, beginning as

$$P_r^{-1} = 1 - z^{-r} Q_r + \dots \quad . \tag{11.29}$$

The matrix $\tilde{B}(z)$ defined by (11.26), therefore, possesses an asymptotic expansion in the sector $\mathcal{S}_r$, cf. (11.25), obtained formally. It is immediately seen from (11.23) and (11.29) that the coefficients of $z^{-\kappa}$ in (11.23) are unchanged for $\kappa < r$ and that the new coefficient of z^{-r} is given by

$$\tilde{B}^{(r)} = B^{(r)} + Q_r B^{(o)} - B^{(o)} Q_r \quad . \tag{11.30}$$

The matrix Q_r can now be so determined that the matrix $\tilde{B}^{(r)}$ in (11.30) is diagonal. Since the matrix $B^{(o)} = A_1^{(o)}$ was assumed to be diagonal with the distinct eigenvalues $\alpha_1, \dots, \alpha_n$ the condition to be satisfied is

$$b_{\mu\nu}^{(r)} + {}_r q_{\mu\nu} \alpha_\nu - \alpha_\mu \, {}_r q_{\mu\nu} = 0 \quad \text{for } \mu \neq \nu \quad , \tag{11.31}$$

where $b_{\mu\nu}^{(r)}$ and ${}_r q_{\mu\nu}$ represent the elements of the matrices $B^{(r)}$ and Q_r respectively. Because of $\alpha_\mu \neq \alpha_\nu$, this condition evidently has the solution

$$ {}_r q_{\mu\nu} = [\alpha_\mu - \alpha_\nu]^{-1} b_{\mu\nu}^{(r)} \quad . \tag{11.32}$$

The diagonal terms ${}_r q_{\nu\nu}$ of Q_r are not determined by the condition and may simply be set equal to zero. Thus the lemma is proved.

Suppose now that the function $U_r(z)$ satisfies the differential equation

$$D_z U_r = z^k A_r(z) U_r \tag{11.33}$$

in which the matrix $A_r(z)$ possesses an expansion of the type (11.11) with $A_r^{(\kappa)}$ diagonal for $\kappa < r$. Then we may apply the Lemma to the matrix $B = A_r$ and construct matrices Q_r, P_r accordingly. Clearly, the column

$$U_{r+1} = P_r U_r \tag{11.34}$$

will satisfy the differential equation

$$D_z U_{r+1} = z^k A_{r+1}(z) U_{r+1} , \tag{11.35}$$

in which

$$A_{r+1} = P_r A_r P_r^{-1} - rz^{-k-r-1} Q_r P_r^{-1} . \tag{11.36}$$

Note that the second part of this expression has an expansion beginning with the term $-rz^{-k-r-1}Q_r$; it is thus of order $k+r+1 \geq r+1$, since $k \geq 0$ was assumed. Consequently, the statements of the Lemma concerning the matrix

$$\tilde{B} = P_r A_r P_r^{-1} \tag{11.37}$$

apply just as well to the matrix A_{r+1}. Consequently, $A_{r+1}^{(r)}$ is diagonal, while, for $\kappa < r$, $A_{r+1}^{(\kappa)} = A_r^{(\kappa)}$ also remains diagonal.

Using a succession of matrices $P_0, P_1, P_2, \ldots$ we thus obtain a succession of matrices $A_1, A_2, A_3, \ldots$ with asymptotic expansions whose κ-th coefficients $A_r^{(\kappa)}$ are the same for all $r \geq \kappa+1$. We may therefore define

$$A_\infty^{(\kappa)} = A_{\kappa+1}^{(\kappa)} = A_{\kappa+2}^{(\kappa)} = \ldots \tag{11.38}$$

and write down a definite formal series

$$\sum_{\kappa=0}^{\infty} z^{-\kappa} A_\infty^{(\kappa)} \tag{11.39}$$

in which all the coefficients are diagonal. For each diagonal term a formal series of the form

$$(11.40)\qquad \sum_{\kappa=0}^{\infty} z^{-\kappa}\,{}_{\infty}a_{\nu}^{(\kappa)} ,$$

where ${}_{\infty}a_{\nu}^{(\kappa)}$ is the ν-th diagonal element of $A_{\infty}^{(\kappa)}$, can be given.

Let us first consider the case in which the expansions (11.11) of the matrices $A_r(z)$ are convergent expansions and the infinite series (11.39) converges to a limit $A_{\infty}(z)$:

$$(11.41)\qquad A_{\infty}(z) = \sum_{\kappa=0}^{\infty} z^{-\kappa} A_{\infty}^{(\kappa)} .$$

Let us further assume that the sequence of transformations $P_0, P_1P_0, P_2P_1P_0, \ldots$ converges uniformly in some sector to a limit transformation T with the inverse S, the limit of the sequence $P_0^{-1}, P_0^{-1}P_1^{-1}, P_0^{-1}P_1^{-1}P_2^{-1}, \ldots$. Then the function

$$(11.42)\qquad U_{\infty}(z) = T(z)U(z)$$

would satisfy the differential equation

$$(11.43)\qquad D_z U_{\infty} = z^k A_{\infty}(z)\, U_{\infty} .$$

Since $A_{\infty}(z)$ is evidently a diagonal matrix, the solution of this equation can be given explicitly. To this end we consider each diagonal term

$$(11.44)\qquad z^k\,{}_{\infty}a_{\nu}(z) = \sum_{\kappa=0}^{\infty} z^{k-\kappa}\,{}_{\infty}a_{\nu}^{(\kappa)}$$

of the matrix $z^k A_{\infty}(z)$, and integrate it. It is necessary to split the integral of $z^k\,{}_{\infty}a_{\nu}(z)$ into two parts, a power series vanishing at infinity, and a polynomial with a logarithmic term added. We set

$$(11.45) \qquad \beta_\nu(z) = \sum_{\kappa=0}^{k} (k-\kappa+1)^{-1} z^{k-\kappa+1} {}_\infty\alpha_\nu^{(\kappa)} + {}_\infty\alpha_\nu^{(k+1)} \log z$$

and

$$(11.46) \qquad \gamma_\nu(z) = \sum_{\kappa=k+2}^{\infty} (k-\kappa+1)^{-1} z^{k-\kappa+1} {}_\infty\alpha_\nu^{(\kappa)}$$

$$= - \sum_{\lambda=1}^{\infty} \lambda^{-1} z^{-\lambda} {}_\infty\alpha_\nu^{(k+1+\lambda)} \quad .$$

Then clearly

$$(11.47) \qquad D_z[\beta_\nu(z) + \gamma_\nu(z)] = z^k {}_\infty\alpha_\nu(z) \quad .$$

According to (11.15), the solution $\underset{\infty}{U}(z)$ of equation (11.43) is then the diagonal matrix $({}_\infty u_\nu(z))$ with diagonal terms

$$(11.48) \qquad {}_\infty u_\nu(z) = e^{\beta_\nu(z)+\gamma_\nu(z)} = e^{\beta_\nu(z)} e^{\gamma_\nu(z)} \quad .$$

It is convenient to introduce the diagonal matrices $E(z)$ and $W(z)$ by giving their ν-th diagonal terms $E_{\nu\nu}(z)$ and $W_{\nu\nu}(z)$ as follows:

$$(11.49) \qquad E_{\nu\nu}(z) = e^{\beta_\nu(z)}$$

$$= z^{[{}_\infty\alpha_\nu^{(k+1)}]} \exp\left\{ \sum_{\kappa=0}^{k} (k-\kappa+1)^{-1} z^{k-\kappa+1} {}_\infty\alpha_\nu^{(\kappa)} \right\} \quad ,$$

$$(11.50) \qquad W_{\nu\nu}(z) = e^{\gamma_\nu(z)} = \exp\left\{ - \sum_{\lambda=1}^{\infty} \lambda^{-1} z^{-\lambda} {}_\infty\alpha_\nu^{(k+1+\lambda)} \right\} \quad .$$

Then we may write

$$(11.51) \qquad \underset{\infty}{U}(z) = W(z)E(z) \quad .$$

Since the function $\gamma_\nu(z)$ is given, by (11.46), in the form of a power series which vanishes at infinity, the function $W(z)$ possesses a power series expansion which approaches the value 1 at ∞:

$$(11.52) \qquad W(z) = 1 + \sum_{\kappa=1}^{\infty} z^{-\kappa} W^{(\kappa)} \quad .$$

The matrix E(z), on the other hand, is an expression involving only exponential functions of polynomials in z and --possibly--fractional powers of z.

With the aid of the transformation S, the limit of the sequence P_0^{-1}, $P_0^{-1}P_1^{-1}$,... the solution U(z) of the original differential equation, connected with the function $U_{\infty}(z)$ by the formula

$$U(z) = S(z)U_{\infty}(z) \quad , \tag{11.53}$$

is given by

$$U(z) = S(z)W(z)E(z) \quad . \tag{11.54}$$

These formulas were derived under the assumption that the series $\sum_{\kappa=0}^{\infty} z^{-\kappa} A_{\infty}^{(\kappa)}$ converges and that the sequences $P_0, P_1P_0, \ldots$ and $P_0^{-1}, P_0^{-1}P_1^{-1}, \ldots$--together with their derivatives--approach limits. If this is not the case the formulas derived have nevertheless a meaning: <u>these formulas give the asymptotic expansion of the solution</u>.

It is convenient to introduce the notion of "formal power series", as an entity assigned to a sequence of coefficients $C^{(\kappa)}$, written symbolically as

$$\tilde{C}(z) = \sum_{\kappa=0}^{\infty} z^{-\kappa} C^{(\kappa)} \quad . \tag{11.55}$$

The operations of addition, multiplication, division if $C^{(0)} \neq 0$, and differentiation can be defined for such series in an obvious manner. The sequence of matrices $A_{\infty}^{(\kappa)}$ which we had introduced earlier, see (11.38), leads to a formal series

$$\tilde{A}_{\infty}(z) = \sum_{\kappa=0}^{\infty} z^{-\kappa} A_{\infty}^{(\kappa)} \quad . \tag{11.56}$$

By the process by which we obtained the matrix W(z) under the assumption that the series $\tilde{A}_{\infty}(z)$ converges, we may define a formal series

(11.57) $$\check{W}(z) = 1 + \sum_{\kappa=1}^{\infty} z^{-\kappa} W^{(\kappa)}(z)$$

without making this assumption. The matrix E(z), on the other hand, is always properly defined, but is not a power series.

However, we want to work solely with power series in the following. For this reason we introduce the function

(11.58) $$V(z) = U(z)E^{-1}(z)$$

instead of U(z). As seen from (11.8), it is to satisfy the equation

(11.59) $$D_z V = z^k A(z)V - VF(z)$$

with

(11.60) $$F(z) = D_z E(z) \cdot E^{-1}(z) \quad .$$

(Note that the matrix

(11.61) $$zF(z) = \sum_{\kappa=0}^{k+1} z^{k+1-\kappa} A_{\infty}^{(\kappa)}$$

is a polynomial of degree k+1.) The desired solution V(z) of (11.59) should satisfy the condition

(11.62) $$V(\infty) = 1$$

and is expected to have an asymptotic power series expansion.

The sequence of transformations

(11.63)
$$T_0 = P_0 ,$$
$$T_1(z) = P_1 P_0 = (1 + z^{-1} Q_1) P_0 ,$$
$$T_2(z) = P_2 P_1 P_0 = (1 + z^{-1} Q_1 + z^{-2} Q_2 + z^{-3} Q_2 Q_1) P_0 ,$$
$$T_3(z) = P_3 P_2 P_1 P_0 = (1 + z^{-1} Q_1 + z^{-2} Q_2 + z^{-3} (Q_2 Q_1 + Q_3) + \ldots) P_0$$
. . . .

also leads to a formal power series; for, the coefficients of powers $\leq r$ in $T_r(z)$ are independent of s for $s \geq r$. The resulting power series will be denoted by $\tilde{T}(z)$:

$$(11.64) \qquad \tilde{T}(z) = (1 + z^{-1}Q_1 + z^{-2}Q_2 + \ldots)P_0 \; ;$$

its inverse will be denoted by $\tilde{S}(z)$:

$$(11.65) \qquad \tilde{S}(z) = (1 - z^{-1}Q_1 + \ldots)P_0$$

$$= 1 + \sum_{\kappa=1}^{\infty} z^{-\kappa} S^{(\kappa)} \quad .$$

The formal series $\tilde{S}(z)\tilde{W}(z)$ will be denoted by $\tilde{V}(z)$,

$$(11.66) \qquad \tilde{V}(z) = \tilde{S}(z)\tilde{W}(z) \quad .$$

If this series converged it would give a solution of equation (11.59), as can be inferred by comparing (11.58) with (11.54). We now maintain: <u>The formal series $\tilde{V}(z)$ satisfies equation (11.59) formally</u>:

$$(11.67) \qquad D_z\tilde{V}(z) = z^k A(z)\tilde{V}(z) - \tilde{V}(z)F(z) \quad .$$

That this is so is clearly indicated by the process by which the series $\tilde{V}(z)$ was derived. Still the statement should be proved. We shall, however, only indicate the steps that should be taken to complete such a proof.

First one should verify the relation

$$(11.68) \qquad D_z\tilde{W} = (z^k \tilde{A}_\infty - F)\tilde{W} \quad .$$

To do this, note that the matrix F consists of the terms of the series $z^k \tilde{A}_\infty$ up to the term in z^{-1}, and that $\tilde{W}(z)$ is therefore identical with the formal expansion of the "formal solution"

$$(11.69) \qquad \exp\left\{ \int^z [\zeta^k \tilde{A}_\infty(\zeta) - F(\zeta)]d\zeta \right\} \quad .$$

Next one should verify the relation

$$(11.70) \qquad D_z\tilde{S} = z^k(A\tilde{S} - \tilde{S}\tilde{A}_\infty) \quad .$$

From relations (11.34), (11.36) we derive by induction that the matrix A_{r+1} can be expressed in terms of the matrix $A_0 = A$ through the relation

$$(11.71) \qquad D_z T_r = z^k(A_{r+1} T_r - T_r A) \quad ,$$

with T_r as defined by (11.63), or equivalently, setting

$$(11.72) \qquad S_r = T_r^{-1} \quad ,$$

through the relation

$$(11.73) \qquad D_z S_r = -S_r \cdot D_z T_r \cdot S_r = z^k(AS_r - S_r A_{r+1}) \quad .$$

In fact, this relation expresses the condition that the function

$$(11.74) \qquad U_{r+1} = T_r U$$

satisfies equation (11.35) whenever U satisfies equation (11.8). Now the matrices A_{r+1} and $\tilde{A}_\infty$ agree in their terms up to the order r; the same is true of S_r and $\tilde{S}$. Consequently, relation (11.70) holds as regards terms of order up to r. Since r is arbitrary, this formal relation holds altogether.

Multiplying relations (11.68) and (11.70) respectively by $\tilde{S}$ on the left and $\tilde{W}$ on the right, and adding the results, we obtain the relation

$$(11.75) \qquad D_z(\tilde{S}\tilde{W}) = z^k A\tilde{S}\tilde{W} - \tilde{S}F\tilde{W} \quad .$$

Using the fact that F and $\tilde{W}$ are diagonal and hence commute, we obtain relation (11.67).

Instead of relation (11.67) we actually need the following, somewhat stronger,

<u>Statement</u>: Suppose that $\hat{V}(z)$ is an analytic function defined in the sector $\mathscr{S}_R$ which there has the formal series $\check{V}(z)$ as its asymptotic expansion, a relation which we indicate by the notation

$$\hat{V}(z) \sim \check{V}(z) \quad , \tag{11.76}$$

and that also

$$D_z\hat{V}(z) \sim D_z\check{V}(z) \tag{11.77}$$

in $\mathscr{S}_R$. Then the function

$$\hat{A}(z) = z^{-k}\{D_z\hat{V}(z) + \hat{V}(z)F(z)\}\hat{V}^{-1}(z) \tag{11.78}$$

has the same asymptotic expansion as $A(z)$:

$$\hat{A}(z) \sim A(z) \quad . \tag{11.79}$$

In other words, the function $\hat{V}(z)$ satisfies an equation

$$D_z\hat{V} = z^k\hat{A}(z)\hat{V} - \hat{V}F(z) \tag{11.80}$$

which differs from equation (11.59) for V only in that the place of the matrix A is taken by a matrix $\hat{A}$ with the same asymptotic expansion.

Again, we only outline the rather obvious steps to be taken in proving this statement.

To every formal series $\tilde{C}(z)$ we assign the sum $[C(z)]^r$ of its terms up to the order r:

$$[C(z)]^r = \sum_{\kappa=0}^{r} z^{-\kappa}C^{(\kappa)} \quad . \tag{11.81}$$

Furthermore we write

$$M_1(z) \underset{s}{\sim} M_2(z) \tag{11.82}$$

if the difference $M_1(z) - M_2(z)$ possesses an asymptotic expansion beginning with terms of order $s+1$.

We then first verify the relation

$$(11.83) \qquad D_z[W]^r \underset{r-k}{\sim} \{z^k[\underset{\infty}{A}]^r - F\}[W]^r \quad ,$$

which follows from the fact that the solution Y(z) of the differential equation

$$(11.84) \qquad D_z Y = \{z^k[\underset{\infty}{A}]^r - F\}Y$$

$$= \sum_{\lambda=2}^{r-k} z^{-\lambda}\underset{\infty}{A}^{(k+\lambda)}Y$$

is given by the diagonal matrix

$$(11.85) \qquad Y = \exp\left\{\sum_{\lambda=1}^{r-k-1}(-\lambda)^{-1}z^{-\lambda}\underset{\infty}{A}^{(k+\lambda+1)}\right\} \quad ,$$

in obvious notation. The terms up to order r-k-1 in the expansion of this matrix are, by virtue of the definition of $\tilde{W}$, exactly the terms up to this order in the expansion of $\tilde{W}$:

$$(11.86) \qquad [Y]^{r-k-1} = [W]^{r-k-1} \quad .$$

Consequently,

$$(11.87) \qquad D_z[W]^r \underset{r-k}{\sim} D_z[Y]^{r-k-1} \underset{r-k}{\sim} D_z Y$$

$$= \{z^k[\underset{\infty}{A}]^r - F\}Y \underset{r-k}{\sim} \{z^k[\underset{\infty}{A}]^r - F\}[W]^{r-k-1}$$

$$\underset{r-k}{\sim} \{z^k[\underset{\infty}{A}]^r - F\}[W]^r \quad .$$

Furthermore, one should verify the relation

$$(11.88) \qquad D_z[S]^r \underset{r-k}{\sim} z^k\{A[S]^r - [S]^r[\underset{\infty}{A}]^r\} \quad .$$

To do this one should observe that the terms up to order r of the transformation S_r supply the corresponding terms of the formal series $\tilde{S}$:

$$(11.89) \qquad [S]^r = [S_r]^r \quad .$$

Furthermore,

(11.90) $$\underset{r}{S} \underset{r}{\sim} [\underset{r}{S}]^r$$

and

(11.91) $$D_z \underset{r}{S} \underset{r+1}{\sim} D_z [\underset{r}{S}]^r \quad .$$

Combining these facts with

(11.92) $$[\underset{\infty}{A}]^r = [\underset{r+1}{A}]^r \quad ,$$

one derives formula (11.88) from relation (11.73).

From formulas (11.83) and (11.88) and definition (11.66), there follows the formula

(11.93) $$D_z [V]^r \underset{r-k}{\sim} z^k A[V]^r - [V]^r F \quad .$$

Thus, bearing definition (11.78) in mind, we have

(11.94) $$\hat{A}(z)\hat{V}(z) \underset{r}{\sim} A[V]^r \quad .$$

Since $\hat{V} \sim \tilde{V}$ and the formal series $\tilde{V}$ has the value 1 at infinity, the inverse function $\hat{V}^{-1}$ exists in a sector $\mathcal{S}_R$ with sufficiently large R, and moreover possesses there the formal inverse series $\tilde{V}^{-1}$ as asymptotic expansion. Hence

(11.95) $$\hat{A}(z) \underset{r}{\sim} A[V]^r \tilde{V}^{-1} \underset{r}{\sim} A \tilde{V} \tilde{V}^{-1} = A(z) \quad ,$$

which, since r is arbitrary, proves our Statement.

Appendix to Section 11

In actual problems it would in general be too cumbersome to carry out the procedure described for determining the asymptotic expansion of a solution. In this procedure, it was necessary to determine successive transformations $\underset{r}{P}$, each of which caused one further term in the expansion of the resulting matrix $A_{r+1}(z)$ to become diagonal. However, it would have been sufficient, as we shall see, to make only the terms up to order k+1 in this expansion diagonal.

Suppose, indeed, this were already the case for the original matrix A(z), so that we might write

$$(11.96) \qquad z^k A(z) = B(z) + C(z) \quad ,$$

with

$$(11.97) \qquad B(z) = \sum_{\kappa=0}^{k+1} z^{k-\kappa} A^{(\kappa)}$$

a diagonal matrix, while

$$(11.98) \qquad C(z) = \sum_{\lambda=2}^{\infty} z^{-\lambda} A^{(k+\lambda)}$$

possesses an asymptotic expansion in negative powers of z.

Since B(z) is diagonal, the diagonal matrix E(z) defined by (11.49) satisfies the equation

$$(11.99) \qquad D_z E(z) = B(z)E(z) \quad .$$

The matrix $V(z) = U(z)E^{-1}(z)$, therefore, satisfies the equation

$$(11.100) \qquad D_z V = -VB + BV + CV \quad ,$$

or

$$(11.101) \qquad BV - VB = D_z V - CV \quad .$$

We know that V(z) possesses an asymptotic power series expansion. Since B is diagonal, it is now seen that the terms $V^{(\kappa)}$ of this series expansion can be determined successively by solving the above equation.

The element $v_{\mu\nu}^{(\kappa)}$ of $V^{(\kappa)}$ should be determined so as to satisfy the equation

$$(11.102) \qquad [a_\mu - a_\nu]v_{\mu\nu}^{(\kappa)} = -\sum_{\sigma=1}^{\kappa} (A^{(\sigma)}V^{(\kappa-\sigma)})_{\mu\nu} + (k-\kappa+1)v_{\mu\nu}^{(\kappa-1-k)} \quad ,$$

where the latter term is to be taken as zero in case $\kappa \leq k$, and the α_ν denote the eigenvalues of $A^{(0)}$; cf. (11.16). Suppose now that the terms $v_{\mu\nu}^{(\lambda)}$ have been determined for $\lambda = 0,1,\ldots,\kappa-1$. Since, by assumption, $\alpha_\mu \neq \alpha_\nu$ for $\mu \neq \nu$, the non-diagonal terms $v_{\mu\nu}^{(\kappa)}$ with $\mu \neq \nu$ can be determined from (11.102) in terms of the $v_{\alpha\beta}^{(\lambda)}$ with $\lambda < \kappa$. For $\mu = \nu$, $\nu = 1,\ldots,n$, relations (11.102), written for $\kappa+1$ instead of κ, involve only the terms $v_{\mu\nu}^{(\lambda)}$ with $\lambda \leq \kappa$, and may now be regarded as equations to determine the n diagonal terms $v_{11}^{(\kappa)},\ldots,v_{nn}^{(\kappa)}$. This can be done, for example, if $k > 0$ and none of the diagonal terms of the matrix $A^{(1)}$ vanishes. Otherwise the procedure is more involved.

If the matrix $B(z)$ is not already diagonal, it can be made so in one step by employing any transformation $P(z)$--a polynomial in z^{-1} or of a form asymptotically expandible in powers of z^{-1}--which diagonalizes the matrix $A(z)$ up to terms of order $k+1$, for example by taking

$$P(z) = T_{k+1}(z) \quad . \tag{11.103}$$

For, then the matrix $PAP^{-1} - z^{-k}D_zP\cdot P^{-1}$ of the new differential equation

$$D_z(PU) = z^k[PAP^{-1} - z^{-k}D_zP\cdot P^{-1}](PU) \tag{11.104}$$

agrees with the transform PAP^{-1} of A up to terms of order $k+1$, since D_zP is at least of second order.

12. Systems of Differential Equations of First Order. Asymptotic Expansions

We proceed to construct a solution of the differential equation (11.8) which has as asymptotic expansion a given formal expansion of the type found in Section 11.

As Wasow has observed, this task is made particularly simple by the use of the following theorem, which goes back to Borel (1895) and for which Ritt (1910) has given a particularly simple proof.

Theorem of Borel-Ritt: To any formal power series $\tilde{V}(z)$ and any arbitrary sector $\mathcal{S}$ there exists an analytic function $\hat{V}(z)$ defined in $\mathcal{S}$ which has the asymptotic expansion

(12.1) $$\hat{V}(z) \sim \tilde{V}(z) \quad \text{in } \mathcal{S},$$

while at the same time its derivative has in $\mathcal{S}$ the asymptotic expansion

(12.2) $$D_z\hat{V}(z) \sim D_z\tilde{V}(z) \quad .$$

Employing the notations of (11.80) and (11.81), we may write relations (12.1), (12.2) in the form

(12.3) $$\hat{V}(z) \underset{r}{\sim} [V(z)]^r \quad ,$$

(12.4) $$D_z\hat{V}(z) \underset{r+1}{\sim} [D_zV(z)]^{r+1} \quad .$$

In order to prove this theorem, we first note that it suffices to give the proof for the case where the coefficients of the expansion $\tilde{V}(z)$ are not matrices but scalars; the more general case can then be treated by combining into a matrix $\hat{V}(z)$ the n^2 scalar functions $\hat{V}_{\nu\mu}(z)$ which have as their respective asymptotic expansions the corresponding entries $\tilde{V}_{\nu\mu}(z)$ of the formal sum $\tilde{V}(z)$.

Thus we let

$$(12.5) \qquad \tilde{v}(z) = \sum_{\kappa=0}^{\infty} z^{-\kappa} v^{(\kappa)}$$

be the given formal expansion, and set

$$(12.6) \qquad \hat{v}(z) = \sum_{\kappa=0}^{\infty} z^{-\kappa}(1 - e^{-b_\kappa z^a})v^{(\kappa)} ,$$

where the positive number $a < 1$ is so chosen that

$$(12.7) \qquad \operatorname{Re}\left(\frac{z}{|z|}\right)^a \geq \varepsilon > 0 \quad \text{in } \mathcal{S} ,$$

while b_κ is defined by

$$(12.8) \qquad b_\kappa |v^{(\kappa)}| = R^\kappa ,$$

where R is some number less than the inner radius of $\mathcal{S}$. Now, for Re $t > 0$ we have

$$(12.9) \qquad |1 - e^{-t}| = \left|\int_0^t e^{-\tau} d\tau\right| \leq \int_0^{|t|} d|\tau| = |t| ;$$

application of this inequality with $t = b_\kappa z^a$ establishes first of all that the series (12.6) defining $\hat{v}(z)$ converges uniformly in the sector $\mathcal{S}$, and secondly that the estimate

$$(12.10) \qquad |z|^r |\hat{v}(z) - [v]^r|$$

$$\leq \sum_{\kappa=0}^{r} |z|^{r-\kappa} e^{-b_\kappa \cdot \varepsilon |z|^a} |v^{(\kappa)}| + \sum_{\kappa=r+1}^{\infty} |z|^{r-\kappa+a} R^\kappa$$

$$= \sum_{\kappa=0}^{r} |z|^{r-\kappa} e^{-\varepsilon b_\kappa |z|^a} |v^{(\kappa)}| + \frac{|z|^a R^{r+1}}{|z| - R}$$

is valid for z in $\mathcal{S}$. Since $0 < a < 1$, both terms of this estimate approach zero as $z \to \infty$; hence the desired relation

$$(12.11) \qquad \hat{v}(z) \underset{r}{\sim} [v]^r$$

holds in $\mathcal{S}$. The relation

$$(12.12) \qquad D_z\hat{v}(z) \underset{r+1}{\sim} [D_z v]^{r+1}$$

is established in a similar manner:

$$(12.13) \quad |z|^{r+1}|D_z\hat{v}(z) - [D_z v]^{r+1}|$$

$$\leq \sum_{\kappa=0}^{r} \kappa|z|^{r-\kappa} e^{-\varepsilon b_\kappa |z|^a} |v^{(\kappa)}|$$

$$+ \sum_{\kappa=r+1}^{\infty} \kappa|z|^{r-\kappa+a} R^{\kappa} + \sum_{\kappa=0}^{\infty} a|z|^{r-\kappa+a} R^{\kappa} e^{-\varepsilon b_\kappa |z|^a}$$

$$\leq \sum_{\kappa=0}^{r} \kappa|z|^{r-\kappa} e^{-\varepsilon b_\kappa |z|^a} |v^{(\kappa)}|$$

$$+ \left\{ \frac{(r+1)R^r|z|^a}{|z| - R} + \frac{R^{r+1}|z|^a}{(|z| - R)^2} \right\}$$

$$+ \left\{ \sum_{\kappa=0}^{r} a|z|^{r-\kappa+a} R^{\kappa} e^{-\varepsilon b_\kappa |z|^a} + \frac{a|z|^a R^{r+1}}{|z| - R} \right\} .$$

Hence the theorem of Borel and Ritt is proved.

We now apply this result to the problem of establishing the existence of a solution $U(z)$ of the equation

$$(12.14) \qquad D_z U = z^k A U$$

with a given asymptotic expansion. We assume that formal series $\tilde{V}$ and $\tilde{A}$ are given such that the function

$$(12.15) \qquad \tilde{U} = \tilde{V}E$$

satisfies the formal equation

$$(12.16) \qquad D_z\tilde{U} = z^k \tilde{A}\tilde{U}$$

formally. While such a formal solution was constructed in the preceding section under the assumption that the eigenvalues $\alpha_\nu^{(o)}$ were distinct, we need not make this assumption from now on. In fact, formal solutions of the form $\tilde{U} = \tilde{V}E$ do exist in many cases in which the eigenvalues are not distinct. In such cases the existence of a solution $U = VE$ with the expansion $\tilde{U} = \tilde{V}E$ can be established just as readily.

Using Ritt's theorem, we may now conclude from the Statement of Section 11 that there are analytic functions $\hat{V}(z)$ and $\hat{A}(z)$ defined and possessing asymptotic expansions in the sector $\mathcal{S}_R$ and having the following properties:

1.

$$(12.17) \qquad \hat{V}(\infty) = 1 \quad ;$$

2. the expansion of $\hat{A}(z)$ is the same as that of $A(z)$; and

3. the function

$$(12.18) \qquad \hat{U}(z) = \hat{V}(z)E(z)$$

satisfies the differential equation

$$(12.19) \qquad D_z\hat{U} = z^k \hat{A}\hat{U} \quad .$$

The function $E(z)$ is here the diagonal matrix

$$(12.20) \qquad E(z) = (\exp\{\beta_\nu(z)\}) \quad ;$$

cf. (11.49).

We note that, since $\hat{V}(\infty) = 1$, the matrix $\hat{V}(z)$ has an inverse $\hat{V}^{-1}(z)$ in an appropriate subsector $\mathcal{S}_{R'}$, described by $|z| \geq R' \geq R$, of $\mathcal{S}_R$. We shall use this inverse to set up an integral equation for the matrix V involved in the solution of the original differential equation (12.14).

We write this equation in the form

$$(12.21) \qquad D_zU - z^k \hat{A}U = z^k(A - \hat{A})U \quad .$$

Evidently, this equation is satisfied by any solution U(z) of the integral equation

$$(12.22)\quad U(z) = \hat{U}(z) + \hat{U}(z) \int_{\infty}^{z} \hat{U}^{-1}(\zeta)\zeta^{k}[A(\zeta) - \hat{A}(\zeta)]U(\zeta)d\zeta \quad ;$$

the integral is to be taken along a path P leading from infinity to the point z in an appropriate way, the precise nature of which will be discussed later on. In fact, each element of the matrix may have its own path of integration.

It will be necessary to work with functions which have asymptotic power series expansions. Therefore we introduce the functions V, $\hat{V}$ instead of U, $\hat{U}$, obtaining the integral equation

$$(12.23)\qquad V(z) = \hat{V}(z) + \hat{V}(z)IV(z) \quad ,$$

where

$$(12.24)\quad IV(z) = \int_{\infty}^{z} E(z)E^{-1}(\zeta)\hat{V}^{-1}(\zeta)\zeta^{k} \cdot [A(\zeta) - \hat{A}(\zeta)]V(\zeta)E(\zeta)E^{-1}(z)d\zeta \quad .$$

Clearly, a solution V(z) of this equation leads to a solution of equation (12.14), and the relation

$$(12.25)\qquad V(\infty) = 1$$

holds.

An integral equation similar to (12.23) was employed by Birkhoff (1908) for the parameter problem. However, Birkhoff did not use the matrix $\hat{A}(z)$ which has the same asymptotic expansion as A(z), but only the matrices $[A(z)]^{r}$. Accordingly, the resulting solution had the desired asymptotic expansion only up to order r-k. Perron (1918) and Tamarkin and Besicowitch (1924) used a thoerem similar to that of Borel-Ritt but employed it only for the initial values of the solution and not to obtain the matrix $\hat{A}(z)$. For references see [C] at the end of Section 15. The present particularly concise argument was given by Wasow [A].

Before we can solve the integral equation (12.23), we must analyze the individual components of the matrix which forms its integrand.

We denote the components of a matrix M by $m_{\lambda\mu}$ or $(M)_{\lambda\mu}$. The diagonal elements of the diagonal matrix E(z) may then be written as

$$(12.26) \qquad e_{\lambda\lambda}(z) = e^{\beta_\lambda(z)} ,$$

with

$$(12.27) \qquad \beta_\lambda(z) = \sum_{\kappa=0}^{k} (k-\kappa+1)^{-1} z^{k-\kappa+1} \, {}_\infty\alpha_\lambda^{(\kappa)} + {}_\infty\alpha_\lambda^{(k+1)} \log z ,$$

cf. (11.45). We shall use the abbreviation

$$(12.28) \qquad \beta_\mu(z) - \beta_\lambda(z) = \beta_{\mu\lambda}(z) .$$

The matrix

$$(12.29) \qquad N = E(z)E^{-1}(\zeta)ME(\zeta)E^{-1}(z)$$

then has the elements

$$(12.30) \qquad n_{\lambda\mu} = e^{\beta_\lambda(z)-\beta_\lambda(\zeta)} m_{\lambda\mu} e^{\beta_\mu(\zeta)-\beta_\mu(z)}$$

$$= m_{\lambda\mu} e^{\beta_{\lambda\mu}(z)-\beta_{\lambda\mu}(\zeta)} .$$

Consequently, the matrix IV(z) has the elements

$$(12.31) \qquad (IV)_{\nu\mu}(z) = \int_{P_{\nu\mu}(z)} e^{\beta_{\nu\mu}(z)-\beta_{\nu\mu}(\zeta)} \zeta^k \cdot \left(\hat{V}^{-1}(\zeta)[A(\zeta) - \hat{A}(\zeta)]V(\zeta)\right)_{\nu\mu} d\zeta$$

We observe that the μ-th column $(IV)^{(\mu)} = \{(IV)_{1\mu},\ldots,(IV)_{n\mu}\}$ of IV depends only on the μ-th column $V^{(\mu)} = \{V_{1\mu},\ldots,V_{n\mu}\}$ of V. In the following we shall treat each such column separately, and accordingly keep the value of μ fixed.

We have indicated in (12.22) that each matrix element has its own path of integration $P_{\nu\mu}(z)$, running from infinity to z. Suppose a sector $\mathcal{S}^{(\mu)} \subseteq \mathcal{S}_0$ to be so chosen that in it paths $P_{\nu\mu}(z)$ could be defined for which the following statements hold:

I.

$$\text{Re}\,[\beta_{\nu\mu}(z) - \beta_{\nu\mu}(\zeta)] \leq 0 \tag{12.32}$$

for all values of ν, all points z in $\mathcal{S}^{(\mu)}$, and all points ζ on $P_{\nu\mu}(z)$.

II. For each m = 1,2,... there is a number $C_m > 0$ such that

$$\int_{P_{\nu\mu}(z)} |\zeta|^{-m-1}|d\zeta| \leq C_m|z|^{-m} \tag{12.33}$$

for all z in $\mathcal{S}^{(\mu)}$.

A sector $\mathcal{S}^{(\mu)}$ in which these two conditions can be met will be called admitted for $U^{(\mu)}$. Later on, we shall show how to choose such sectors $\mathcal{S}^{(\mu)}$. At present, we shall assume that this can be done and derive from these conditions the fact that the integral equation (12.23) possesses in $\mathcal{S}^{(\mu)}$ a solution V with the same asymptotic expansion as $\hat{V}$.

It is convenient for our purposes to assign to a matrix M and its column $M^{(\mu)}$ the local norms

$$|M| = \max_{\lambda,\mu} |m_{\lambda\mu}| \quad , \qquad |M^{(\mu)}| = \max_{\lambda} |m_{\lambda}^{(\mu)}| \quad . \tag{12.34}$$

Then, as is easily verified,

$$|M_1M_2| \leq n|M_1||M_2| \quad , \qquad |M_1M_2^{(\mu)}| \leq n|M_1||M_2^{(\mu)}| \quad , \tag{12.35}$$

where n is the number of elements in a column. If $M = M(z)$ is a function of z in a sector $\mathcal{S}$, we assign to it and to its μ-th column $M^{(\mu)}(z)$ the global norms

$$(12.36)\qquad \|M\| = \underset{z\varepsilon\mathcal{S}}{\text{l.u.b}}\ |M(z)| \quad , \quad \|M^{(\mu)}\| = \underset{z\varepsilon\mathcal{S}}{\text{l.u.b}}\ |M^{(\mu)}(z)| \quad .$$

Clearly, the matrices $\hat{V}(z)$ and $\hat{V}^{-1}(z)$ have finite global norms:

$$(12.37)\qquad \|\hat{V}\| < \infty \quad , \quad \|\hat{V}^{-1}\| < \infty \quad ;$$

in fact, we have shown that the sector $\mathcal{S}$ can be so chosen that this is the case. Furthermore we know that each of the matrices $z^{m+1}[A(z) - \hat{A}(z)]$ has a finite global norm:

$$(12.38)\qquad \|z^{m+1}[A - \hat{A}]\| < \infty \quad ;$$

indeed, this statement says exactly that $A(z)$ and $\hat{A}(z)$ have the same asymptotic expansion. The last relation evidently implies the relation

$$(12.39)\qquad |A(z) - \hat{A}(z)| \leq p_m |z|^{-m-1} \quad \text{for } z \text{ in } \mathcal{S} \quad ,$$

where

$$(12.40)\qquad p_m = \|z^{m+1}[A - \hat{A}]\| < \infty \quad .$$

For the matrix

$$(12.41)\qquad M(z) = \hat{V}^{-1}(z) z^k [A(z) - \hat{A}(z)] V(z) \quad ,$$

we consequently have

$$(12.42)\qquad |M^{(\mu)}(z)| \leq n^2 \|\hat{V}^{-1}\|\, p_m \|V^{(\mu)}\|\, |z|^{k-m-1} \quad .$$

We next estimate the elements

$$(12.43)\qquad n_{\nu\mu}(z,\zeta) = m_{\nu\mu} e^{\beta_{\nu\mu}(z) - \beta_{\nu\mu}(\zeta)}$$

of the matrix

(12.44) $$N(z,\zeta) = E(z)E^{-1}(\zeta)M(\zeta)E(\zeta)E^{-1}(z) \quad ,$$

cf. (12.29). Since by assumption the real parts of $\beta_{\nu\mu}(z) - \beta_{\nu\mu}(\zeta)$ are negative on $P_{\nu\mu}(z)$, we have

(12.45) $$|n_{\nu\mu}(z,\zeta)| \leq |m_{\nu\mu}(\zeta)| \leq n^2\|\hat{V}^{-1}\| p_m \|v^{(\mu)}\| \, |\zeta|^{k-m-1}$$

for ζ on $P_{\nu\mu}(z)$. After integration over $P_{\nu\mu}$, we find, making use of assumption II, that for $m > k$

(12.46) $$(IV(z))_{\nu\mu} \leq q_m \|v^{(\mu)}\| \, |z|^{k-m} \quad ,$$

or

(12.47) $$|IV^{(\mu)}(z)| \leq n q_m \|v^{(\mu)}\| \, |z|^{k-m} \quad ,$$

where

(12.48) $$q_m = n^2\|\hat{V}^{-1}\| p_m c_{m-k} \quad .$$

Finally, we obtain

(12.49) $$|\hat{V}(z)IV^{(\mu)}(z)| \leq Q_m \|v^{(\mu)}\| \, |z|^{-m} \quad \text{for} \quad m \geq 1 \quad ,$$

with

(12.50) $$Q_m = \|\hat{V}\| n^2 q_{m+k} < \infty \quad .$$

This inequality (12.49) implies that <u>any solution</u> $V(z)$ <u>of the integral equation</u> (12.23) <u>has the same asymptotic expansion as the function</u> $\hat{V}(z)$, provided only that its global norm $\|V\|$ is finite.

In order to prove that such a solution V with finite norm actually exists in a sector $\mathcal{S}_R$ with a sufficiently large value of R, we employ the inequality for m = 1, and assume

$$R = \theta^{-1} Q_1 , \quad 0 < \theta < 1 . \tag{12.51}$$

Then the inequality (12.49) reads

$$|\hat{V}(z) I V^{(\mu)}(z)| \leq \theta \| V^{(\mu)} \| \tag{12.52}$$

for $|z| \geq R$; consequently

$$\| \hat{V}(IV)^{\mu} \| \leq \theta \| V^{(\mu)} \| . \tag{12.53}$$

This inequality is sufficient to insure that the iteration scheme

$$\begin{cases} V_0^{(\mu)} = \hat{V}^{(\mu)} , \\ V_{\sigma+1}^{(\mu)} = \hat{V}^{(\mu)} + \hat{V}(IV_\sigma)^{(\mu)} \end{cases} \tag{12.54}$$

converges, and further that the limit function $V^{(\mu)} = V_\infty^{(\mu)}$ is analytic and satisfies

$$\| (IV_\sigma)^{(\mu)} - (IV)^{(\mu)} \| \longrightarrow 0 \quad \text{as} \quad \sigma \longrightarrow \infty . \tag{12.55}$$

Hence this limit function has finite norm and satisfies the integral equation (12.23), and therefore leads to a solution $U^{(\mu)}$ of the differential equation (12.14). If, therefore, a sector $\mathcal{S}$ is contained in an admitted sector $\mathcal{S}^{(\mu)}$ for each $\mu = 1,\ldots,n$, a full matrix solution $U(z) = V(z)E(z)$ is defined in $\mathcal{S}$ and possesses there the same asymptotic expansion as the function $\hat{U}(z)$ defined by (12.18).

13. Admitted Sectors and Paths

We now investigate the nature of admitted sectors, i.e. sectors in which paths can be defined such that the conditions I and II of Section 12 are met. To this end we consider the functions

$$(13.1)\qquad \beta_{\nu\mu}(z) = \sum_{\kappa=0}^{k} (k-\kappa+1)^{-1} z^{k-\kappa+1} {}_{\infty}a_{\nu\mu}^{(\kappa)} + {}_{\infty}a_{\nu\mu}^{(k+1)} \log z ,$$

where

$$(13.2)\qquad {}_{\infty}a_{\nu\mu}^{(\kappa)} = {}_{\infty}a_{\nu}^{(\kappa)} - {}_{\infty}a_{\mu}^{(\kappa)} .$$

It would not be necessary here for us to assume that the condition

$$(13.3)\qquad a_{\nu\mu} = {}_{\infty}a_{\nu\mu}^{(0)} = a_{\nu} - a_{\mu} \neq 0 \quad \text{for} \quad \nu \neq \mu$$

is satisfied, as we had done in developing the formal expansion in Section 11. Nevertheless, we make this assumption for the sake of simplicity, as it would otherwise be somewhat awkward to carry out the following discussion, though in principle nothing prevents us from doing so.

As we shall show later on, the asymptotic behavior of the function $\beta_{\nu\mu}(z)$ will be determined by its leading term

$$(13.4)\qquad (k+1)^{-1} z^{k+1} a_{\nu\mu} .$$

It is therefore convenient to introduce the quantities

$$(13.5)\qquad \hat{z} = z^{k+1} , \qquad \hat{\zeta} = \zeta^{k+1} ,$$

and choose the paths $P_{\nu\mu}$ in such a way that their images $\hat{P}_{\nu\mu}$ in the $\hat{\zeta}$-plane are straight lines

$$(13.6)\qquad \hat{\zeta} = \hat{z} + \sigma \eta_{\nu\mu} , \qquad 0 \leq \sigma < \infty ,$$

where the $\eta_{\nu\mu}$ are appropriately chosen complex numbers of absolute value unity:

$$(13.7) \qquad |\eta_{\nu\mu}| = 1 \quad .$$

These $\eta_{\nu\mu}$ will be so chosen that:

1) the path $\hat{P}_{\nu\mu}$ lies in the sector defined by

$$(13.8) \qquad \hat{\Phi}_- \leq \arg \hat{z} \leq \hat{\Phi}_+ \quad ,$$

where $\hat{\Phi}_\pm$ is to be defined later, cf. (13.12);

2) the backward prolongation of $\hat{P}_{\nu\mu}$, given by formula (13.6) with $\sigma < 0$, intersects one of the bounding rays of this sector; and

3) the relation

$$(13.9) \qquad \mathrm{Re}\, a_{\nu\mu}\, \eta_{\nu\mu} > 0$$

holds.

The possibility of choosing the $\eta_{\nu\mu}$, hence the nature of admitted domains and paths, depends on the relative positions of the vectors representing the complex numbers $\bar{a}_{\nu\mu}$, the conjugates of the numbers $a_{\nu\mu}$. Among the values of $\nu \neq \mu$ we select one, renumber it $\nu = 1$, fix a determination of the corresponding angle $\arg \bar{a}_{1\mu}$. Among the possible determinations of the angles $\arg \bar{a}_{\nu\mu}$ corresponding to the other vectors $\bar{a}_{\nu\mu}$ with $\nu \neq 1$ and $\nu \neq \mu$, we then choose that one for which

$$(13.10) \qquad \arg \bar{a}_{1\mu} \leq \arg \bar{a}_{\nu\mu} < \arg \bar{a}_{1\mu} + 2\pi \quad .$$

Next we renumber these values of ν as $2,3,\ldots,n-1$ in such a way that

$$(13.11) \qquad \arg \bar{a}_{2\mu} \leq \arg \bar{a}_{3\mu} \leq \cdots \leq \arg \bar{a}_{n-1,\mu} \quad .$$

We then introduce a pair of angles $\hat{\Phi}_-$, $\hat{\Phi}_+$ such that

$$(13.12) \qquad \hat{\Phi}_- > \arg \bar{a}_{n-1,\mu} - \frac{3\pi}{2} \,, \quad \hat{\Phi}_+ < \arg \bar{a}_{1\mu} + \frac{3\pi}{2}$$

and

(13.13) $$\pi < \hat{\Phi}_{+} - \hat{\Phi}_{-} < 2\pi \quad .$$

Finally, we set

(13.14) $$\Phi_{\pm} = (k+1)^{-1} \hat{\Phi}_{\pm}$$

and maintain that <u>the sector $\mathcal{S}^{(\mu)}$ given by</u>

(13.15) $$\Phi_{-} \leq \arg z \leq \Phi_{+} \quad , \quad |z| \geq R$$

<u>is admitted</u> for $U^{(\mu)}$ if R is large enough, provided that, as we assume from now on, the original sector $\mathcal{S}_0$ of asymptotic expansibility of A(z) is large enough to contain it.

We note that there is thus some leeway in the choice of admitted sectors, even if the determinations of $\arg \bar{a}_{\nu\mu}$ are fixed. Those sectors that belong to the same set of determinations may be called "equivalent". The totality of all such equivalent admitted sectors forms the sector $\mathcal{S}^{(\mu)}$:

(13.16) $$\Theta_{-} = \frac{1}{k+1}\left(\arg \bar{a}_{n-1,\mu} - \frac{3\pi}{2}\right) < \arg z$$

$$< \frac{1}{k+1}\left(\arg \bar{a}_{1,\mu} + \frac{3\pi}{2}\right) = \Theta_{+} \quad ,$$

which is called a <u>maximal admissibility sector</u>. The lines $\arg z = \Theta_{\pm}$ forming the boundary of this maximal admissibility sector will be called edges or "Stokes lines". In the special case n = 2 the maximal admissibility sector covers the angle

(13.17) $$\Theta_{+} - \Theta_{-} = \frac{3\pi}{k+1} \quad .$$

For k = 0 this result is in agreement with the well-known property of the asymptotic expansion of the Bessel functions.

To prove the statement that the sector $\mathcal{S}^{(\mu)}$ given by (13.15) is admitted, we assign to each value of $\nu \neq n$ a unit vector $\eta_{\nu\mu}$ in such a way that the two conditions

$$(13.18) \qquad \arg \bar{a}_{\nu\mu} - \frac{\pi}{2} < \arg \eta_{\nu\mu} < \arg \bar{a}_{\nu\mu} + \frac{\pi}{2}$$

and

$$(13.19) \qquad \hat{\Phi}_+ - \pi < \arg \eta_{\nu\mu} < \hat{\Phi}_- + \pi$$

are satisfied. This can be done, since by virtue of (13.10), (13.11), and (13.12) the inequalities

$$(13.20) \qquad \arg \bar{a}_{\nu\mu} - \frac{\pi}{2} \leq \arg \bar{a}_{n-1,\mu} - \frac{\pi}{2} < \hat{\Phi}_- + \pi$$

and

$$(13.21) \qquad \hat{\Phi}_+ - \pi \leq \arg \bar{a}_{1\mu} + \frac{\pi}{2} \leq \arg \bar{a}_{\nu\mu} + \frac{\pi}{2}$$

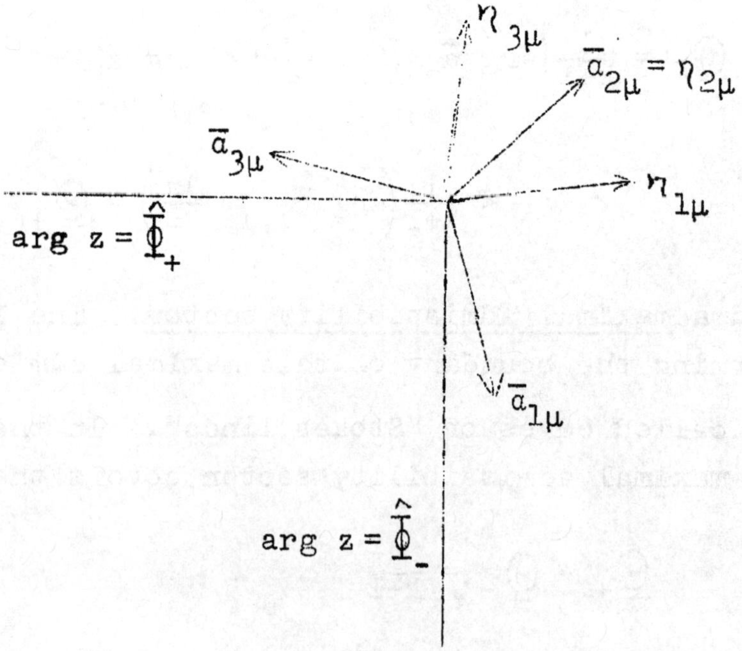

Figure 4

Determination of the vectors η in the case $n = 4$

hold, while from (13.13) the inequality

$$(13.22) \qquad \hat{\Phi}_{+} - \pi < \hat{\Phi}_{-} + \pi$$

follows.

Condition (13.9), the third of the three desired properties of $\eta_{\nu\mu}$ expressed above, is seen to be a consequence of relation (13.18). The second of these properties is a consequence of relation (13.19), as is immediately verified, while the first follows from the fact that because of the first inequality of (13.13), the vector $\eta_{\nu\mu}$ itself lies in the sector given by (13.8).

The sector $\hat{\mathcal{S}}^{(\mu)}$ in the $\hat{z}$-plane which corresponds to the sector $\mathcal{S}^{(\mu)}$ in the z-plane is cut out of the sector (13.8) by the condition

$$(13.23) \qquad |\hat{z}| \geq \hat{R} = R^{k+1} \quad .$$

This condition has the effect that for the points z in two certain "shadow regions" (whose images in the $\hat{z}$-plane are

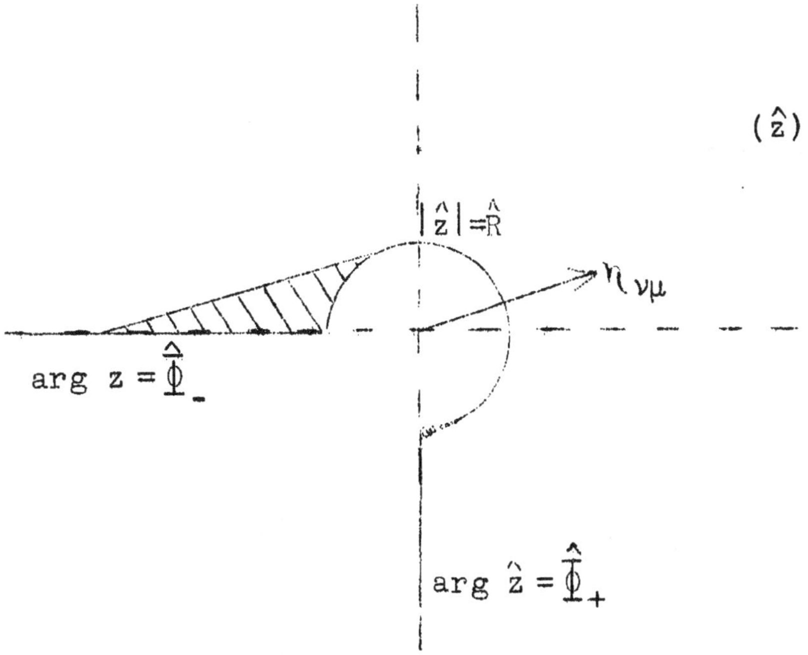

Figure 5

"Shadow Regions" in the determination of admitted paths

shown in Figure 5) the path $\hat{P}_{\nu\mu}$ given by (13.6) intersects the circle $|\hat{z}| = \hat{R}$. We shall exclude these two regions without further referring to them; instead, we also might have defined the paths $P_{\nu\mu}$ differently for points z in these regions, as we did in Section 4.

In order to prove that the two requirements I and II (cf. (12.32), (12.33)) are met for the sector $\mathcal{S}^{(\mu)}$, we first state the

<u>Lemma</u>: There is a constant $\delta > 0$ such that

$$\left|\frac{\zeta}{z}\right| \geq \delta \tag{13.24}$$

on each path $P_{\nu\mu}$.

In fact,

$$\begin{aligned} |\hat{\zeta}/\hat{z}|^2 &= 1 + 2\sigma \operatorname{Re}\,(\eta_{\nu\mu}\hat{z}^{-1}) + \sigma^2 |\hat{z}|^{-2} \\ &\geq 1 + 2\sigma |\hat{z}|^{-1} \operatorname{Re}\, e^{i\phi} + \sigma^2 |\hat{z}|^{-2} \\ &\geq 1 - (\operatorname{Re}\, e^{i\phi})^2 \quad , \end{aligned} \tag{13.25}$$

where

$$0 < \phi = \max \left| \hat{\Phi}_{\pm} - \arg \eta_{\nu\mu} \right| < \pi \quad . \tag{13.26}$$

Thus we can take

$$\delta = \left| 1 - (\operatorname{Re}\, e^{i\phi})^2 \right|^{1/2(k+1)} > 0 \quad . \tag{13.27}$$

From this lemma we easily derive requirement II. For, we have

$$|z|^m \int_{P_{\nu\mu}(z)} |\zeta|^{-m-1} |d\zeta| = \int_{P_{\nu\mu}(\frac{z}{|z|})} |\tilde{\zeta}|^{-m-1} |d\tilde{\zeta}| \quad . \tag{13.28}$$

We may split up the latter integral into a term contributed by the portion of the path lying within the unit circle and a term due to the remainder of the path. As the starting-point $z/|z|$ itself lies on this circle, the first of these terms may be estimated by

$$2\delta^{-m-1} , \tag{13.29}$$

while the second can be no greater than

$$\int_1^\infty x^{-m-1}dx = m^{-1} \leq 1 . \tag{13.30}$$

Thus in (12.33) we may take

$$C_m = 1 + 2\delta^{-m-1} < \infty . \tag{13.31}$$

Finally, we verify requirement I. We write

$$\beta_{\nu\mu}(z) - \beta_{\nu\mu}(\zeta) = (k+1)^{-1} \alpha_{\nu\mu} (\hat{z} - \hat{\zeta})\, h_{\nu\mu}(z,\zeta) , \tag{13.32}$$

with

$$h_{\nu\mu}(z,\zeta) = \sum_{\kappa=0}^{k} \frac{k+1}{k-\kappa+1} \alpha_{\nu\mu}^{-1}\, {}_{\infty}\alpha_{\nu\mu}^{(\kappa)} \frac{\hat{z}^{\frac{k+1-\kappa}{k+1}} - \hat{\zeta}^{\frac{k+1-\kappa}{k+1}}}{\hat{z} - \hat{\zeta}} + \alpha_{\nu\mu}^{-1} \frac{{}_{\infty}\alpha_{\nu\mu}^{(\kappa+1)}}{\hat{z} - \hat{\zeta}} \log (\hat{z}/\hat{\zeta}) . \tag{13.33}$$

Now

$$\left| \frac{\hat{z}^{\frac{k+1-\kappa}{k+1}} - \hat{\zeta}^{\frac{k+1-\kappa}{k+1}}}{\hat{z} - \hat{\zeta}} \right| \tag{13.34}$$

$$= \left| \frac{1}{\sigma} \int_0^\sigma \frac{k+1-\kappa}{k+1} (\hat{z} + \vartheta \eta_{\nu\mu})^{-\frac{\kappa}{k+1}} d\vartheta \right| \leq (\delta |\hat{z}|)^{-\frac{\kappa}{k+1}} ,$$

which for $\kappa > 0$ approaches zero as $|z| \to \infty$. Consequently,

$$(13.35) \qquad h_{\nu\mu}(z,\zeta) \to 1 \text{ as } |z| \to \infty .$$

Therefore one can make the radius R so large that for $|z| \geq R$

$$(13.36) \qquad |\alpha_{\nu\mu}\eta_{\nu\mu}(h_{\nu\mu} - 1)| < \operatorname{Re} \alpha_{\nu\mu}\eta_{\nu\mu} .$$

As a consequence,

$$(13.37) \quad \operatorname{sgn} \operatorname{Re} [\beta_{\nu\mu}(z) - \beta_{\nu\mu}(\zeta)] = \operatorname{sgn} \operatorname{Re} \alpha_{\nu\mu}(\hat{z} - \hat{\zeta})h_{\nu\mu}(z,\zeta)$$

$$= - \operatorname{sgn} \operatorname{Re} \alpha_{\nu\mu}\eta_{\nu\mu}h_{\nu\mu}(z,\zeta)$$

$$= - \operatorname{sgn} \operatorname{Re} \alpha_{\nu\mu}\eta_{\nu\mu} < 0 ,$$

by (13.9). Thus requirement II is met.

14. Analytic Continuation. Dominant and Recessive Solutions. Stokes Phenomenon

A solution $U^{(\mu)}(z)$ can be characterized by the condition that

$$(14.1) \qquad U^{(\mu)}(z)e^{-\beta_\mu(z)} \to 1^{(\mu)}$$

if z approaches infinity in a direction within the maximal sector of admissibility; here $1^{(\mu)}$ is the column with the components

$$(14.2) \qquad 1_\nu^{(\mu)} = \delta_{\nu\mu} = 0 \text{ if } \nu \neq \mu$$

$$= 1 \text{ if } \nu = \mu .$$

According to our construction (Section 13) there are several solutions $U^{(\mu)}(z)$, each with a different maximal sector of admissibility. In fact, there are in general

$(k+1)(n-1)$ solutions $U^{(\mu)}(z)$, since any one of the n-1 subscripts $\nu \neq \mu$ could be chosen as the first one, $\nu = 1$, and any of the k+1 determinations of $z = \hat{z}^{1/(k+1)}$ could be adopted. All these solutions carry the same exponential factor $e^{\beta_\mu(z)}$; they will be said to be of the same "asymptotic type".

Since two of these maximal admissibility regions may overlap, it may happen that two different solutions $U^{(\mu)}(z)$ of the same type are defined in the same subsection. We may ask what relationship exists between them.

To discuss this question it is convenient to introduce the notion of "dominance". Any of the solutions $U^{(\mu)}(z)$ behaves like $e^{a_\mu z^{k+1}/(k+1)}$ as $|z| \to \infty$. Such a solution is said to dominate the solution $U^{(\nu)}(z)$ in the direction η if

$$\text{(14.3)} \qquad \operatorname{Re} a_{\nu\mu} \hat{\eta} < 0 \quad \text{for} \quad \hat{\eta} = \eta^{k+1} ,$$

for then $U_\mu(z)/U_\nu(z) \to \infty$ as $z \to \infty$ in the direction η. If $U^{(\mu)}(z)$ dominates all other solutions $U^{(\nu)}(z)$ in a direction η it is said to be "dominant" in this direction. If $U^{(\mu)}(z)$ is dominated by all other solutions in the direction η it is said to be "recessive" in the direction η.

Suppose all the vectors $\bar{a}_{\nu\mu}$, $\nu \neq \mu$, lie in one quadrant. Then for every direction $\hat{\eta}$ in this quadrant condition (14.3), with μ and ν interchanged, is satisfied. Consequently, $U^{(\mu)}(z)$ is recessive in every direction $\eta = \hat{\eta}^{1/(k+1)}$. If the opposite direction $-\hat{\eta} = \hat{\eta} e^{\pm i\pi}$ lies in the maximal $\hat{z}$-domain of admissibility, the solution $U^{(\mu)}(z)$ is dominant in the direction $(-\hat{\eta})^{1/(k+1)} = (\hat{\eta} e^{\pm i\pi})^{1/(k+1)}$.

Consider two solutions $U^{(\mu)}(z)$, both being defined in the intersection of their maximal admissibility sectors. The difference of these two solutions, being itself a solution, may be expressed as a linear combination of any n linearly independent solutions. Clearly, this difference is dominated by either of the original solutions, since the leading term cancels out in taking the difference. If there were no other solution dominated by $U^{(\mu)}(z)$ the two solutions would have to be identical, but there always is a dominated solution. In any case the remark made restricts the possibilities of expressing the difference of two solutions $U^{(\mu)}(z)$ in terms of other solutions.

Suppose one were able to express one solution $U^{(\mu)}(z)$ in terms of another one $\overset{(1)}{U}{}^{(\mu)}(z)$ and some dominated solutions $U^{(\nu)}(z)$, and suppose that the sectors of admissibility of $\overset{(1)}{U}{}^{(\mu)}(z)$ and the $U^{(\nu)}(z)$ employed include in their interiors the edge of the domain of maximal admissibility of $U^{(\mu)}(z)$. Then this formula could be used to continue the solution $U^{(\mu)}(z)$ analytically across this edge.

Let $U^{(\nu_1)}(z), U^{(\nu_2)}(z), \ldots, U^{(\nu_s)}(z)$ be a set of linearly independent solutions dominated by $U^{(\mu)}(z)$ near the edge and so chosen that $U^{(\nu_1)}$ dominates the others there. These solutions should also be so chosen that they can be continued across the edge. Consequently we may express $\overset{(1)}{U}{}^{(\mu)}(z)$ in the form

$$U^{(\mu)}(z) = \overset{(1)}{U}{}^{(\mu)}(z) + c_1 U^{(\nu_1)}(z) + \ldots + c_s U^{(\nu_s)}(z) \quad . \tag{14.4}$$

As we shall show below, beyond the edge the solution $U^{(\nu_1)}(z)$ dominates $\overset{(1)}{U}{}^{(\mu)}(z)$ as well as $U^{(\nu_2)}(z), \ldots, U^{(\nu_s)}(z)$. The asymptotic behavior of the analytic continuation $\underset{\sim}{U}^{(\mu)}(z)$ beyond the edge is therefore given by

$$\underset{\sim}{U}^{(\mu)}(z) \sim c_1 U^{(\nu_1)}(z) \quad , \tag{14.5}$$

provided $c_1 \neq 0$. If this coefficient c_1 were determined, <u>the jump in the asymptotic expansion of $U^{(\mu)}(z)$ would be determined.</u>

Consider a direction $\hat{\eta}$ near the edge of the image in the $\hat{z}$-plane of the domain of maximal admissibility of $U^{(\mu)}$; e.g., let

(14.6) $$\arg \hat{\eta} = \arg \bar{a}_{1\mu} + \frac{3\pi}{2} - \varepsilon \quad .$$

Then

(14.7) $$\operatorname{Re} a_{1\mu} \hat{\eta} = |a_{1\mu}| \operatorname{Im} e^{-i\varepsilon} < 0 \quad .$$

Therefore $U^{(\mu)}(z)$ dominates $U^{(1)}(z)$ in the corresponding direction $\eta = \hat{\eta}^{1/(k+1)}$.

Thus near the edge of its maximal domain of admissibility a solution dominates at least one other; it will in general dominate several other solutions, if not all.

Of course, this statement makes sense only if there exists one solution $U^{(1)}(z)$ which is defined in the neighborhood of the edge $\mathcal{E}$; i.e. for which this edge lies within the maximal admissibility sector. This is in fact the case. We need only choose in the determination of $U^{(1)}(z)$ the subscript μ as the "first" one, i.e. use determinations of $\arg \bar{a}_{\lambda 1}$, $\lambda \neq 1$, such that

(14.8) $$\arg \bar{a}_{\mu 1} < \arg \bar{a}_{\lambda 1} \quad , \quad \lambda \neq \mu \quad .$$

A little discussion shows that then the edge $\mathcal{E}$ lies in the maximal domain of admissibility of $U^{(1)}(z)$.

Note that the edge $\mathcal{E}$ is perpendicular to the direction $\bar{a}_{1\mu} = -\bar{a}_{\mu 1}$. Hence the solution $U^{(1)}(z)$, which is dominated by $U^{(\mu)}(z)$ along a direction ahead of the edge, dominates any solution $\overset{(1)}{U}{}^{(\mu)}(z)$ beyond the edge.

For simplicity, we assume that all the angles arg $\bar{\alpha}_{\mu\nu}$, $\nu \neq \mu$ are different from each other. We then may conclude that none of the solutions $U^{(\nu)}(z)$ for $\nu \neq \mu$, $\nu \neq 1$ changes its dominance relative to $U^{(\mu)}(z)$ and $U^{(1)}(z)$ at the edge $\mathcal{E}$. Since the solutions $U^{(\nu)}(z)$ occurring in the expression (14.4) are dominated by $\overset{(1)}{U}{}^{(\mu)}(z)$ ahead of the edge, these same solutions, except for $U^{(1)}(z)$, are dominated by $\overset{(1)}{U}{}^{(\mu)}(z)$ beyond the edge; hence they are dominated by $U^{(1)}(z)$ beyond the edge, and consequently they are also dominated by $U^{(1)}(z)$ ahead of the edge.

Thus we see that we can take $U^{(1)}(z)$ as the solution denoted by $U^{(\nu_1)}(z)$ in formula (14.4). We, therefore, have <u>characterized precisely the solution</u> $U^{(\nu_1)}(z) = U^{(1)}(z)$ <u>whose contribution is responsible for the jump in the asymptotic expansion of the solution</u> $U^{(\mu)}(z)$ <u>when it is continued analytically across an edge of its maximal domain of admissibility</u>.

For the discussions in this section see the work of Birkhoff [D] and Turrittin [B].

15. Special Cases

As was observed at the beginning of Section 11, a differential equation of any order for a single function can be reduced to a system of equations of the first order. To do this for an equation of the second order this equation should be written in the form

$$(15.1) \qquad D_z^2 w + z^k a(z) D_z w + z^{2k} b(z) w = 0 \quad ,$$

in which the functions a(z), b(z) possess asymptotic power series expansions

(15.2) $a(z) \sim \sum_{\kappa=0}^{\infty} a^{(\kappa)} z^{-\kappa}$, $b(z) \sim \sum_{\kappa=0}^{\infty} b^{(\kappa)} z^{-\kappa}$.

Setting

(15.3) $$w = u_1 \quad , \quad D_z w = z^k u_2 \quad ,$$

one finds that equation (15.2) is equivalent with the system

(15.4) $$\begin{aligned} D_z u_1 &= z^k u_2 \\ D_z u_2 &= -z^k b(z) u_1 - z^k [a(z) + k z^{-k-1}] u_2 \quad , \end{aligned}$$

which is of the form (11.8) with

(15.5) $$A(z) = \begin{pmatrix} 0 & 1 \\ -b(z) & -a(z) - kz^{-k-1} \end{pmatrix} .$$

The eigenvalues of the matrix

(15.6) $$A^{(0)} = \begin{pmatrix} 0 & 1 \\ -b^{(0)} & -a^{(0)} \end{pmatrix}$$

are

(15.7) $$\alpha_{1,2}^{(0)} = \frac{1}{2} \left\{ -a^{(0)} \pm \sqrt{[a^{(0)}]^2 - 4b^{(0)}} \right\} .$$

If

(15.8) $$[a^{(0)}]^2 \neq 4b^{(0)} \quad ,$$

the theory developed in Sections 11 to 13 is applicable.

To obtain the matrix E(z) which characterizes the asymptotic types of the solutions, one should expand the eigenvalues of the matrix

(15.9) $$\sum_{\kappa=0}^{k+1} z^{-\kappa} A^{(\kappa)}$$

up to terms of the order z^{-k-1}, which we do not want to carry out in general.

For the special equation of second order treated in Section 10, we evidently may take $k = 0$. In this case it is sufficient to expand the eigenvalue $\alpha_{1,2}(z)$ of the matrix

$$(15.10) \quad A^{(0)} + z^{-1}A^{(1)} = \begin{pmatrix} 0 & 1 \\ -b^{(0)} & -a^{(0)} \end{pmatrix} + z^{-1}\begin{pmatrix} 0 & 0 \\ -b^{(1)} & -a^{(1)} \end{pmatrix} .$$

We find

$$(15.11) \quad \alpha_{1,2}(z) = \frac{1}{2}\Big\{-a^{(0)} - z^{-1}a^{(1)} \pm \sqrt{[a^{(0)}+z^{-1}a^{(1)}]^2 - 4b^{(0)} - 4z^{-1}b^{(1)}}\Big\} ;$$

hence $\alpha_{1,2}^{(0)}$ is given by (15.7) and $\alpha_{1,2}^{(1)}$ by

$$(15.12) \quad \alpha_{1,2}^{(1)} = -\frac{1}{2}\, a^{(1)} \pm \frac{1}{2}\{[a^{(0)}]^2 - 4b^{(0)}\}^{-1/2}\{a^{(0)}a^{(1)} - 2b^{(1)}\} .$$

The two solutions $w^{(1,2)}$ are therefore of the form

$$(15.13) \quad w^{(1,2)}(z) = v^{(1,2)}(z) z^{\alpha_{1,2}^{(1)}} \exp\{\alpha_{1,2}^{(0)} z\} ,$$

in which the functions $v^{(1,2)}(z)$ possess asymptotic power series expansions.

In Section 10 we considered the case that one solution $w(z)$ which itself had an asymptotic power series expansion existed. We now see that this case arises if

$$(15.14) \quad \alpha_1^{(o)} = \alpha_1^{(1)} = 0 ,$$

or if

$$(15.14)' \quad \alpha_2^{(o)} = \alpha_2^{(1)} = 0 .$$

From formulas (15.7), (15.12) one deduces that this happens if and only if

$$b^{(o)} = 0 \quad \text{and} \quad b^{(1)} = 0 \quad . \tag{15.15}$$

These are precisely the conditions found in Section 10, cf. (10.5).

An important special differential equation of the second order is Airy's equation

$$D_z^2 w - zw = 0 \quad , \tag{15.16}$$

whose solutions are the Airy integrals, cf. Section 9. To bring this equation into the form (15.1) we must set $k = 1$. The coefficients $a(z)$ and $b(z)$ for this equation are then $a(z) = 0$ and $b(z) = -z^{-1}$. The matrix $A^{(o)}$ becomes

$$A^{(o)} = \begin{pmatrix} 0 & 1 \\ 0 & 0 \end{pmatrix} ,$$

which not only has the double eigenvalue $\alpha_{1,2}^{(o)} = 0$, but in addition has a non-simple elementary divisor. The theory of Sections 11 to 13 is, therefore, not applicable without modification.

In this case it is easy to see which modifications are needed. From the discussion in Section 9 we know that the exponential function which enters the asymptotic description of the solutions has the exponent $\pm \frac{2}{3} z^{3/2}$. It is, therefore, clear that an asymptotic description of the type found in Section 11 cannot obtain in the present case since this description involved polynomials of z in the exponent. On the other hand, it is expected that such an asymptotic description will obtain if

$$\tilde{z} = z^{1/2} \tag{15.17}$$

is introduced as new variable in place of z. By doing this one brings the differential equation into the form

$$D_{\tilde{z}}^2 w - \tilde{z}^{-1} D_{\tilde{z}} w - 4\tilde{z}^4 w = 0 \quad . \tag{15.18}$$

Evidently, k = 2 now. The matrix $A^{(o)}$ is

$$A^{(o)} = \begin{pmatrix} 0 & 1 \\ 4 & 0 \end{pmatrix} ; \tag{15.19}$$

it has two distinct eigenvalues $\alpha^{(o)} = \pm 2$. The leading term in the exponent is then found to be

$$\frac{\alpha^{(o)}}{k+1} \tilde{z}^{k+1} = \pm \frac{2}{3} \tilde{z}^3 = \pm \frac{2}{3} z^{3/2} \tag{15.20}$$

in agreement with the results of Section 9.

The theory of Section 13 shows that there should be $k+1 = 3$ solutions of each of the two types, each solution having a maximal admissibility sector of $3\pi/(k+1) = \pi$ in the $\tilde{z}$-plane. The angle of the admissibility sector in the z-plane then equals 2π, in agreement with the results of Section 9. There, however, we described only three solutions, while there should be six solutions altogether according to the present theory. To resolve the apparent discrepancy we need only observe that each of the solutions described in Section 9 as functions of z leads to two functions of $\tilde{z}$ according to the determination of arg $\tilde{z}$; the two functions of $\tilde{z}$ then obtained are defined in different sectors and are of different types.

We also recall that each solution was recessive in the middle third of its sector of admissibility and dominant in the two outer thirds. Further we recall that the basic identity between Airy functions allowed us to express in such an outer third a solution as a linear combination of another solution of the same type and a third solution of the other type and that the continuation across the Stokes line could then be performed, the third solution becoming dominant on the other side of this line.

References for Sections 11-15

[A] Wasow, W.: Introduction to the Asymptotic Theory of Ordinary Linear Differential Equations. National Bureau of Standards, Los Angeles, California, 1953.

[B] Turrittin, H. L.: Asymptotic Expansions of Solutions of Systems of Ordinary Linear Differential Equations Containing a Parameter. Contribution to the Theory of Non-Linear Oscillations. vol. II, Annals of Mathematical Studies 29, Princeton Univ. Press, 1952, pp. 81-116.

[C] Antosiewicz, H. A., Davis, P. and Oberhettinger, F.: Selected Topics in the Theory of Asymptotic Expansions. National Bureau of Standards Report 2392, March 1953.

[D] Birkhoff, G. D.: Singular Points of Ordinary Linear Differential Equations. Transactions of the American Mathematical Society, vol. 10, pp. 436-470 (1909).
Equivalent Singular Points of Ordinary Linear Differential Equations. Mathematische Annalen, vol. 74, p. 134 (1913).

16. Method of Laplace Transformation

If the coefficient matrix $A(z)$ in the differential equation (11.8) is a polynomial in z^{-1}, integral representations of the solutions can be given which allow a detailed study of the analytic continuation of the solutions beyond the Stokes lines. Under favorable circumstances this continuation can be given explicitly. The method of obtaining such special solutions is the Laplace transformation already employed by Poincaré in his first paper on asymptotic integration.

We confine ourselves to the case in which $k = 0$ and the matrix A is a polynomial of the first degree. Instead of $A(z)$ we write $A + z^{-1}B$ with constant A and B, so that the differential equation becomes

$$D_z w = (A + z^{-1}B)w \quad . \tag{16.1}$$

The matrix A will be assumed diagonal:

$$A = (\alpha_\nu) \quad , \tag{16.2}$$

with distinct eigenvalues α_ν.

In the method of Laplace transformation one represents solutions $w(z)$ in the form

$$w(z) = \int_{\mathcal{P}} \phi(t) e^{tz} dt \tag{16.3}$$

with the aid of appropriate functions $\phi(t)$. The path $\mathcal{P}$ should be so chosen that

$$\int_{\mathcal{P}} \frac{d}{dt} [\phi(t) e^{tz}] dt = 0 \tag{16.4}$$

and

$$\int_{\mathcal{P}} \frac{d}{dt} [t\phi(t) e^{tz}] dt = 0 \quad . \tag{16.5}$$

If these conditions are satisfied there follows

$$(16.6) \qquad z(D_z - A)w(z) = z \int_{\mathcal{P}} (D_z - A)[\phi(t)e^{tz}]dt$$

$$= \int_{\mathcal{P}} (t - A)\phi(t) z e^{tz} dt$$

$$= \int_{\mathcal{P}} (t - A)\phi(t) \frac{d}{dt}(e^{tz})dt$$

$$= - \int_{\mathcal{P}} \frac{d}{dt}[(t - A)\phi(t)]e^{tz}dt$$

$$= - \int_{\mathcal{P}} [(t - A)\frac{d}{dt}\phi(t) + \phi(t)]e^{tz}dt \quad .$$

Hence we have

$$(16.7) \qquad zD_z w - (zA + B)w = - \int_{\mathcal{P}} [(t - A)\frac{d}{dt}\phi(t) + (B + 1)\phi(t)]e^{tz}dt$$

for the function $w(z)$ given by (16.3). Therefore, this function satisfies the differential equation (16.1) if the function $\phi(t)$ satisfies the differential equation

$$(16.8) \qquad [t - A]\frac{d}{dt}\phi(t) + [B + 1]\phi(t) = 0 \quad ,$$

in addition to conditions (16.4) and (16.5).

Differential equation (16.8) has singularities at the eigenvalues α_ν of the matrix A, but these singularities are regular ones. Since the eigenvalues are simple, we infer from the standard theory of such singularities that there is just one solution $\phi^{(\mu)}(t)$ of equation (16.8) which near the point $t = \alpha_\mu$ is of the form

$$(16.9) \qquad \phi^{(\mu)}(t) = (t - \alpha_\mu)^{-\rho_\mu} \psi^{(\mu)}(t)$$

with $\psi^{(\mu)}(t)$ analytic and regular at $t = \alpha_\mu$. The exponent ρ_μ is given by

$$\rho_\mu = 1 + b_{\mu\mu} \quad , \tag{16.10}$$

as is easily verified by substitution.

The path $\mathcal{P} = \mathcal{P}_\mu$ should come from infinity in a direction $\bar{\xi}$, encircle the point $t = \alpha_\mu$ once in the positive direction, and return to infinity in the direction $-\bar{\xi}$; it should, of course, avoid all singularities $t = \alpha_\nu$. The function

$$w^{(\mu)}(z) = \int_{\mathcal{P}_\mu} \phi^{(\mu)}(t) e^{tz} dt \tag{16.11}$$

is then defined in the sector

$$|\arg z - \arg \xi| < \frac{\pi}{2} \quad . \tag{16.12}$$

The analytic continuation of the solution $w(z)$ thus obtained can now be performed by simply turning the vector ξ and, accordingly, deforming the path $\mathcal{P}_\mu$.

Before determining the asymptotic expansion of the solution $w^{(\mu)}(z)$ we impose a restriction on the path $\mathcal{P}_\mu$, namely that, except in the neighborhood of the point $t = \alpha_\mu$, it lie entirely in the half-plane

$$\operatorname{Re} \eta t < 0 \tag{16.13}$$

for an appropriate vector η.

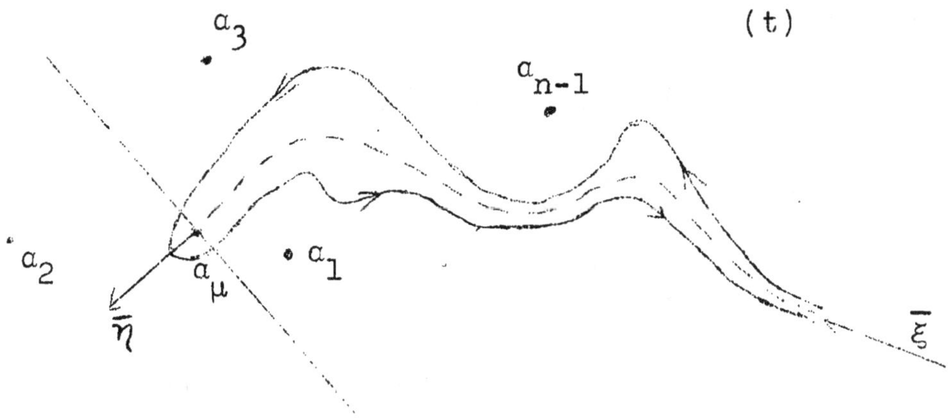

Figure 6

A Possible Restricted Path $\mathcal{P}_\mu$

From the results concerning the Bromwich integral derived in Section 7, in particular from formula (7.23), we may then infer that $w^{(\mu)}(z)$ possesses an asymptotic expansion of the form

$$w^{(\mu)}(z) \sim e^{a_\mu z} z^{\rho_\mu - 1} v^{(\mu)}(z) \quad , \tag{16.14}$$

in which $v^{(\mu)}(z)$ is a formal series in powers of z^{-1}. This expansion is valid if arg $\bar{z}$ is within $\pi/2$ of a possible direction of approach of the path $\mathcal{P}_\mu$ toward a_μ, i.e. for z in the sector

$$|\arg z - \arg \eta| < \pi \ , \quad |z| \geq R \quad , \tag{16.15}$$

with a sufficiently large value of R.

The direction of η may still be chosen to a large extent arbitrarily, but within certain limits. Turning η in the positive direction, we approach a situation in which the path $\mathcal{P}_\mu$ is squeezed between a certain eigenvalue, which we call a_1, and the line Re $\eta t = 0$. Thus η is limited by the condition

$$(16.16) \qquad \arg \eta < \arg (\bar{\alpha}_1 - \bar{\alpha}_\mu) + \frac{\pi}{2} ,$$

and similarly by

$$(16.17) \qquad \arg \eta > \arg (\bar{\alpha}_{n-1} - \bar{\alpha}_\mu) - \frac{\pi}{2}$$

for a properly chosen α_{n-1}. The limitation on z is then

$$(16.18) \qquad \arg (\bar{\alpha}_{n-1} - \bar{\alpha}_\mu) - \frac{3\pi}{2} < \arg z < \arg (\bar{\alpha}_1 - \bar{\alpha}_\mu) + \frac{3\pi}{2} ,$$

in agreement with the results of Section 14.

It is clear in the present case how to express the analytic continuation of a solution $w^{(\mu)}$ as the sum of a solution of the same asymptotic type and a solution of the type $w^{(1)}$ or $w^{(n-1)}$ respectively. Indeed, to continue such a solution analytically across a Stokes line, one needs only to deform both branches of the path $\mathcal{P}_\mu$ of integration through the singularity at α_1 or α_{n-1}. The continuation of the original solution $u^{(\mu)}$ will then be the sum of the Laplace integral along this new path, which is of the same asymptotic type as $u^{(\mu)}$, and two "residual integrals" over paths associated with the branch point α_1 (or α_{n-1}), which are of the asymptotic type belonging to this branch point.

17. The Parameter Problem. Formal Expansions

We shall consider a differential equation

$$D_z u = \rho^p A(z,\rho) u \tag{17.1}$$

for a function $u = u(z) = \{u_1, \ldots, u_n\}$, in which the matrix $A(z,\rho)$ is an analytic function of the independent variable z and the "parameter" ρ. This matrix is assumed to be defined when z lies in an appropriate open domain $\mathcal{R}_0$ of the z-plane and ρ lies in a sector $\mathcal{T}$ given by

$$\tau_- \leq \arg \rho \leq \tau_+ , \quad |\rho| \geq \rho_0 \quad . \tag{17.2}$$

Specifically, we assume that for any z in $\mathcal{R}_0$ the matrix $A(z,\rho)$ possesses an asymptotic expansion

$$A(z,\rho) \sim \sum_{\kappa=0}^{\infty} \rho^{-\kappa} A^{(\kappa)}(z) \tag{17.3}$$

in negative powers of ρ, valid for ρ in $\mathcal{T}$, with coefficients $A^{(\kappa)}(z)$ which are analytic functions of z, and that this expansion holds uniformly for z in any closed bounded subset $\mathcal{R}$ of $\mathcal{R}_0$. The number p is a non-negative integer.

The problem is first to find formal series in ρ which satisfy equation (17.1) formally, then to prove the existence of actual solutions of this equation which possess these given formal series as asymptotic expansions valid in bounded closed subsets $\mathcal{R}$ of $\mathcal{R}_0$. Finally, of course, the relationship between the various solutions found should be investigated.

Clearly, this problem is a counterpart to the problem considered in the preceding sections in which the asymptotic expansion referred to powers of z^{-1}. In fact, it would at first sight seem that the problem treated before, involving the differential equation

$$(17.4) \qquad D_z u = z^k A(z) u \quad ,$$

could be interpreted as a special case of the problem considered now, simply by substituting ρz for z in equation (17.4). In fact, this equation would then attain the form

$$(17.5) \qquad D_z u = \rho^{k+1} z^k A(\rho z) u \quad ,$$

and the asymptotic expansion

$$(17.6) \qquad A(z) \sim \sum_{\kappa=0}^{\infty} z^{-\kappa} A^{(\kappa)}$$

would yield the asymptotic expansion

$$(17.7) \qquad z^k A(\rho z) \sim \sum_{\kappa=0}^{\infty} \rho^{-\kappa} z^{k-\kappa} A^{(\kappa)} \quad ,$$

which is of the form (17.3).

There is, however, a difference in the two problems. The sector in the z-plane in which the asymptotic expansion was established in the previous sections corresponds--after substituting ρz for z --to a sector in the z-plane whose inner radius depends on the value of ρ. In the limit, as $\rho \to \infty$, it covers the full sector

$$(17.8) \qquad \Theta_- \leq \arg z \leq \Theta_+ \ , \quad |z| > 0 \ .$$

On the other hand, a bounded set $\mathcal{R}'$ in the z-plane of the present problem corresponds to a set in the z-plane of the previous problem which depends on the value of ρ in such a way that it disappears towards infinity as $\rho \to \infty$.

Thus we see that if one wanted to derive the asymptotic expansions of the previous problem from those of the present problem, it would not be sufficient to establish the latter expansions only in closed bounded sets. We therefore shall try to obtain estimates of the remainder terms in the asymptotic expansions to be established in such a way that the results of the previous theory can be derived--at least to a certain degree.

For the sake of simplicity we shall confine ourselves to the case

$$p = 1 \quad , \tag{17.9}$$

which corresponds to the case $k = 0$ in the previous problem.

The problem of a single differential equation of nth order can easily be reduced to the problem of a system of the first order. We assume the single equation to be given in the form

$$D_z^n f + \rho a_1(z,\rho) D_z^{n-1} f + \ldots + \rho^n a_n(z,\rho) f = 0 \quad , \tag{17.10}$$

which is no serious restriction. Then we need only set

$$u_1 = f \quad , \tag{17.11a}$$

$$u_\nu = \rho^{-\nu+1} D_z^{\nu-1} f \quad \text{for} \quad \nu = 2,\ldots,n \quad , \tag{17.11b}$$

and rewrite equation (17.10) in the form

$$\begin{cases} D_z u_1 = \rho u_2 \quad , \\ D_z u_2 = \rho u_3 \quad , \\ \cdot \; \cdot \; \cdot \; \cdot \; \cdot \; \cdot \; \cdot \\ D_z u_{n-1} = \rho u_n \quad , \\ D_z u_n = -\rho [a_n u_1 + \ldots + a_1 u_{n-1}] \quad , \end{cases} \tag{17.12}$$

which evidently is of the form of equation (17.1) with $p = 1$. It should be mentioned, though, that there are cases in which a method different from (17.11) of introducing the functions $u_1,\ldots,u_n$ proves more economical.

The parameter problem was treated as early as 1837 by Liouville, who considered a single equation of second order. A mathematically complete asymptotic theory for this type of equation was given in 1899 by Horn. For a differential equation of nth order the asymptotic theory was developed by Birkhoff (1908), Noaillon (1912), Perron (1918), Tamarkin and Besicovitch (1917 and 1922); the corresponding theory for systems of equations is due to Trjitzinsky and Turrittin (1936).

In order to obtain formal expansions satisfying equation (17.1), we could employ, as Turrittin did, a method similar to that explained in Section 11. We prefer, instead, to proceed in a less elegant but more transparent way.

We first factor out from $u(z,\rho)$ an exponential function by setting

$$u(z,\rho) = v(z,\rho)e^{\rho h(z)} \tag{17.13}$$

in which the function $h(z)$ is to be appropriately chosen. We set

$$D_z h(z) = g(z) \tag{17.14}$$

and write the equation for $v(z,\rho)$ in the form

$$D_z v = \rho\{A(z,\rho) - g(z)\}v \quad , \tag{17.15}$$

in which the symbol $g(z)$ stands for the identity matrix multiplied by the function $g(z)$.

We now seek to determine this function $g(z)$ in such a way that equation (17.15) possesses a formal solution $\tilde{v}(z,\rho)$ of the form

$$\tilde{v}(z,\rho) = \sum_{\kappa=0}^{\infty} \rho^{-\kappa} v^{(\kappa)}(z) \quad . \tag{17.16}$$

Inserting this expansion into equation (17.15), and making use of the expansion (17.3) of $A(z,\rho)$, we obtain the conditions

(17.17) $$\{A^{(0)}(z) - g(z)\}v^{(0)}(z) = 0 \quad ,$$

(17.18) $$D_z v^{(\kappa-1)}(z) = \{A^{(0)}(z) - g(z)\}v^{(\kappa)}(z) + \sum_{\lambda=0}^{\kappa-1} A^{(\kappa-\lambda)}(z)v^{(\lambda)}(z) \quad \text{for } \kappa = 1,2,3,\ldots \quad .$$

Relation (17.17) implies that $g(z)$ is an eigenvalue of the matrix $A^{(0)}(z)$, and therefore a root of the equation

(17.19) $$\det\{A^{(0)}(z) - g\} = 0 \quad ;$$

furthermore, $v^{(0)}(z)$ is an associated eigenfunction.

Let us assume that there exists in the domain $\mathcal{R}_0$ a regular analytic transformation $T(z)$ possessing there a regular analytic inverse $T^{-1}(z)$ such that the matrix

(17.20) $$B^{(0)}(z) = T(z)A^{(0)}(z)T^{-1}(z)$$

is diagonal. This assumption implies that the matrix $A^{(0)}(z)$ has for every z in $\mathcal{R}_0$ simple elementary divisors. For convenience we shall denote the columns $T(z)\tilde{v}(z,\rho)$ by $\tilde{w}(z,\rho)$ and the matrices $T(z)A^{(\kappa)}T^{-1}(z)$ by $B^{(\kappa)}$:

(17.21) $$\tilde{w}(z,\rho) = T(z)\tilde{v}(z,\rho) \quad ,$$

(17.22) $$B^{(\kappa)}(z) = T(z)A^{(\kappa)}(z)T^{-1}(z) \quad .$$

Let $g = g(z)$ be one of the eigenvalues of $A^{(0)}(z)$, or equivalently of $B^{(0)}(z)$, and let r be its multiplicity. We assume that this multiplicity is constant in the whole region $\mathcal{R}_0$; i.e., we exclude the occurrence of eigenvalues which are multiple only in proper subsets of $\mathcal{R}_0$. We may suppose that the r-dimensional space of eigenvectors of the matrix $B^{(0)}(z)$ associated with this eigenvalue is precisely the space spanned by the first r unit coordinate vectors, so that the associated eigenfunctions are characterized by the condition that their $(r+1)^{st}$ through n^{th} components all vanish. We denote the r-dimensional column consisting of the first r components of $\tilde{w}$ by $\tilde{w}_1$; similarly, the column formed by the remaining n-r components will be called $\tilde{w}_2$. Accordingly, we may write

$$\tilde{w} = \{\tilde{w}_1, \tilde{w}_2\} \quad . \tag{17.23}$$

Correspondingly, we split each matrix $B^{(\kappa)}$ into four submatrices $B^{(\kappa)}_{\alpha\beta}$ $(\alpha, \beta = 1,2)$ such that--in obvious notation--

$$\begin{aligned} (B^{(\kappa)}\tilde{w})_1 &= B^{(\kappa)}_{11}\tilde{w}_1 + B^{(\kappa)}_{12}\tilde{w}_2 \quad , \\ (B^{(\kappa)}\tilde{w})_2 &= B^{(\kappa)}_{21}\tilde{w}_1 + B^{(\kappa)}_{22}\tilde{w}_2 \quad . \end{aligned} \tag{17.24}$$

We may then write

$$B^{(\kappa)} = \begin{pmatrix} B^{(\kappa)}_{11} & B^{(\kappa)}_{12} \\ B^{(\kappa)}_{21} & B^{(\kappa)}_{22} \end{pmatrix} \quad . \tag{17.25}$$

The condition that the matrix $B^{(0)}(z)$ --or equivalently the matrix $B^{(0)}(z) - g(z)$ --is diagonal is then that the latter matrix be of the form

$$B^{(0)}(z) - g(z) = \begin{pmatrix} 0 & 0 \\ 0 & \Gamma(z) \end{pmatrix} \quad , \tag{17.26}$$

where $\Gamma(z)$ is a diagonal matrix with eigenvalues different from zero. Actually all that is needed of this matrix $\Gamma(z)$ is that it possesses an inverse $\Gamma^{-1}(z)$ defined as a regular analytic function in the region $\mathcal{R}_0$.

In our notation, equation (17.17) evidently reduces simply to the equation

$$\Gamma(z) w_2^{(0)}(z) = 0 \quad . \tag{17.27}$$

Equation (17.18) splits into two equations which we write in the form

$$D_z w_1^{(\kappa-1)} - \left[B_{11}^{(1)} + S_{11}\right] w_1^{(\kappa-1)} = \left[B_{12}^{(1)} + S_{12}\right] w_2^{(\kappa-1)} + \sum_{\lambda=0}^{\kappa-2} \left[B_{11}^{(\kappa-\lambda)} w_1^{(\lambda)} + B_{12}^{(\kappa-\lambda)} w_2^{(\lambda)}\right] , \tag{17.28}$$

$$\Gamma(z) w_2^{(\kappa)} = D_z w_2^{(\kappa-1)} - S_{21} w_1^{(\kappa-1)} - S_{22} w_2^{(\kappa-1)} - \sum_{\lambda=0}^{\kappa-1} \left[B_{21}^{(\kappa-\lambda)} w_1^{(\lambda)} + B_{22}^{(\kappa-\lambda)} w_2^{(\lambda)}\right] , \tag{17.29}$$

for $\kappa = 1,2,3,\ldots$, where we have set

$$D_z T \cdot T^{-1}(z) = S(z) = \begin{pmatrix} S_{11} & S_{12} \\ S_{21} & S_{22} \end{pmatrix} , \tag{17.30}$$

with the same mode of subdivision as in (17.25).

It is now immediately seen that the functions $w_2^{(0)}(z)$, $w_1^{(0)}(z)$, $w_2^{(1)}(z)$, $w_1^{(1)}(z), \ldots$ can be successively determined. Since the matrix $\Gamma(z)$ possesses an inverse, equation (17.27) implies that

$$w_2^{(0)}(z) = 0 \quad . \tag{17.31}$$

Using this result, equation (17.28) reduces for $\kappa = 1$ to

$$D_z w_1^{(0)} - \left[B_{11}^{(1)} + S_{11}\right] w_1^{(0)} = 0 \quad . \tag{17.32}$$

As is known from the theory of differential equations equation (17.32) possesses a solution $w_1^{(o)}$ in any simply connected region in which the coefficients are regular. We need not discuss here how to describe such a solution either explicitly or approximately. But we know that it is determined if its values at any points are prescribed. Take $w_1^{(o)}$ as such a solution. The function $w_2^{(1)}(z)$ is then uniquely determined from equation (17.29), which becomes for $\kappa = 1$ simply

$$\Gamma(z)w_2^{(1)} = -\left[B_{21}^{(1)} + S_{21}\right] w_1^{(o)} \quad . \tag{17.33}$$

It is clear that the process described can be continued. It is also clear that <u>the sequence of functions</u>

$$w^{(\kappa)} = \left\{ w_1^{(\kappa)},\ w_2^{(\kappa)} \right\} \tag{17.34}$$

thus found <u>leads to a formal solution</u>

$$\tilde{w} = \sum_{\kappa=0}^{\infty} \rho^{-\kappa} w^{(\kappa)} \tag{17.35}$$

of the transform

$$D_z w - S(z)w = \rho\left\{B(z,\rho) - g(z)\right\} w \tag{17.36}$$

of the differential equation (17.15).

It is on occasion opportune to modify the procedure described. Instead of defining the function g(z) as solution of equation (17.19), one may let it depend on ρ in such a way that it possesses an expansion with respect to powers of ρ^{-1} with the leading term a root of (17.19). Also a transformation $T(z,\rho)$ may be chosen in many ways such that its leading term diagonalizes the leading term $A^{(o)}(z)$ of A(z). The resulting formal series for u(z) is independent of these modifications, as one readily verifies.

We maintain that in the manner described we can find r linearly independent formal solutions of equation (17.1) of the same asymptotic type. We need only prescribe r arbitrary linearly independent values for the solutions $w_1^{(0)}$ of equation (17.28) for $\kappa = 1$ at an arbitrarily chosen point z_o and for $\lambda > 0$ prescribe $w_1^{(\lambda)} = 0$ at this point.

Clearly, this process can be carried out for each root g of equation (17.19). The n formal solutions $u(z,\rho)$ obtained in this fashion may be combined in a matrix

$$\tilde{U}(z,\rho) = \tilde{V}(z,\rho)E(z,\rho) \quad . \tag{17.37}$$

in which the diagonal matrix $E(z,\rho)$ is given by

$$E(z,\rho) = \left(e^{\rho h_\nu(z)}\right) = \exp\{\rho H(z)\} \quad ; \tag{17.38}$$

cf. (17.13), (17.14). From the construction of the columns $\tilde{w}^{(\nu)}(z,\rho)$ of the matrix

$$\tilde{W}(z,\rho) = T(z)\tilde{V}(z,\rho) \tag{17.39}$$

it is clear that the functions $\tilde{W}(z,\rho)$, and hence $\tilde{V}(z,\rho)$, are linearly independent at the point z_o and hence everywhere in $\mathcal{R}_o$.

It is naturally of interest to find out in detail how the process just described leads to the formal asymptotic solution of a differential equation of second order for a single function $f(z,\rho)$. We write the equation

$$D_z^2 f + \rho a_1(z) D_z f + \rho^2 a_2(z) f = 0 \tag{17.40}$$

in the form

$$\begin{cases} D_z u_1 = \rho u_2 \quad , \\ D_z u_2 = -\rho[a_2 u_1 + a_1 u_2] \quad . \end{cases} \tag{17.41}$$

For simplicity we assume that a_1 and a_2 are independent of ρ. As function $g(z)$ we choose one of the eigenvalues g of the matrix

(17.42) $$A(z) = \begin{pmatrix} 0 & 1 \\ -a_2(z) & -a_1(z) \end{pmatrix} ;$$

i.e., a solution of the equation

(17.43) $$g(g+a_1) + a_2 = 0 \quad .$$

The two roots of equation (17.43) are equal if $a_1^2 = 4a_2$. The matrix A cannot be diagonalized if this relation holds, for it is then already in the Jordan normal form. Therefore we require

(17.44) $$4a_2(z) \neq a_1^2(z) \quad \text{in } \mathcal{R}_0 \quad .$$

We then have

(17.45) $$g(z) = -\frac{1}{2} a_1(z) + \frac{1}{2} d(z) \quad ,$$

with

(17.46) $$d(z) = [a_1^2(z) - 4a_2(z)]^{1/2} \quad ;$$

furthermore

(17.47) $$h(z) = \int^z g(z)dz \quad .$$

After factoring out the exponential function $\rho h(z)$:

(17.48) $$u_1 = v_1 e^{\rho h} \quad , \quad u_2 = v_2 e^{\rho h} \quad ,$$

the equation becomes

$$(17.49) \qquad \begin{cases} D_z v_1 = \rho[-g v_1 + v_2] \quad ; \\ D_z v_2 = -\rho[a_2 v_1 + (a_1 + g) v_2] \quad . \end{cases}$$

The diagonalization of the leading matrix may be effected by the transformation

$$(17.50) \qquad \begin{cases} d v_1 = w_1 + w_2 \quad , \\ d v_2 = g w_1 - (a_1 + g) w_2 \quad , \end{cases}$$

with the inverse

$$(17.51) \qquad \begin{cases} w_1 = (a_1 + g) v_1 + v_2 \quad , \\ w_2 = g v_1 - v_2 \quad . \end{cases}$$

Note that

$$(17.52) \qquad d = a_1 + 2g$$

and that

$$(17.53) \qquad d^2 = a_1^2 - 4a_2 \neq 0 \quad \text{in} \quad \mathcal{R}_0 \quad .$$

The equations for w_1 and w_2 become

$$(17.54) \qquad \begin{cases} D_z w_1 = d^{-1} D_z(a_1 + g) \cdot (w_1 + w_2) \quad , \\ D_z w_2 = -\rho d w_2 + d^{-1} D_z g \cdot (w_1 + w_2) \quad . \end{cases}$$

The expansion coefficients of w_1 and w_2 may then be found successively:

$$(17.55)\qquad w_2^{(0)} = 0 \ ,$$

$$w_1^{(0)} = \exp\left\{ \int^z d^{-1} D_z (a_1 + g)\, dz \right\} \ ,$$

$$w_2^{(1)} = d^{-2} D_z g \cdot \exp\left\{ \int^z d^{-1} D_z (a_1 + g)\, dz \right\} \ ,$$

and so on.

From (17.50) we then have

$$(17.56)\qquad v_1^{(0)} = d^{-1} \exp\left\{ \int^z d^{-1} D_z (a_1 + g)\, dz \right\} \ ,$$

$$= \exp\left\{ - \int^z d^{-1} D_z g \cdot dz \right\} \ ,$$

and finally from (17.48)

$$(17.57)\qquad f^{(0)} = u_1^{(0)} = \exp\left\{ - \int^z d^{-1} D_z g \cdot dz \right\} \exp\left\{ \rho \int^z g\, dz \right\} \ .$$

In the special case in which $a_1 = 0$ this formula reduces to

$$(17.58)\qquad f^{(0)} = c(-a_2)^{-1/4} \exp\left\{ \rho \int^z (-a_2)^{1/2}\, dz \right\}$$

with an appropriate constant c.

It is true that if the aim had been only to derive this formula, we could have done it much more quickly. Setting

$$(17.59)\qquad f = v e^{\rho h}$$

one finds immediately for v the equation

$$(17.60)\qquad d D_z v + D_z g \cdot v = -\rho^{-1} D_z^2 v \ ,$$

whose solution in lowest order is just (17.56). Nevertheless, if one desires to derive terms of higher order or to treat more general problems, the procedure as outlined seems preferable.

18. Solutions with a given Asymptotic Expansion

The main result obtained in the preceding section was that the differential equation

$$(18.1) \qquad D_z u = \rho A(z,\rho) u$$

possesses a formal solution $\tilde{u}(z)$ of the form

$$(18.2) \qquad \tilde{u}(z) = \tilde{v}(z) e^{\rho h_\mu(z)} \quad ,$$

in which $\tilde{v}(z)$ was a formal power series

$$(18.3) \qquad \tilde{v}(z) = \sum_{\kappa=0}^{\infty} \rho^{-\kappa} v^{(\kappa)}(z)$$

and $h_\mu(z)$ was a function whose derivative

$$(18.4) \qquad g_\mu(z) = D_z h_\mu(z)$$

was one of the eigenvalues of the matrix $A^{(0)}(z)$, the first term in the expansion

$$(18.5) \qquad A(z,\rho) \sim \sum_{\kappa=0}^{\infty} \rho^{-\kappa} A^{(\kappa)}(z) \quad .$$

For this, it was assumed that the matrix $A^{(0)}(z)$ could be diagonalized with the aid of a transformation which is regular analytic in the region $\mathcal{R}_0$ considered.

The solution $\tilde{u}(z)$ given by (18.2) was said to have the same "asymptotic type" as $e^{\rho h_\mu(z)}$, or simply to be of the μth type. We found, in fact, r linearly independent solutions of the μth type, where $r = r_\mu$ is the multiplicity of the eigenvalue $g_\mu(z)$.

Altogether, there were $n = \sum_\mu r_\mu$ linearly independent formal solutions of the form (18.2), which could be used to set up a formal "fundamental solution"

(18.6) $$\tilde{U}(z,\rho) = \tilde{V}(z,\rho)e^{\rho H(z)} ,$$

where H(z) was the diagonal matrix

(18.7) $$H(z) = (h_\nu(z)) .$$

This formal fundamental solution satisfied the equation

(18.8) $$D_z \tilde{U} = \rho A \tilde{U}$$

and the formal power series $\tilde{V}(z,\rho)$ satisfied the equation

(18.9) $$D_z \tilde{V} = \rho A \tilde{V} - \rho \tilde{V} G ,$$

where G(z) was the diagonal matrix

(18.10) $$G(z) = (g_\nu(z)) .$$

We may choose the leading term $V^{(0)}(z)$ of $\tilde{V}(z,\rho)$ so that it has an inverse at one point in the region $\mathcal{R}_o$. We assume --although this could be proved to be so--that $V^{(0)}(z)$ has an inverse in all of $\mathcal{R}_o$. Then $\tilde{V}(z,\rho)$ has a formal inverse $\tilde{V}^{-1}(z,\rho)$ given by a series

(18.11) $$\tilde{V}^{-1}(z,\rho) = \sum_{\kappa=0}^{\infty} \rho^{-\kappa} V^{(\kappa)}(z) .$$

We now use a slight extension of the Borel-Ritt theorem:

<u>Lemma</u>: To any given formal series

(18.12) $$\tilde{V}(z,\rho) = \sum_{\kappa=0}^{\infty} \rho^{-\kappa} V^{(\kappa)}(z)$$

defined in a closed bounded region $\mathcal{R}$ in the z-plane and a sector $\mathcal{T}$ in the ρ-plane there exists an analytic function $\hat{V}(z,\rho)$ defined in $\mathcal{R} \times \mathcal{T}$ which has the formal series (18.12) as asymptotic expansion and whose z-derivative has as asymptotic expansion the z-derivative of this series:

$$\hat{V}(z,\rho) \underset{\rho}{\sim} \tilde{V}(z,\rho) \quad , \quad D_z\hat{V}(z,\rho) \underset{\rho}{\sim} D_z\tilde{V}(z,\rho) \quad . \tag{18.13}$$

To prove this statement one may proceed as in the proof of the Borel-Ritt theorem, using estimates involving

$$\max_z |v^{(\kappa)}(z)| + \max_z |D_z v^{(\kappa)}(z)| \quad . \tag{18.14}$$

Of course, one must consider ρ instead of z as the independent variable and z as a parameter. The uniformity of all estimates with respect to z is easily established.

Since the leading term $v^{(0)}(z)$ of $\hat{V}(z,\rho)$ has an inverse for z in $\mathcal{R}$, the same is true of $\hat{V}(z,\rho)$ for $|\rho| \geq \rho_0$ if ρ_0 is chosen large enough. Clearly, this inverse has the asymptotic expansion

$$\hat{V}^{-1}(z,\rho) \sim \tilde{V}^{-1}(z,\rho) \quad . \tag{18.15}$$

It follows that the function $D_z\hat{V}\cdot\hat{V}^{-1}$ has the asymptotic expansion $D_z\tilde{V}\cdot\tilde{V}^{-1}$. We now define the matrix $\hat{A}(z,\rho)$ by

$$\hat{A}(z,\rho) = \hat{V}(z,\rho)G(z)\hat{V}^{-1}(z,\rho) + \rho^{-1}D_z\hat{V}(z,\rho)\cdot\hat{V}^{-1}(z,\rho) \quad . \tag{18.16}$$

Since, as seen from (18.9), the matrix $A(z,\rho)$ satisfies the asymptotic relation

$$A(z,\rho) \sim \tilde{V}(z,\rho)G(z)\tilde{V}^{-1}(z,\rho) + \rho^{-1}D_z\tilde{V}(z,\rho)\cdot\tilde{V}^{-1}(z,\rho) \quad , \tag{18.17}$$

we may conclude that $\hat{A}(z,\rho)$ and $A(z,\rho)$ have the same asymptotic expansion:

$$\hat{A}(z,\rho) \sim A(z,\rho) \quad . \tag{18.18}$$

By virtue of the definition (18.16) of $\hat{A}$, the matrix $V(z,\rho)$ satisfies the equation

$$D_z\hat{V} = \rho\hat{A}\hat{V} - \rho\hat{V}G \quad ; \tag{18.19}$$

the function

$$\hat{U} = \hat{V} E \quad , \tag{18.20}$$

with

$$E(z,\rho) = e^{\rho H(z)} \quad , \tag{18.21}$$

cf. (18.7), therefore satisfies the equation

$$D_z \hat{U} = \rho \hat{A} \hat{U} \quad . \tag{18.22}$$

Thus the column

$$\hat{u}_{(\mu)} = \hat{v}_{(\mu)} e^{h_\mu(z)} \quad , \tag{18.23}$$

of the μth asymptotic type, satisfies the equation

$$D_z \hat{u}_{(\mu)} = \rho \hat{A} \hat{u}_{(\mu)} \quad . \tag{18.24}$$

As in Section 12, we shall determine the solution u of equation (18.1) as solution $u_{(\mu)}$ of the integral equation

$$u_{(\mu)}(z) = \hat{u}_{(\mu)}(z) + \hat{U}(z) \int_{\mathcal{P}(z)} \hat{U}^{-1}(\zeta) \rho [A(\zeta) - \hat{A}(\zeta)] u_{(\mu)}(\zeta) d\zeta \quad , \tag{18.25}$$

where the path $\mathcal{P}(z)$, which may depend on the matrix element, leads from a fixed point to the point z. Clearly, every solution of this integral equation satisfies the differential equation (18.1). Furthermore, this equation for $u_{(\mu)}(z)$ is equivalent with the integral equation

$$v_{(\mu)}(z) = \hat{v}_{(\mu)}(z) + \hat{V}(z) \int_{\mathcal{P}(z)} E(z) E^{-1}(\zeta) \hat{V}^{-1}(\zeta) \cdot \rho [A(\zeta) - \hat{A}(\zeta)] e^{\rho [h_\mu(\zeta) - h_\mu(z)]} v_{(\mu)}(\zeta) d\zeta \tag{18.26}$$

for the function $v_{(\mu)}(z)$. We write this equation in the form

$$v_{(\mu)} = \hat{v}_{(\mu)} + \hat{V} I^{(\mu)} v \quad , \tag{18.27}$$

where specifically the λth element of the column $I^{(\mu)}v$ is given by

$$\{I^{(\mu)}v(z)\}_{\lambda} = \int_{\mathcal{P}_{\lambda\mu}(z)} e^{\rho[h_{\lambda\mu}(z) - h_{\lambda\mu}(\zeta)]} \cdot \sum_{\nu=1}^{n} \hat{\underline{v}}_{\lambda\nu}(\zeta)\{\rho[A(\zeta) - \hat{A}(\zeta)]v_{(\mu)}(\zeta)\}_{\nu} d\zeta \quad , \tag{18.28}$$

with

$$h_{\lambda\mu}(z) = h_{\lambda}(z) - h_{\mu}(z) \quad ; \tag{18.29}$$

where the $\hat{\underline{v}}_{\lambda\nu}$ are elements of the matrix $\hat{V}^{-1}$.

Having chosen a subscript μ to characterize the asymptotic type of a desired solution, we impose upon the domain $\mathcal{R}$ the restriction that there should exist for every subscript λ and every point z in $\mathcal{R}$ a path $\mathcal{P}_{\lambda\mu}(z)$ lying in $\mathcal{R}$ such that

$$\text{I.} \quad \text{Re}[h_{\lambda\mu}(\zeta) - h_{\lambda\mu}(z)] \geq 0 \tag{18.30}$$

for every ζ on $\mathcal{P}_{\lambda\mu}(z)$, and

$$\text{II.} \quad \int_{\mathcal{P}_{\lambda\mu}(z)} |d\zeta| \leq \ell \tag{18.31}$$

for some fixed positive constant ℓ independent of z and λ. A region $\mathcal{R}$ which is permitted under this restriction will be called <u>admissible for the μth asymptotic type</u>.

Assume now that conditions I and II are satisfied, and that ρ is real and positive. Then we state that to every integer $m > 0$ there exists a finite constant C_m such that

$$(18.32)\qquad \|I^{(\mu)}v\| \le C_m\rho^{-m}\|v_{(\mu)}\| \quad .$$

Here the norm $\|v\|$ is defined as

$$(18.33)\qquad \|v\| = \max_z \max_\lambda |v_\lambda(z)| \quad .$$

The validity of this statement follows immediately from properties I and II and the facts that the matrices A and $\hat{A}$ are asymptotically equal and that the inverse $\hat{V}^{-1}(z,\rho)$ is bounded in $\mathcal{R}$ for $|\rho| \ge \rho_0$.

Inequality (18.32 for m = 1 is sufficient to show that the natural iteration process converges provided ρ is sufficiently large. Thus the existence of a solution $v = v_{(\mu)}$ of the integral equation (18.26), and therefore of a corresponding solution $u_{(\mu)} = v_{(\mu)}e^{\rho h_\mu}$ of the differential equation (18.1), has been established.

Furthermore, the validity of inequality (18.32) for all m is precisely equivalent to the fact that the functions $v_{(\mu)}(z,\rho)$ and $\hat{v}_{(\mu)}(z,\rho)$ have the same asymptotic expansions:

$$(18.34)\qquad v_{(\mu)}(z,\rho) \sim \hat{v}_{(\mu)}(z,\rho) \quad .$$

From (18.13) we then conclude that

$$(18.35)\qquad v_{(\mu)}(z,\rho) \sim \tilde{v}_{(\mu)}(z,\rho) \quad .$$

Thus under conditions I and II the solution $u_{(\mu)} = v_{(\mu)}^{\rho h_\mu}$ has the formal series $\tilde{u}$ given by (18.2) as asymptotic expansion.

Condition II implies that the region $\mathcal{R}$ is bounded. If the domain $\mathcal{R}$ were allowed to extend to infinity, it would be necessary to modify condition II. This would not be difficult; indeed, the modified condition would be similar to the condition numbered II imposed in Section 12. For simplicity we shall not do this here.

As a typical case illustrating the application of condition I, one may imagine the region $\mathcal{R}$ to be bounded by a "curved polygon" consisting of arcs $\ell^{(1)}, \ell^{(2)}, \ldots$ such that to each subscript λ for which $g_{\lambda\mu}(z)$ is not identically zero there is one such arc, $\ell^{(\lambda)}$, on which

$$\text{Re}\, h_{\lambda\mu}(z) = \text{const.} = c_\lambda \quad , \tag{18.36}$$

while for every other point z of $\mathcal{R}$

$$\text{Re}\, h_{\lambda\mu}(z) \leq c_\lambda \quad . \tag{18.37}$$

Assume further that each set Re $h_{\lambda\mu}(z)$ = const consists of a single arc in $\mathcal{R}$ --although, as we shall see, this condition is too strong. Then one need only choose for each subscript λ a point z_λ on the arc $\ell^{(\lambda)}$, so that

$$\text{Re}\, h_{\lambda\mu}(z_\lambda) = c_\lambda \quad . \tag{18.38}$$

Then each point z in $\mathcal{R}$ can be connected with the point z_λ by a path $\mathcal{P}_{\lambda\mu}(z)$ such that

$$\text{Re}\, h_{\lambda\mu}(\zeta) \geq \text{Re}\, h_{\lambda\mu}(z) \tag{18.39}$$

for ζ on $\mathcal{P}_{\lambda\mu}(z)$.

19. Solutions near a Turning Point

A better insight into the possible shapes of admissible regions will be gained by considering such regions in relation to points at which two eigenvalues coalesce.

Let us first suppose that the order n is 2. Assume that the two eigenvalues $g_1(z)$ and $g_2(z)$ become equal at the point $z = z_0$; for simplicity we take $z_0 = 0$. We consider a neighborhood $\mathfrak{N}$ of the point $z = 0$ in which $g_1(z) = g_2(z)$ only for $z = 0$. Clearly, the derivative $g_{12}(z)$ of the function $h_{12}(z)$ vanishes at the point $z = 0$:

(19.1) $$D_z h_{12}(0) = g_{12}(0) = 0 \quad .$$

For simplicity, we assume that the zero of $g_{12}(z)$ at $z = 0$ is of first order, so that $D_z^2 h_{12}(0) \neq 0$. As a consequence of this assumption, two curves $\operatorname{Re} h_{12}(z) = \operatorname{Re} h_{12}(0) = \text{constant}$ pass through the point $z = 0$, crossing at right angles there. We shall call these curves "transition lines".

Without restriction we may assume that

(19.2) $$\operatorname{Re} h_{12}(0) = 0 \quad .$$

The neighborhood $\mathfrak{N}$ is then divided by the transition lines into four regions, in each of which either $\operatorname{Re} h_{12}(z) \geq 0$ or $\operatorname{Re} h_{12}(z) \leq 0$. We denote these regions, including their boundary lines, by $\mathfrak{N}_a$, $\mathfrak{N}_b$, $\mathfrak{N}_c$, $\mathfrak{N}_d$ --later on a, b, c, d shall denote points in the respective regions--and choose the notation such that

(19.3) $$\begin{cases} \operatorname{Re} h_{12}(z) \geq 0 & \text{in } \mathfrak{N}_a \text{ and } \mathfrak{N}_c \quad , \\ \operatorname{Re} h_{12}(z) \leq 0 & \text{in } \mathfrak{N}_b \text{ and } \mathfrak{N}_d \quad . \end{cases}$$

We further suppose that the neighborhood $\mathfrak{N}$ is chosen so small that each set of points z in each of these regions on which $\operatorname{Re} h_{12}(z)$ is constant is either a single arc or a point.

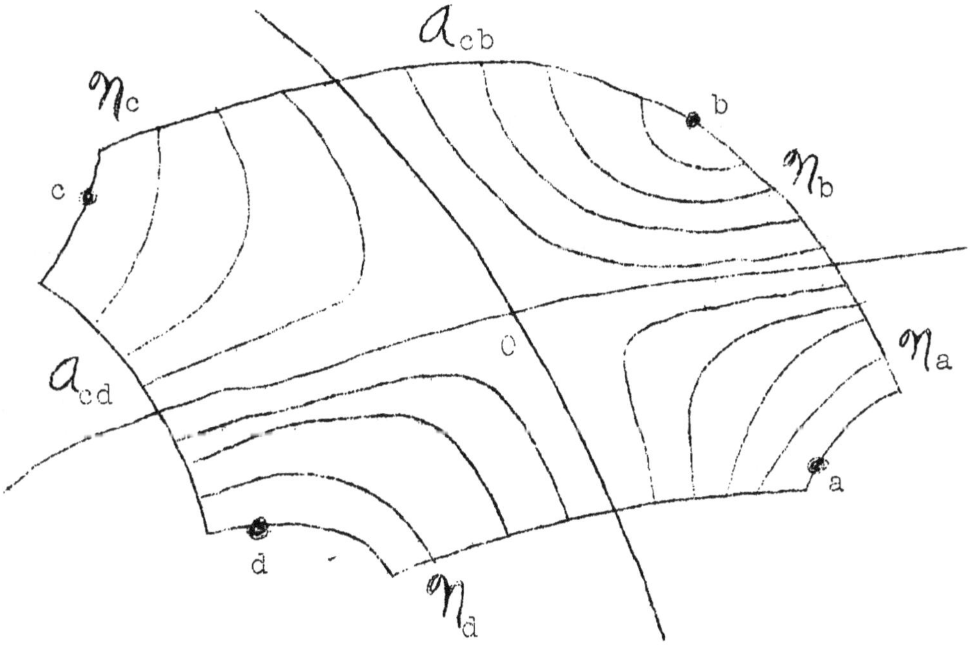

Figure 7

Configuration near a Turning Point

We intend to show that admissible regions $\mathcal{R}_a$ may be obtained from the neighborhood η by excluding approximate open neighborhoods of the "sector" η_a. These neighborhoods $\mathcal{M}_a$ of η_a can be chosen arbitrarily close to η_a, i.e., given any $\varepsilon > 0$, $\mathcal{M}_a$ can be chosen so as to consist only of points at distance less than ε from η_a. Thus the admissible region

$$\mathcal{R}_a = \eta - \mathcal{M}_a \tag{19.4}$$

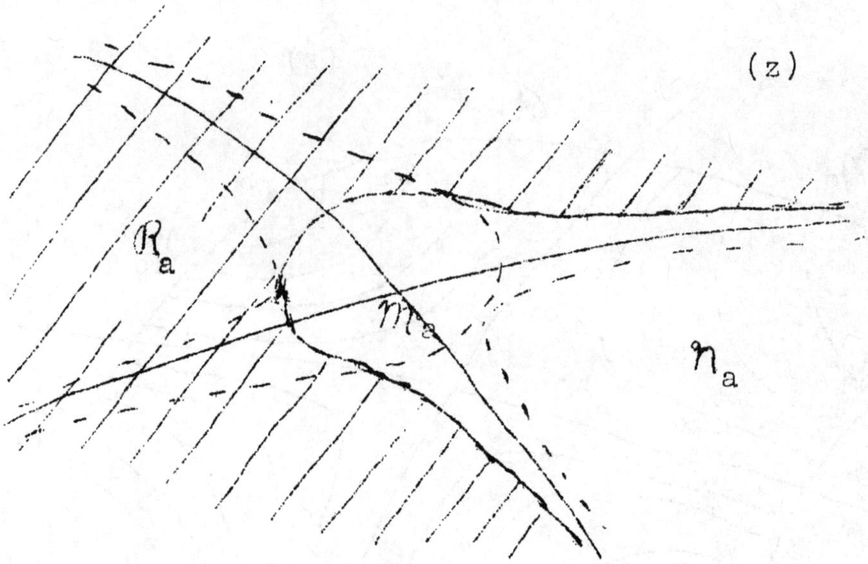

Figure 8

Admissible Region near a Turning Point

consists essentially of the three remaining sectors. Specifically, the region $\mathcal{R}_a$ will be admissible for the second asymptotic type, $\mu = 2$. Similarly, we shall construct regions

(19.5) $$\mathcal{R}_c = \mathcal{N} - \mathcal{M}_c$$

which are also admissible for the second asymptotic type, and regions

(19.6) $$\mathcal{R}_b = \mathcal{N} - \mathcal{M}_b , \quad \mathcal{R}_d = \mathcal{N} - \mathcal{M}_d$$

which are admissible for the first asymptotic type, $\mu = 1$.

To show that this can be done, we select in the regions $\mathcal{N}_a, \mathcal{N}_b, \mathcal{N}_c, \mathcal{N}_d$ fixed points a, b, c, d such that

(19.7)
$$\begin{aligned} \operatorname{Re} h_{12}(z) &\le \operatorname{Re} h_{12}(a) && \text{for } z \text{ in } \mathcal{N}_a , \\ &\ge \operatorname{Re} h_{12}(b) && \text{for } z \text{ in } \mathcal{N}_b , \\ &\le \operatorname{Re} h_{12}(c) && \text{for } z \text{ in } \mathcal{N}_c , \\ &\ge \operatorname{Re} h_{12}(d) && \text{for } z \text{ in } \mathcal{N}_d . \end{aligned}$$

Clearly, these points lie on the boundary of $\mathcal{N}$. Also, it is clear that the point c can be connected with the points b and d by arcs $\mathcal{A}_{cb}$ and $\mathcal{A}_{cd}$ on which Re $h_{12}(z)$ decreases and which are such that each curve Re $h_{12}(z)$ = const. in $\mathcal{N}_b + \mathcal{N}_c$ intersects $\mathcal{A}_{cb}$ and each such curve in $\mathcal{N}_c + \mathcal{N}_d$ intersects $\mathcal{A}_{cd}$. Therefore, the point c can be connected with any point z in $\mathcal{N}_b + \mathcal{N}_c + \mathcal{N}_d$ by a path $\mathcal{P}_{12}(z)$ which consists of a segment of $\mathcal{A}_{cb}$ or $\mathcal{A}_{cd}$ and a segment consisting of points ζ with Re $h_{12}(\zeta)$ = Re $h_{12}(z)$. Thus it is seen that conditions I and II can be satisfied in $\mathcal{R}_a$ and, similarly, in $\mathcal{R}_c$.

It is not sufficient, however, to insure that these two conditions are satisfied. We must also make sure that there exist as formal solutions power series in ρ^{-1} with coefficients which are bounded in $\mathcal{R}_a$. In addition, the leading term $V^{(o)}(z)$ in the expansion of $\tilde{V}(z,\rho)$ should have a bounded inverse in $\mathcal{R}_a$.

In order to achieve this it will--in general--be necessary to exclude a neighborhood of the singular point $z = 0$. If this is done, points in a certain neighborhood of the boundary of $\mathcal{N}_a$ can no longer be connected with the point c on a path of points ζ for which Re $h_{12}(\zeta) \geq$ Re $h_{12}(z)$. This neighborhood should therefore also be excluded. Once this is done, a region $\mathcal{R}_a$ is obtained in which all requirements are met.

In such a region $\mathcal{R}_a$, then, a solution $u^a_{(2)} = \overset{a}{u}$ exists which has as asymptotic expansion the given expansion of the second asymptotic type. Similarly, regions $\mathcal{R}_c$ can be described in which solutions $u^c_{(2)} = \overset{c}{u}$ exist which again have expansions of the second asymptotic type.

Interchanging the roles of the subscripts 1 and 2 we can describe regions $\mathcal{R}_b$ and $\mathcal{R}_d$ in which solutions $u^b_{(1)} = \overset{b}{u}$ and $u^d_{(1)} = \overset{d}{u}$ exist which have asymptotic expansions of the first asymptotic type.

Consider the solutions $\overset{c}{u}$ and $\overset{d}{u}$ in that part of the region $\mathcal{N}_b$ in which they are both defined. Since Re $h_2(z) \geq$ Re $h_1(z)$ in this region, the function $e^{\rho h_2(z)}$ dominates the function $e^{\rho h_1(z)}$ there. (Note that $\rho > 0$ was assumed.) Since the former exponential function characterizes the second asymptotic type, it is clear that <u>the solution $\overset{c}{u}$ dominates the solution $\overset{d}{u}$ in the region $\mathcal{N}_b$</u>.

Quite generally, we may assign to each of the four regions $\mathcal{R}_a$, $\mathcal{R}_b$, $\mathcal{R}_c$, $\mathcal{R}_d$ an "inner" portion and two "outer" portions, the "inner" portion of $\mathcal{R}_a$, for example, being $\mathcal{N}_c$. Then we may say that <u>a solution of one asymptotic type dominates the solutions of the other asymptotic type in the two outer portions of its domain of definition and is dominated by them in the inner portion</u>.

Consider, furthermore, two solutions $\overset{a}{u}$ and $\overset{c}{u}$ in the part of the region $\mathcal{N}_b$ in which both are defined. This part belongs to the outer domain of each of these solutions. Hence they each dominate the solution $\overset{d}{u}$ in $\mathcal{N}_b$. Since the three solutions $\overset{a}{u}$, $\overset{c}{u}$, and $\overset{d}{u}$ must be linearly dependent, constants c_1, c_3, c_4 exist such that

$$c_1\overset{a}{u} + c_3\overset{c}{u} + c_4\overset{d}{u} \equiv 0 \quad . \tag{19.8}$$

Of course, the coefficients c_1, c_3, c_4 are functions of ρ. Neither c_1 nor c_3 can be zero, since the two remaining solutions would be of different asymptotic type. We, therefore, may assume $c_1 = -1$ and write

$$\overset{a}{u} = c_3\overset{c}{u} + c_4\overset{d}{u} \quad . \tag{19.9}$$

Since both the solutions $\overset{c}{u}$ and $\overset{d}{u}$ can be continued into the region $\mathcal{N}_a$, the asymptotic expansion of the analytic continuation of $\overset{a}{u}$ can be performed if the coefficients c_3 and

c_4 are known. Since $\overset{d}{u}$ dominates $\overset{c}{u}$ in the region $\mathcal{M}_a$, the term $c_4\overset{d}{u}$ will supply the asymptotic expansion, unless the coefficient c_3 happens to depend on ρ in such a way that the term $c_3\overset{c}{u}$ actually dominates.

Aside from the latter possibility, the problem of determining the asymptotic expansion of a solution outside of its region of admissibility is reduced to the determination of the coefficient c_4. In general, $c_4 \neq 0$. In that case a <u>Stokes phenomenon</u> will occur upon crossing the transition lines, which form part of the boundary of the maximum admissibility regions. These transition lines are then <u>Stokes lines</u>. The problem of determining the asymptotic expansion of the analytic continuation of a solution around a turning point is referred to as the "turning point problem".

The problem of second order we have discussed was selected because it is the simplest problem involving a turning point. It is not the most important such problem arising in Mathematical Physics, however, as often the difference of two eigenvalues has a branch point at the turning point, and frequently additional degeneracies occur. We shall discuss such problems in a later section.

At present we shall mention only the case in which the system is of higher than second order, but only one pair of eigenvalues coalesce at the point $z = 0$. In fact, we shall consider only the third order case in which the eigenavlues $g_1(z)$, $g_2(z)$, $g_3(z)$ are such that

$$(19.10) \qquad g_{12}(0) = 0 \ , \quad D_z g_{12}(0) \neq 0 \ ,$$

$$(19.11) \qquad g_{13}(0) \neq 0 \ , \quad g_{23}(0) \neq 0 \ , \quad D_z g_{13}(0) \neq 0 \ , \ D_z g_{23}(0) \neq 0.$$

To obtain solutions of the first--or second--type near $z = 0$ we may proceed as before by selecting three adjacent "sectors" and choosing paths $\mathcal{P}_{21}(z)$ of points ζ along which

$$(19.12) \qquad \operatorname{Re} h_{21}(\zeta) \geq \operatorname{Re} h_{21}(z) \quad .$$

We maintain that paths $_{31}(z)$ can then always be chosen on which

$$\text{(19.13)} \qquad \operatorname{Re} h_{31}(\zeta) \geq \operatorname{Re} h_{31}(z)$$

provided we restrict ourselves to a sufficiently small neighborhood of $z = 0$. As indicated in the figures, one may

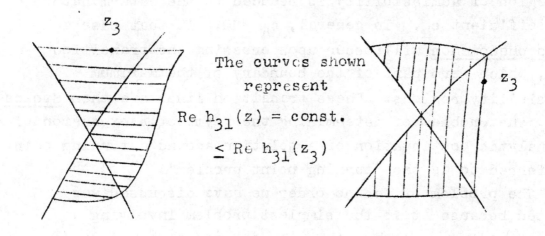

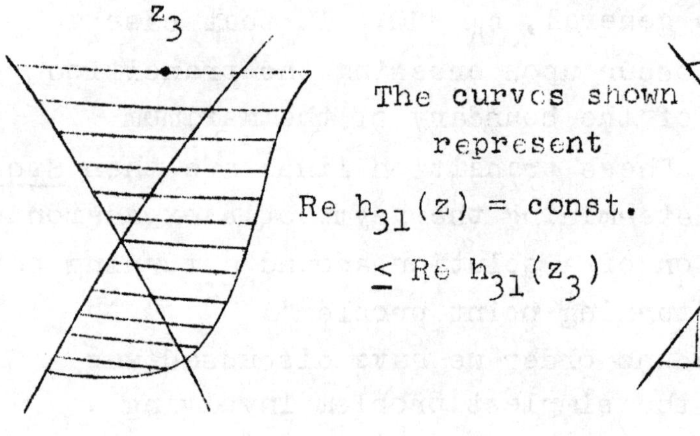

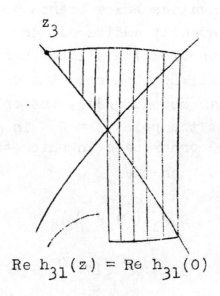

Figure 9

Turning Point for a Third-Order Problem

regions

Admissibility for the solution $W^{(1)}(z)$ are shown in three diferent cases, depending on the behavior of the curves

$$\operatorname{Re} h_{31}(z) = \text{const.} \leq \operatorname{Re} h_{31}(z_3) .$$

not always choose this neighborhood $\mathcal{N}$ and a point z_3 in it such that every point z in $\mathcal{N}$ can be connected to z_3 by a path $\mathcal{P}_{31}(z)$ on which Re $h_{31}(\zeta)$ does not increase from $\zeta = z_3$ to $\zeta = z$. The exception arises if the set Re $h_{31}(z) \geq$ Re $h_{31}(0)$ is disconnected within the "three sectors" in which we seek to define $u_{(1)}$. In that case, only one of the components of this set may be retained. Since there are two such components--if the neighborhood is properly chosen--there are two possible solutions of the first type having the same inner sector. In each case, an additional Stokes line occurs, namely one of the two rays

(19.14) $$\text{Re } h_{31}(z) = \text{Re } h_{31}(0) \quad .$$

Solutions of the third type may be defined in a full neighborhood of the point $z = 0$, since the functions Re $h_{13}(z)$ and Re $h_{23}(z)$ have no saddle point there. The curve Re $h_{13}(z)$ = Re $h_{23}(z)$ is distinguished by the fact that the relative dominance of the solutions of first and third types changes on crossing it. In particular, if the additional Stokes line shown in the third figure is crossed in the direction of the arrow indicated, the solution of the third type becomes dominant over the solution of the first type. Of course, one expects this to happen at a Stokes line.

20. A Typical Turning Point Problem

Before treating the turning point problem in general, we shall treat a typical case in which all questions can be answered explicitly. We consider the system of second order

(20.1) $$D_z u = (\rho z P + \rho \overset{\circ}{P} + Q)u \quad ,$$

in which the 2 by 2 matrices P, $\overset{\circ}{P}$, and Q are constant and $\overset{\circ}{P}$ is such that the matrix $zP + \overset{\circ}{P}$ has for all z the same eigenvalues as zP. We assume that the eigenvalues of the matrix P are distinct.

With the aid of various elementary transformations one may bring this system into the form

$$\text{(20.2)}\qquad \begin{cases} D_z u_1 = \rho z u_1 + \rho \overset{o}{p}_{12} u_2 + q_{12} u_2 \ , \\ D_z u_2 = q_{21} u_1 \ , \end{cases}$$

with a real parameter ρ. To do this we first diagonalize the matrix P. Then, as is easily seen from our requirement on the eigenvalues of $\overset{o}{P}$,

$$\text{(20.3)}\qquad \overset{o}{p}_{11} = \overset{o}{p}_{22} = 0 \text{ and } \overset{o}{p}_{12}\overset{o}{p}_{21} = 0 \ ;$$

we assume without restriction that $\overset{o}{p}_{21} = 0$. Next we factor out of u the function $e^{\frac{1}{2}\rho z^2 p_2}$, where p_2 is the second eigenvalue of P; by doing this we reduce the second eigenvalue of the new matrix P to zero. By factoring out the function $e^{q_{22} z}$, we further achieve that $q_{22} = 0$ for the new matrix Q so obtained. We then substitute $p_{11}^{-1/2} z$ for z in order to make $p_{11} = 1$, and finally make $q_{11} = 0$ by substituting $z - \rho^{-1} q_{11}$ for this new z.

We shall assume that

$$\text{(20.4)}\qquad a = q_{12}q_{21} + \rho \overset{o}{p}_{12} = a_1 + \rho a_o \neq 0 \ ,$$

since otherwise the problem is rather trivial. Furthermore, we shall set

$$\text{(20.5)}\qquad a_o = \overset{o}{p}_{12} = 0 \ ,$$

although the case in which $a_o \neq 0$ could be handled just as easily.

Clearly, $g_1 = z$ and $g_2 = 0$, and hence

$$\text{(20.6)}\qquad h_1 = \tfrac{1}{2} z^2 \ , \quad h_2 = 0 \ , \quad h_{12} = \tfrac{1}{2} z^2 \ .$$

The four regions, denoted by $\mathcal{S}_1$, $\mathcal{S}_i$, $\mathcal{S}_{-1}$, $\mathcal{S}_{-i}$, in the neighborhood of the turning point $z = 0$, are therefore as indicated in the figure.

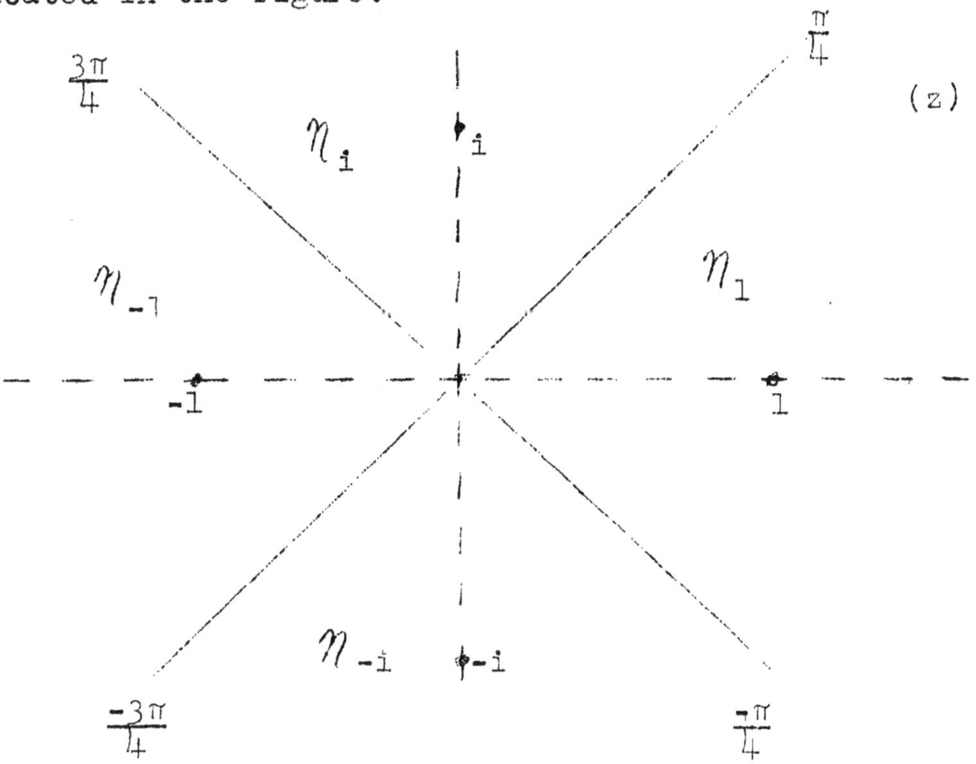

Figure 10

Admissible Regions for the Special Turning-Point Problem

In order to treat equation (20.2), it is convenient to eliminate u_1. We find the single equation

$$D_z^2 w - \rho z D_z w - aw = 0 \tag{20.7}$$

of second order for the single function

$$w = u_2 \quad . \tag{20.8}$$

We first determine the formal solution

$$\tilde{w}(z,\rho) = \sum_{\kappa=0}^{\infty} \rho^{-\kappa} w^{(\kappa)}(z) \tag{20.9}$$

of the second asymptotic type. The coefficients $w^{(\kappa)}(z)$ are successively found from the recursion formula

$$zD_z w^{(\kappa)} = (D_z^2 - a)w^{(\kappa-1)} \quad , \tag{20.10}$$

in which one may for convenience take $w^{(-1)} = 0$; this formula, though easily derived from equation (20.7), also results when the systematic treatment of Section 17 is applied to the special case under consideration. Choosing

$$w^{(0)} = 1 \quad , \tag{20.11}$$

we find from (20.10) that

$$w^{(1)} = -a \log z \tag{20.12}$$

and

$$w^{(2)} = -\frac{a}{2} z^{-2} + \frac{a^2}{2} \log^2 z \quad , \tag{20.13}$$

except for additional arbitrary constants which we have set equal to zero.

In order to determine the formal solution of the first asymptotic type, we find it convenient to introduce the function

$$v = we^{-\frac{1}{2}\rho z^2} \quad , \tag{20.14}$$

which satisfies the differential equation

$$D_z^2 v + \rho D_z(zv) - av = 0 \quad . \tag{20.15}$$

Assuming the formal expansion

$$\tilde{v}(z,\rho) = \sum_{\kappa=0}^{\infty} \rho^{-\kappa} v^{(\kappa)}(z) \quad , \tag{20.16}$$

we find the recursion formula

$$D_z(zv^{(\kappa)}) = -(D_z^2 - a)v^{(\kappa-1)} \quad , \tag{20.17}$$

where again one sets $v^{(-1)} = 0$. Taking

$$v^{(o)} = z^{-1} \quad , \tag{20.18}$$

we obtain

$$v^{(1)} = z^{-3} + az^{-1} \log z \tag{20.19}$$

and

$$v^{(2)} = 3z^{-5} + az^{-3} \log z - \tfrac{3}{2} a z^{-3} + \tfrac{1}{2} a^2 z^{-1} \log^2 z \quad , \tag{20.20}$$

again except for additional arbitrary constants which have been set equal to zero.

We find it convenient to introduce the quantity

$$\varepsilon = \rho^{-1} \tag{20.21}$$

and to write our two formal solutions as

$$\tilde{w}_{(1)}(z,\rho) = e^{\frac{1}{2}\rho z^2} \Big\{ z^{-1} + \varepsilon[z^{-3} + az^{-1} \log z] + \varepsilon^2[3z^{-5} + az^{-3} \log z - \tfrac{3}{2} az^{-3} + \tfrac{1}{2} a^2 z^{-1} \log^2 z] + \dots \Big\} \tag{20.22}$$

and

$$\tilde{w}_{(2)}(z,\rho) = 1 - \varepsilon a \log z - \tfrac{1}{2} \varepsilon^2 [az^{-2} - a^2 \log^2 z] + \dots \quad . \tag{20.23}$$

From the general theory developed in the preceding sections, we then know that the differential equation (20.7) possesses two solutions $\overset{1}{w}(z,\rho)$ and $\overset{-1}{w}(z,\rho)$ of the second asymptotic type having (20.23) as asymptotic expansion, and in addition two solutions $\overset{\pm i}{w}(z,\rho)$ of the first asymptotic type with (20.22) as asymptotic expansion. These four solutions are recessive in the respective "inner" regions $\mathcal{S}_1$, $\mathcal{S}_{-1}$, $\mathcal{S}_i$, $\mathcal{S}_{-i}$, and are dominant in the two adjoining "outer" regions.

The solutions of the problem under consideration can be given <u>explicitly</u> with the aid of the <u>Laplace transformation</u>.

We set

$$(20.24) \qquad w(z) = \int_{\mathcal{P}} e^{zt}\phi(t)dt$$

as in Section 16, and find $\phi(t)$ as the solution

$$(20.25) \qquad \phi(t) = ct^{\varepsilon a-1} e^{-\frac{1}{2}\varepsilon t^2}$$

of the differential equation

$$(20.26) \qquad D_t(t\phi) = \varepsilon(a - t^2)\phi \quad .$$

The constant $c = c(\varepsilon)$ and the path $\mathcal{P}$ will be determined in such a manner that the solutions

$$(20.27) \qquad w(z) = c\int_{\mathcal{P}} e^{zt - \frac{1}{2}\varepsilon t^2} t^{\varepsilon a-1} dt$$

given by (20.24) have the expansions (20.22) or (20.23) as asymptotic expansions.

First we choose the paths $\mathcal{P} = \mathcal{P}_{\pm 1}$ as indicated in Figure 11. The function $t^{\varepsilon a}$ will be taken as positive for real positive values of t when these values are approached via values with a positive imaginary part; i.e.,

$$(20.28) \qquad t^{\varepsilon a} = \begin{cases} e^{\varepsilon a \log t} & \text{on } \mathcal{P}_1 \ , \\ e^{\varepsilon a[\log(-t) + i\pi]} & \text{on } \mathcal{P}_{-1} \ , \end{cases}$$

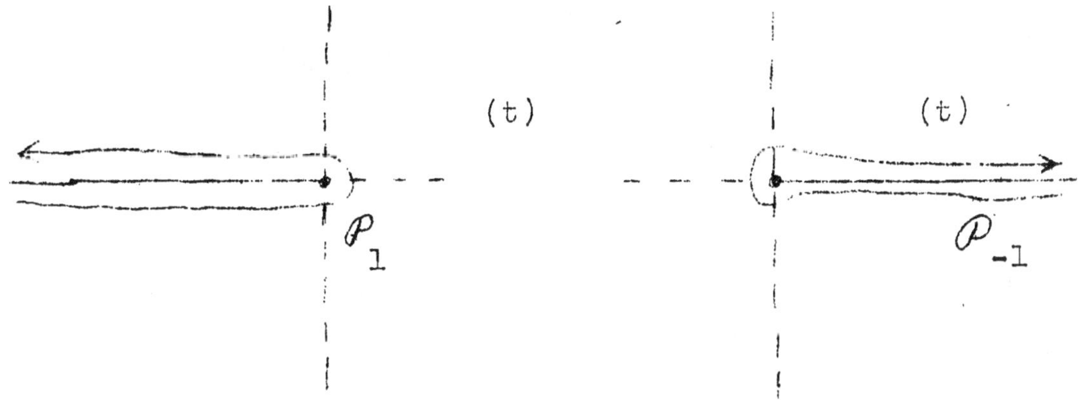

Figure 11

The Paths $\mathcal{P}_1$ and $\mathcal{P}_{-1}$

where that value of the logarithm is chosen whose imaginary part is as small as possible in absolute value.

In order to determine the asymptotic expansion of the resulting function $\frac{1}{w}(z,\rho)$, we introduce the new variable

$$\tau = zt \quad . \tag{20.29}$$

The function $\frac{1}{w}$ may then be expressed in the form

$$\frac{1}{w}(z,\rho) = c_1(\varepsilon)z^{-\varepsilon a} \int_{\mathcal{P}_1(z)} e^{\tau} \tau^{\varepsilon a-1} e^{-\frac{1}{2}\varepsilon z^{-2}\tau^2} d\tau \quad , \tag{20.30}$$

where the path $\mathcal{P}_1(z)$ agrees with the path $\mathcal{P}_1$ if z is real positive, while for complex z it is to be obtained by rotation of $\mathcal{P}_1$ through an angle δ so chosen that

$$|\delta| < \frac{\pi}{2} \tag{20.31}$$

and

(20.32) $$|\delta - \arg z| < \frac{\pi}{4} \quad .$$

Condition (20.31) insures that the integral (20.30) is defined for $\varepsilon = 0$, while (20.32) guarantees the convergence of this integral for positive ε. A δ satisfying these conditions can always be found if

(20.33) $$|\arg z| < \frac{3\pi}{4} \quad .$$

For the function $\overset{1}{w}(z,\rho)$ we then find the expansion

(20.34) $$\overset{1}{w}(z,\rho) = c_1(\varepsilon)z^{-\varepsilon a} \int_{\mathcal{P}_1(z)} e^{\tau}\tau^{\varepsilon a-1}[1 - \tfrac{1}{2}\varepsilon z^{-2}\tau^2 + \tfrac{1}{8}\varepsilon^2 z^{-4}\tau^4 + \ldots]d\tau \quad .$$

Making use of the well-known formula

(20.35) $$\int_{\mathcal{P}_1} e^{\tau}\tau^{\varepsilon a+r}d\tau = (-1)^r(\varepsilon a+r)!(e^{-i\pi\varepsilon a} - e^{i\pi\varepsilon a})$$
for integral r ,

we choose the constant $c_1(\varepsilon)$ as

(20.36) $$c_1(\varepsilon) = [(\varepsilon a-1)!(e^{i\pi\varepsilon a} - e^{-i\pi\varepsilon a})]^{-1}$$
$$= [2i(\varepsilon a-1)! \sin \pi\varepsilon a]^{-1}$$

and find that

(20.37) $$\overset{1}{w}(\rho,z) \sim z^{-\varepsilon a}[1 - \tfrac{1}{2}\varepsilon^2 a(\varepsilon a+1)z^{-2} + \tfrac{1}{8}\varepsilon^3 a(\varepsilon a+1)(\varepsilon a+2)(\varepsilon a+3)z^{-4} + \ldots] \quad .$$

Expanding the function $z^{-\varepsilon a}$ as

$$(20.38)\quad z^{-\varepsilon a} = e^{-\varepsilon a \log z}$$

$$= 1 - \varepsilon a \log z + \tfrac{1}{2}\varepsilon^2 a^2 \log^2 z - \dots ,$$

and writing the contents of the bracket as a power series in ε, we finally obtain

$$(20.39)\quad \overset{1}{w}(z,\rho) \sim 1 - \varepsilon a \log z - \tfrac{1}{2}\varepsilon^2 a z^{-2} + \tfrac{1}{2}\varepsilon^2 a^2 \log^2 z + \dots ,$$

in agreement with (20.23). Since z was restricted by condition (20.33), this expansion holds in the sector $\mathcal{S}_{-i} + \mathcal{S}_1 + \mathcal{S}_i$.

Similarly, performing the transformation

$$(20.40)\qquad \tau = -zt ,$$

using the formula

$$(20.41)\qquad \int_{\mathcal{P}_{-1}} e^{-\tau}\tau^{\varepsilon a+r}\, d\tau = (\varepsilon a+r)!(1 - e^{2\pi i\varepsilon a}) ,$$

and choosing $c(\varepsilon) = c_{-1}(\varepsilon)$ as

$$(20.42)\qquad c_{-1}(\varepsilon) = [(\varepsilon a-1)!(1 - e^{2\pi i\varepsilon a})]^{-1}\, e^{-i\pi\varepsilon a} ,$$

we obtain the expansion

$$(20.43)\quad \overset{-1}{w}(z,\rho) \sim e^{-i\pi\varepsilon a}(-z)^{-\varepsilon a}[1 - \tfrac{1}{2}\varepsilon^2 a(\varepsilon a+1)z^{-2} + \dots] ,$$

valid for

$$(20.44)\qquad |\arg(-z)| < \frac{3\pi}{4} ,$$

i.e. for z in the sector $\mathcal{S}_i + \mathcal{S}_{-1} + \mathcal{S}_{-i}$. In this sector, we have

$$(20.45)\quad (-z)^{-\varepsilon a} = e^{-\varepsilon a \log(-z)} = e^{-\varepsilon a[\log z - i\pi]}$$

and therefore

(20.46) $$e^{-i\pi\varepsilon a}(-z)^{-\varepsilon a} = e^{-\varepsilon a \log z}$$

$$= 1 - \varepsilon a \log z + \frac{1}{2}\varepsilon^2 a^2 \log^2 z - \dots \quad ,$$

where log z has been so determined that

(20.47) $$\frac{\pi}{4} < \operatorname{Im} \log z < \frac{7\pi}{4} \quad .$$

Thus we obtain from (20.43) the same expansion for $\overset{-1}{w}(z,\rho)$ as we did in (20.39) for $\overset{1}{w}(z,\rho)$.

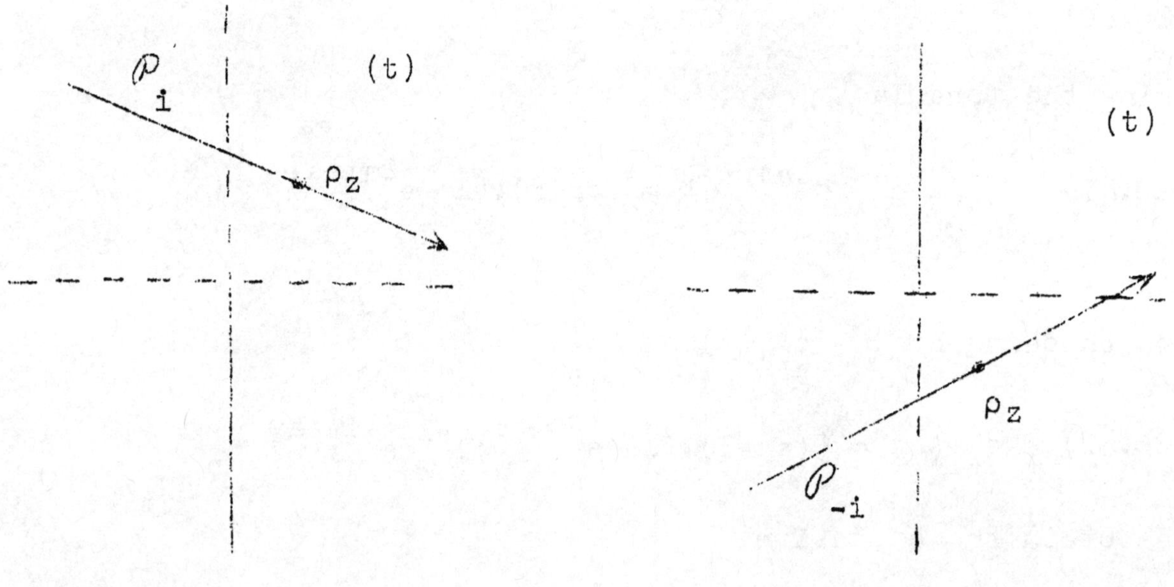

Figure 12

The Paths $\mathcal{P}_i$ and $\mathcal{P}_{-i}$

To obtain representations of the functions $\overset{i}{w}$ and $\overset{-i}{w}$, we choose the paths $\mathcal{P}_i$ and $\mathcal{P}_{-i}$ as indicated in Figure 12. Specifically, we place the paths $\mathcal{P}_i$ and $\mathcal{P}_{-i}$ through the respective saddle points $t = \rho z$ of the exponent in the integral (20.27). Instead of t we then introduce the new variable of integration

$$\sigma = \varepsilon t - z \quad . \tag{20.48}$$

The expressions for $\overset{\pm i}{w}$ can then be written as

$$\overset{\pm i}{w}(z,\rho) = c_{\pm i}(\varepsilon)\rho^{\varepsilon a} z^{\varepsilon a-1} e^{\frac{1}{2}\rho z^2} \int_{\mathcal{P}_{\pm i}(z)} e^{-\frac{1}{2}\rho\sigma^2} [1 + z^{-1}\sigma]^{\varepsilon a-1} d\sigma \quad , \tag{20.49}$$

where the paths $\mathcal{P}_{\pm i}(z)$ may be taken as straight lines through the origin and forming with the positive real axis an angle

$$\delta = \arg \sigma \tag{20.50}$$

which satisfies the conditions

$$|\delta| < \frac{\pi}{4} \tag{20.51}$$

and

$$|\delta - \arg z \pm \frac{\pi}{2}| < \frac{\pi}{2} \quad . \tag{20.52}$$

Condition (20.51) insures that the integral (20.49) is defined, while condition (20.52) insures that as z is moved into $\pm i$ the path $\mathcal{P}_{\pm i}(z)$ can be deformed continuously into the image in the σ-plane of the horizontal path $\mathcal{P}_{\pm i}$ corresponding to $z = \pm i$ without crossing the branch point $\sigma = -z$.

We now make use of the formulae

$$\int_{\mathcal{P}_{\pm i}} e^{-\frac{1}{2}\rho\sigma^2} \sigma^{2m} d\sigma = (m - \tfrac{1}{2})! \left(\frac{\rho}{2}\right)^{-m-\frac{1}{2}} \quad , \tag{20.53}$$

$$(20.54) \qquad \int_{\mathcal{P}_{\pm i}} e^{-\frac{1}{2}\rho\sigma^2} \sigma^{2m+1}\, d\sigma = 0 \quad ,$$

and choose $c(\varepsilon) = c_{\pm i}(\varepsilon)$ as

$$(20.55) \qquad c_{\pm i}(\varepsilon) = (2\pi\varepsilon)^{-1/2}\, \varepsilon^{\varepsilon a} \quad .$$

We find first

$$(20.56) \quad \overset{\pm i}{w}(z,\rho) \sim z^{\varepsilon a-1} e^{\frac{1}{2}\rho z^2} \Big\{ 1 + \frac{1}{2}\, \varepsilon(1-\varepsilon a)(2-\varepsilon a) z^{-2}$$

$$+ \frac{3}{4!}\, \varepsilon^2 (1-\varepsilon a)(2-\varepsilon a)(3-\varepsilon a)(4-\varepsilon a) z^{-4} + \dots \Big\}$$

and then

$$(20.57) \quad \overset{\pm i}{w}(z,\rho) \sim z^{-1} e^{\frac{1}{2}\rho z^2} \Big\{ 1 + \varepsilon [z^{-2} + a \log z]$$

$$+ \varepsilon^2 [3z^{-4} - \tfrac{3}{2} a z^{-2} + a z^{-2} \log z + \tfrac{1}{2} a^2 \log^2 z] + \dots \Big\} \quad ,$$

in evident agreement with (20.22). The expansion (20.57) of $\overset{i}{w}(z,\rho)$ holds if z lies in the sector $\mathcal{S}_1 + \mathcal{S}_i + \mathcal{S}_{-1}$ and the corresponding expansion of $\overset{-i}{w}(z,\rho)$ holds for z in $\mathcal{S}_{-1} + \mathcal{S}_{-i} + \mathcal{S}_1$, since a δ satisfying conditions (20.51) and (20.52) exists if and only if z lies in the sector mentioned.

We observe that the functions $w^{(\kappa)}(z)$ which enter the asymptotic expansions (20.39) and (20.57) are singular at the turning point z = 0. The actual solutions $w(z,\rho)$, however, are not singular there. One should expect that the values $w(0,\rho)$ of these solutions also possess expansions with respect to $\varepsilon = \rho^{-1}$; however, these expansions can not be read off from the formulas (20.39), (20.57).

The values $w(0,\rho)$ can easily be determined for the solutions of the special problem (20.7) considered in this section. From formula (20.27), we have

$$(20.58)\qquad w(0,\rho) = c(\varepsilon)\int_{\mathcal{P}} e^{-\frac{1}{2}\varepsilon t^2}\, t^{\varepsilon a-1}\, dt \quad .$$

We first choose $\mathcal{P} = \mathcal{P}_1$ and $c = c_1(\varepsilon)$ by (20.36). Setting

$$(20.59)\qquad t = (2\rho\sigma)^{1/2}\, e^{\pm i\pi} \quad ,$$

we find that

$$(20.60)\qquad \overset{1}{w}(0,\rho) = \tfrac{1}{2}(2\rho)^{\varepsilon a/2}[(\varepsilon a-1)!]^{-1}\int_0^\infty e^{-\sigma}\sigma^{\varepsilon a/2-1}\, d\sigma$$

or

$$(20.61)\qquad \overset{1}{w}(0,\rho) = (2\rho)^{\varepsilon a/2}\, \tfrac{\varepsilon a}{2}!/(\varepsilon a)! \quad ,$$

Similarly, by choosing $\mathcal{P} = \mathcal{P}_{-1}$ and using (20.42) we find

$$(20.62)\qquad \overset{-1}{w}(0,\rho) = e^{-i\pi\varepsilon a}(2\rho)^{\varepsilon a/2}\, \tfrac{\varepsilon a}{2}!/(\varepsilon a)! \quad .$$

Finally, choosing $\mathcal{P} = \mathcal{P}_{\pm i}$ and using (20.55), we obtain

$$(20.63)\qquad \overset{\pm i}{w}(0,\rho) = (1 - e^{\pm i\pi\varepsilon a})(\varepsilon a)^{-1}(2\pi\varepsilon)^{-1/2}(2\varepsilon)^{\varepsilon a/2}\, \tfrac{\varepsilon a}{2}! \quad .$$

By similar calculations, we would find the expressions

$$(20.64)\qquad D_z\overset{1}{w}(0,\rho) = -\sqrt{\tfrac{\varepsilon}{2}}\, a(2\rho)^{\varepsilon a/2}\, \tfrac{\varepsilon a-1}{2}!/(\varepsilon a)! \quad ,$$

$$(20.65)\qquad D_z\overset{-1}{w}(0,\rho) = \sqrt{\tfrac{\varepsilon}{2}}\, a\, e^{-i\pi\varepsilon a}(2\rho)^{\varepsilon a/2}\, \tfrac{\varepsilon a-1}{2}!/(\varepsilon a)! \quad ,$$

$$(20.66)\qquad D_z\overset{\pm i}{w}(0,\rho) = \tfrac{1}{2}(1 + e^{\pm i\pi\varepsilon a})\pi^{-1/2}\, \rho(2\varepsilon)^{\varepsilon a/2}\, \tfrac{\varepsilon a-1}{2}! \quad .$$

For later purposes it is desirable to give one or two terms of the expansions of $\overset{1}{w}(0,\rho)$ and $D_z\overset{1}{w}(0,\rho)$ with respect to ε. Using the well-known relation

$$(20.67)\qquad \zeta! = 1 - c\zeta + \dots \quad ,$$

in which

$$(20.68)\qquad C = -\int_0^{\infty} e^{-\sigma}\log\sigma \, d\sigma$$

is the Euler constant, cf. (6.7), we find that

$$(20.69)\qquad \overset{1}{w}(0,\rho) \sim 1 - \frac{1}{2}\,\varepsilon a \log \varepsilon + \frac{1}{2}\,\varepsilon a\,(C + \log 2) + \dots$$

and

$$(20.70)\qquad D_z\overset{1}{w}(0,\rho) \sim -a\sqrt{\frac{\pi\varepsilon}{2}}\,(1 + \dots) \quad .$$

Note that these expansions are not strict power series in ε.

With the aid of the values of $w(0,\rho)$ and $D_z w(0,\rho)$ found above, we can immediately solve the continuation problem for the solutions of the equation considered here.

Suppose we want to find the asymptotic expansion of the continuation of the solution $\overset{1}{w}(z)$ into the sector $\mathcal{S}_{-1}$. We know that to do this we need only express this solution $\overset{1}{w}(z)$ as a linear combination of the solutions $\overset{-1}{w}(z)$ and $\overset{i}{w}(z)$, whose asymptotic expansions in the region $\mathcal{S}_{-1}$ are already known. Since all three of these functions $w(z)$ are solutions of the same second order differential equation, they must satisfy for sufficiently large ρ some linear relation

$$(20.71)\qquad \overset{1}{w}(z,\rho) = \overset{1}{p}_{-1}(\varepsilon)\,\overset{-1}{w}(z,\rho) + \overset{1}{p}_{i}(\varepsilon)\,\overset{i}{w}(z,\rho)$$

with coefficients depending possibly on ε but not on z. To find these coefficients, we set $z = 0$ and solve the system of simultaneous linear equations

$$(20.72)\qquad \begin{cases} \overset{1}{w}(0,\rho) = \overset{1}{p}_{-1}(\varepsilon)\,\overset{-1}{w}(0,\rho) + \overset{1}{p}_{i}(\varepsilon)\,\overset{i}{w}(0,\rho) \quad , \\ D_z\overset{1}{w}(0,\rho) = \overset{1}{p}_{-1}(\varepsilon)\,D_z\overset{-1}{w}(0,\rho) + \overset{1}{p}_{i}(\varepsilon)\,D_z\overset{i}{w}(0,\rho) \quad , \end{cases}$$

using the values of $w(0,\rho)$ and $D_z w(0,\rho)$ obtained above. We find

$$(20.73) \qquad \overset{1}{p}_{-1}(\varepsilon) = 1 \quad ,$$

$$(20.74) \qquad \overset{1}{p}_{i}(\varepsilon) = -\sqrt{2\pi\varepsilon}\;\varepsilon a\, e^{-i\pi\varepsilon a}\, \rho^{\varepsilon a}/(\varepsilon a)! \quad .$$

Thus we may write

$$(20.75) \qquad \overset{1}{w}(z,\rho) = \overset{-1}{w}(z,\rho) + \overset{1}{p}_{i}(\varepsilon)\overset{i}{w}(z,\rho) \quad ,$$

with $\overset{1}{p}_{i}(\varepsilon)$ as given by (20.74).

Since $\overset{-1}{w}(z,\rho)$ is recessive in the sector $\mathcal{S}_{-1}$, the asymptotic expansion of the continuation of $\overset{1}{w}(z,\rho)$ into this sector is the same as the expansion of $\overset{1}{p}_{i}(\varepsilon)\overset{i}{w}(z,\rho)$, namely

$$(20.76) \quad \overset{1}{w}(z,\rho) \sim -\sqrt{2\pi\varepsilon}\;\varepsilon a\, e^{\frac{1}{2}\rho z^2}\, z^{-1}$$

$$\left\{1 + \varepsilon[aC - i\pi a + z^{-2} + a \log z] - \varepsilon a \log \varepsilon + \dots\right\} \quad .$$

Thus it is seen that in $\mathcal{S}_{-1}$ the solution $\overset{1}{w}(z,\rho)$ is of the dominant "first" type, but with a coefficient of the order $\varepsilon^{3/2}$.

In a similar manner we may obtain the asymptotic expansion of $\overset{i}{w}(z,\rho)$ in the sector $\mathcal{S}_{-i}$. We write

$$(20.77) \qquad \overset{i}{w}(z,\rho) = \overset{-i}{w}(z,\rho) + \overset{i}{p}_{1}(\varepsilon)\overset{1}{w}(z,\rho)$$

and find that

$$(20.78) \quad \overset{i}{p}_{1}(\varepsilon) = -(e^{i\pi\varepsilon a} - e^{-i\pi\varepsilon a})(\varepsilon a)^{-1}(2\pi\varepsilon)^{-1/2}\varepsilon^{\varepsilon a}(\varepsilon a)! \quad .$$

Clearly, we then have

$$(20.79) \quad \overset{i}{w}(z,\rho) \sim -i(2\pi\rho)^{1/2}\left\{1 - \varepsilon a(C + \log z) + \varepsilon a \log \varepsilon + \dots\right\}$$

in $\mathcal{S}_{-i}$. Hence in this sector the solution $\overset{i}{w}(z,\rho)$ is of the second, "balanced" type; it is not bounded, however, but grows like $\rho^{1/2}$.

21. The Continuation and Connection Problems

We proceed to describe the connection problem for a general differential equation

$$(21.1) \qquad D_z u = \rho A(z,\rho)u$$

of second order. (The case of an equation of higher order can be handled in a similar manner.) Suppose the equation has a turning point at $z = 0$; i.e., the two eigenvalues of the matrix $A^{(0)}(z)$ coalesce there and are otherwise distinct. Let $u_{(1)}(z,\rho)$ be a solution of (21.1) which possesses a given asymptotic expansion in a sector $\mathcal{S}^{(1)}$ with vertex at the turning point, and suppose that this solution is recessive in a subsector $\mathcal{S}_o^{(1)}$, so that it is uniquely determined by this expansion. The problem of finding an expansion of the value $u^{(1)}(0,\rho)$ of this solution at the turning point will be called the connection problem.

Just as in the last section, so in the general case can the continuation problem be reduced to the connection problem. Suppose that the asymptotic expansion of the solution $u_{(1)}(z,\rho)$ is to be found in a sector beyond the Stokes line bounding an outer sector $\mathcal{S}_+^{(1)}$ of this solution. To do this, we seek two other solutions: one, $u_{(2)}(z,\rho)$, is to have the sector $\mathcal{S}_+^{(1)}$ as inner sector,

$$(21.2) \qquad \mathcal{S}_+^{(1)} = \mathcal{S}_o^{(2)} ,$$

and is to be recessive there, while the other, $u_{(3)}(z,\rho)$, should have the sector $\mathcal{S}_+^{(1)}$ as outer sector,

$$(21.3) \qquad \mathcal{S}_+^{(1)} = \mathcal{S}_-^{(3)} ,$$

and should be recessive in a sector

$$(21.4) \qquad \mathcal{S}_o^{(3)} = \mathcal{S}_+^{(2)}$$

beyond the Stokes line in question. This done, two constants $p_2^{(1)}$ and $p_3^{(1)}$, both depending on ρ, may be found such that the relation

$$(21.5) \qquad u_{(1)}(z,\rho) = p_2^{(1)}(\rho)u_{(2)}(z,\rho) + p_3^{(1)}(\rho)u_{(3)}(z,\rho)$$

holds.

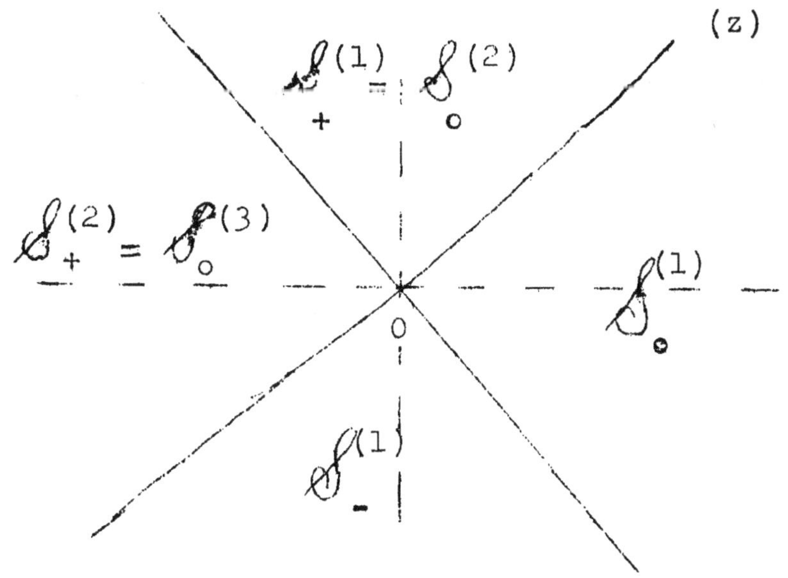

Figure 13

The Continuation Problem

Once these coefficients are found the asymptotic expansion of $u^{(1)}(z,\rho)$ in the sector $\mathcal{S}_+^{(2)}$ can be determined, since the expansions of $u_{(2)}(z,\rho)$ and $u_{(3)}(z,\rho)$ are known. In general, it will be given by

$$(21.6) \qquad u_{(1)}(z,\rho) \sim p_2^{(1)} u_{(2)}(z,\rho) \quad ,$$

since $u_{(3)}(z,\rho)$ is recessive in the region $\mathcal{S}_+^{(2)}$.

In order to determine the coefficients $p_2^{(1)}(\rho)$ and $p_3^{(1)}(\rho)$, it suffices to establish relation (21.5) at the point $z = 0$:

$$(21.7)\quad u_{(1)}(0,\rho) = p_2^{(1)}(\rho)u_{(2)}(0,\rho) + p_3^{(1)}(\rho)u_{(3)}(0,\rho) \quad ,$$

$$(21.8)\quad D_z u_{(1)}(0,\rho) = p_2^{(1)}(\rho)D_z u_{(2)}(0,\rho) + p_3^{(1)}(\rho)D_z u_{(3)}(0,\rho) \quad .$$

This can be done as soon as the values of the three functions u and of their z-derivatives at the turning point z = 0 are known. Hence the continuation problem can indeed be reduced to the connection problem.

In order to solve the connection problem we introduce a new independent variable. We assume that one eigenvalue of $A^{(0)}(z)$ is identically zero and that the other eigenvalue $g(z)$ is regular at z = 0 and vanishes there to first order:

$$(21.9)\qquad g(0) = 0 \quad , \quad g'(0) \neq 0 \quad .$$

We introduce the new variable

$$(21.10)\qquad \zeta = [2\rho h(z)]^{1/2} \quad ,$$

where

$$(21.11)\qquad D_z h(z) = g(z)$$

and

$$(21.12)\qquad h(0) = 0 \quad .$$

For simplicity, let us assume that

$$(21.13)\qquad A^{(0)}(z) = zB \quad ,$$

where B is a constant matrix with eigenvalues 0 and 1, so that

$$(21.14)\qquad g(z) = z \quad , \quad h(z) = \frac{1}{2}z^2 \quad ,$$

and

$$(21.15)\qquad \zeta = \rho^{1/2} z \quad .$$

Our differential equation (21.1) then becomes

$$D_\zeta u = \zeta B u + \sum_{\kappa=1}^{\infty} \varepsilon^{\kappa-1/2} A^{(\kappa)}(\varepsilon^{1/2}\zeta)u \quad . \tag{21.16}$$

This equation will be called the "stretched" differential equation.

In every finite ζ-neighborhood of the point $\zeta = 0$ the right member of the equation (21.16) is a regular function of ζ and of $\varepsilon^{1/2}$. Consequently, this differential equation possesses solutions $u(\zeta) = \underset{*}{u}(\zeta)$ of the form

$$\underset{*}{u}(\zeta) = \sum_{\lambda=0}^{\infty} \varepsilon^{\lambda/2} \underset{\lambda}{u}(\zeta) \quad . \tag{21.17}$$

Equation (21.16) enables one to express the quantity

$$(D_\zeta - \zeta B)\underset{\lambda}{u}(\zeta) \tag{21.18}$$

in terms of functions $\underset{\mu}{u}(\zeta)$ with $\mu < \lambda$. We note that the equation

$$(D_\zeta - \zeta B)u = f \tag{21.19}$$

can be solved explicitly. This would be apparent if the matrix B had been brought into normal form. We could also employ the symbolic solution

$$u = \exp\left\{\tfrac{1}{2}\zeta^2 B\right\}$$

to write down the solution symbolically but explicitly. In any case, the terms $\underset{\lambda}{u}(\zeta)$ can be found explicitly. Of course, each of these terms depends on the choice of two arbitrary constants, which may be taken as the components of the initial value $\underset{\lambda}{u}(0) = \{\underset{\lambda}{u_1}(0), \underset{\lambda}{u_2}(0)\}$.

Clearly, the function $\underset{*}{u}(\sqrt{\rho}\, z)$ is a solution of the original differential equation (21.1). It is now our aim to identify this solution with a solution of a given asymptotic type. For example, we may want to identify it with the solution $\overset{1}{u}(z,\rho)$ which is balanced in the sectors $\mathcal{S}_1$ and $\mathcal{S}_{\pm i}$. That is, we want to determine the initial values $u_\lambda(0)$--as functions of ε--in such a way that

$$(21.20)\qquad u_*(\sqrt{\rho}\, z) = \overset{1}{u}(z,\rho) \quad .$$

If we succeed in finding suitable values $u_\lambda(0)$, we shall automatically have found the value

$$(21.21)\qquad \overset{1}{u}(0,\rho) = u_*(0)$$

of $\overset{1}{u}(z,\rho)$ at the turning point in its dependence on ε.

Naturally, we will be satisfied to determine the appropriate value of $u_\lambda(0)$ asymptotically, by giving asymptotic expansions of this function of ε near $\varepsilon = 0$. When ε is small, the asymptotic expansion of $\overset{1}{u}(z)$ is valid very near the turning point. On the other hand, if ε is sufficiently small, any point z away from the turning point corresponds to a point ζ near infinity. Thus it seems plausible that the identification of the function $u_*(\sqrt{\rho}\, z)$ with the function $\overset{1}{u}(z,\rho)$ may be effected by identifying the function $u_*(\sqrt{\rho}\, z)$ for large values of $\zeta = \sqrt{\rho}\, z$ with the function $\overset{1}{u}(z,\rho)$ for small values of ε.

We shall first describe a <u>formal procedure</u> which accomplishes this. We try to obtain an asymptotic expansion near $\zeta = \infty$ of each of the terms $u_\lambda(\zeta)$ in the series (21.17). Leaving open what type of expansion we seek, we write

$$(21.22)\qquad u_\lambda(\zeta) \sim \sum_\mu u_{\lambda\mu}(\zeta) \quad .$$

Actually, each term $u_{\lambda\mu}(\zeta)$ will be of the form

$$(21.23)\qquad u_{\lambda\mu}(\zeta) = \zeta^{a_{\lambda\mu}} (\log \zeta)^{b_{\lambda\mu}} [c_{\lambda\mu} + d_{\lambda\mu}\, e^{\frac{1}{2}\zeta^2}] \quad .$$

In the resulting formula

$$\underset{*}{u}(\zeta) \sim \sum_{\lambda,\mu} \varepsilon^{\lambda/2} \underset{\lambda\mu}{u}(\zeta) \tag{21.24}$$

we substitute $\zeta = \sqrt{\rho}\, z$. There will then result a series involving terms of the form

$$u_{\alpha\beta}(z) = z^{\alpha}(\log z)^{\beta} \tag{21.25}$$

and

$$u'_{\alpha\beta}(z) = z^{\alpha}(\log z)^{\beta}\, e^{\frac{1}{2}z^2} \quad . \tag{21.26}$$

Each of these terms will receive many contributions. Each coefficient resulting from these contributions will form a series in powers of ε and of $\log \varepsilon$. This coefficient must then be identified with the coefficient of the same term $u_{\alpha\beta}(z)$ or $u'_{\alpha\beta}(z)$ resulting from the asymptotic expansion of the function $\overset{1}{u}(z,\rho)$. The coefficients of the $u'_{\alpha\beta}(z)$, in particular, should vanish, since these terms do not occur in the expansion of the balanced solution $\overset{1}{u}(z,\rho)$.

Note that the coefficients of $u_{\alpha\beta}(z)$ and $u'_{\alpha\beta}(z)$ resulting from the expansion of $\underset{*}{u}(\zeta)$ depend on the initial values $\underset{\lambda}{u}(0)$. The condition that these coefficients agree with those resulting from the expansion of $\overset{1}{u}(z)$ should then determine the values $\underset{\lambda}{u}(0)$ as functions of ε. Once these values are determined, the connection problem is solved.

It is to be noted that in this procedure the solution $\overset{1}{u}(z,\rho)$ is characterized by its asymptotic expansion. Actually, in the sector $\mathscr{S}_1$ this solution is determined by its expansion only within multiples of the solution $\overset{i}{u}(z,\rho)$ which are asymptotically zero. For example, if the sector $\mathscr{S}_1$ is restricted to lie in the circle $|z| \leq z_0$, the multiple $c(\varepsilon)\, \overset{i}{u}(z,\rho)$ is asymptotically zero there if the function $c(\varepsilon)$

is such that $c(\varepsilon)e^{\frac{1}{2}\rho|z_0^2|}$ is asymptotically zero. Since the value of $c(\varepsilon)\overset{i}{u}(0,\rho)$ is also asymptotically zero, the values of $\overset{1}{u}(0,\rho)$ and $\overset{1}{u}(0,\rho)+c(\varepsilon)\overset{i}{u}(0,\rho)$ are asymptotically the same.

To exemplify the formal procedure, we consider the special equation

$$(21.27)\qquad \begin{cases} D_z u_1 = \rho z u_1 + a u_2 + b z u_2 , \\ D_z u_2 = u_1 , \end{cases}$$

in which a and b are constants; for b = 0 this equation reduces to the special problem treated in Section 20. The asymptotic expansion of the solution $\overset{1}{u}(z)$ which is balanced in the sectors $\mathcal{S}_1$ and $\mathcal{S}_{\pm i}$ begins with

$$(21.28)\qquad \begin{aligned} \overset{1}{u}_1(z,\rho) &\sim -\varepsilon a z^{-1} - \varepsilon b + \dots , \\ \overset{1}{u}_2(z,\rho) &\sim 1 - \varepsilon a \log z - \varepsilon b z + \dots , \end{aligned}$$

as is easily verified.

The stretched differential equation obtained by introducing $\zeta = \sqrt{\rho}\, z$ as new variable is

$$(21.29)\qquad \begin{cases} (D_\zeta - \zeta)u_1 = \sqrt{\varepsilon}\, a u_2 + \varepsilon b \zeta u_2 , \\ D_\zeta u_2 = \sqrt{\varepsilon}\, u_1 . \end{cases}$$

For the terms in the series

$$(21.30)\qquad \underset{*}{u}(\zeta) = \sum_{\lambda=0}^{\infty} \varepsilon^{\lambda/2} \underset{\lambda}{u}(\zeta)$$

we find first

$$(21.31) \qquad \begin{aligned} {}_{0}u_1(\zeta) &= {}_{0}c_1\, e^{\frac{1}{2}\zeta^2} \;, \\ {}_{0}u_2(\zeta) &= {}_{0}c_2 \;, \end{aligned}$$

with constant ${}_{0}c_1$, ${}_{0}c_2$. Since the asymptotic expansion of ${}_{0}u(\zeta)$ near $\zeta = \infty$ should not contain the term $e^{\frac{1}{2}\zeta^2}$, we should set ${}_{0}c_1 = 0$. Furthermore we set ${}_{0}c_2 = 1$, so that the term ${}_{0}u(\zeta)$ agrees with the leading term in the expansion of $\overset{1}{u}(z,\rho)$. Thus

$$(21.32) \qquad \begin{aligned} {}_{0}u_1(\zeta) &= 0 \;, \\ {}_{0}u_2(\zeta) &= 1 \;. \end{aligned}$$

For the term ${}_{1}u(\zeta)$ we obtain

$$(21.33) \qquad \begin{aligned} {}_{1}u_1(\zeta) &= a\, e^{\frac{1}{2}\zeta^2} \int^{\zeta} e^{-\frac{1}{2}\alpha^2}\, d\alpha \;, \\ {}_{1}u_2(\zeta) &= {}_{1}c_2 \;. \end{aligned}$$

We take infinity as the lower limit of the integral in (21.33), in order to insure that no term $e^{\frac{1}{2}\zeta^2}$ occurs in the asymptotic expansion of ${}_{1}u_1(\zeta)$ near $\zeta = \infty$. Integrating by parts, we obtain

$$(21.34) \qquad {}_{1}u_1(\zeta) = -a\zeta^{-1} - a\, e^{\frac{1}{2}\zeta^2} \int_{\infty}^{\zeta} \alpha^{-2}\, e^{-\frac{1}{2}\alpha^2}\, d\alpha \;,$$

whence follows

$$(21.35) \qquad {}_{1}u_1(\zeta) \sim -a[\zeta^{-1} - \zeta^{-3} + \dots] \;.$$

Inserting $\zeta = \sqrt{\rho}\, z$, we find

$$\sqrt{\varepsilon}\;\underset{1}{u}_1(\sqrt{\rho}\,z) \sim -\varepsilon a z^{-1} + \varepsilon^2 a z^{-3} + \dots ,$$

(21.36)

$$\sqrt{\varepsilon}\;\underset{1}{u}_2(\sqrt{\rho}\,z) \sim \sqrt{\varepsilon}\;\underset{1}{c}_2 + \dots .$$

The term $-\varepsilon a z^{-1}$ agrees with the first term in the expansion of $\overset{1}{u}_1(z,\rho)$ in (21.28). Since no term $c\sqrt{\varepsilon}$ occurs in the expansion of $\overset{1}{u}_2(z,\rho)$, we may set $\underset{1}{c}_2 = 0$. Thus

$$\underset{1}{u}_1(\zeta) = a e^{\frac{1}{2}\zeta^2} \int_{\infty}^{\zeta} e^{-\frac{1}{2}\alpha^2}\, d\alpha ,$$

(21.37)

$$\underset{1}{u}_2(\zeta) = 0 .$$

For $\underset{2}{u}(\zeta)$ we find

$$\underset{2}{u}_1(\zeta) = -b ,$$

(21.38)

$$\underset{2}{u}_2(\zeta) = a \int^{\zeta} e^{\frac{1}{2}\alpha^2} \int_{\infty}^{\alpha} e^{-\frac{1}{2}\beta^2}\, d\beta\, d\alpha + \text{const.}$$

In finding $\underset{2}{u}_1(\zeta)$, we have anticipated the absence of a term $e^{\frac{1}{2}\zeta^2}$. The term

(21.39) $$\varepsilon\,\underset{2}{u}_1(\sqrt{\rho}\,z) = -\varepsilon b$$

agrees with the second term in the expansion of $\overset{1}{u}_1(z,\rho)$ given in (21.28).

In the expression for $\underset{2}{u}_2(\zeta)$, we cannot take ∞ as the lower limit of the first integral, since $\underset{1}{u}_1(\zeta)$ behaves asymptotically like $-a\zeta^{-1}$. We find it convenient to write

(21.40) $$\underset{2}{u}_2(\zeta) = a \int_0^{\zeta} e^{\frac{1}{2}\alpha^2} \int_{\infty}^{\alpha} e^{-\frac{1}{\beta}\beta^2}\, d\beta\, d\alpha + \underset{2}{c}_2$$

and to determine the constant c_{2_2} appropriately. To this end we write $u_{2_2}(\zeta)$ in a different form, introducing $\xi = \beta - \alpha$ as new independent variable in place of β. We find

$$(21.41)\qquad u_{2_2}(\zeta) = -a \int_0^{\zeta} \int_0^{\infty} e^{-\frac{1}{2}\xi^2 - \alpha\xi}\, d\xi\, d\alpha + c_{2_2}$$

$$= -a \int_0^{\infty} e^{-\frac{1}{2}\xi^2} [1 - e^{-\zeta\xi}]\xi^{-1} d\xi + c_{2_2}$$

$$= -a \int_0^{\infty} e^{-\frac{1}{2}\xi^2} [\xi(1 - e^{-\zeta\xi}) - \zeta e^{-\zeta\xi}] \log \xi \, d\xi + c_{2_2}$$

$$= -a \int_0^{\infty} \xi e^{-\frac{1}{2}\xi^2} (1 - e^{-\zeta\xi}) \log \xi \, d\xi$$

$$+a \int_0^{\infty} e^{-\frac{1}{2}\eta^2\zeta^{-2}} e^{-\eta} \log (\eta \zeta^{-1}) d\eta + c_{2_2} \;.$$

The asymptotic behavior of $u_{2_2}(\zeta)$ near $\zeta = \infty$ is then seen to be given by

$$(21.42)\qquad u_{2_2}(\zeta) \sim -a \int_0^{\infty} \xi e^{-\frac{1}{2}\xi^2} \log \xi \, d\xi$$

$$+a \int_0^{\infty} e^{-\eta} \log (\eta \zeta^{-1}) d\eta + c_{2_2} \quad ,$$

at least in the sector $\mathcal{S}_1$ where $e^{-\zeta\xi}$ decreases exponentially. Using now the formulas

$$(21.43)\qquad \int_0^{\infty} e^{-\eta} d\eta = 1 \quad ,$$

$$(21.44) \qquad \int_0^\infty e^{-\eta} \log \eta \, d\eta = -C \quad ,$$

$$(21.45) \qquad \int_0^\infty \xi e^{-\frac{1}{2}\xi^2} \log \xi \, d\xi = \tfrac{1}{2}[\log 2 - C] \quad ,$$

involving the Euler constant C, we find that

$$(21.46) \qquad \underset{2}{u}_2(\zeta) \sim -a \log \zeta - \tfrac{a}{2}[\log 2 + C] + \underset{2}{c}_2$$

in $\mathcal{S}_1$. Comparison with (21.28), after substituting $\zeta = \sqrt{\rho}\, z$, shows that the constant $\underset{2}{c}_2$ should be taken as

$$(21.47) \qquad \underset{2}{c}_2 = \tfrac{1}{2}\, a \log \rho + \tfrac{1}{2}\, a[\log 2 + C] \quad .$$

Although it is possible to continue in this fashion, it would be somewhat tedious to do so.

We can now determine the expansion of $\overset{1}{u}(z,\rho)$ at the turning point z = 0. From (21.32), (21.37), (21.38), (21.40), we have

$$(21.48) \qquad \begin{array}{lll} \underset{0}{u}_1(0) = 0 \ , & \underset{1}{u}_1(0) = -a\sqrt{\frac{\pi}{2}} \ , & \underset{2}{u}_1(0) = -b \ , \\ \underset{0}{u}_2(0) = 1 \ , & \underset{1}{u}_2(0) = 0 \ , & \underset{2}{u}_2(0) = \underset{2}{c}_2, \ldots, \end{array}$$

whence

$$(21.49) \qquad \begin{aligned} \overset{1}{u}_1(0,\rho) &\sim -a\sqrt{\frac{\pi\varepsilon}{2}} - \varepsilon b + \ldots \ , \\ \overset{1}{u}_2(0,\rho) &\sim 1 + \tfrac{1}{2}\, \varepsilon a \log \rho + \tfrac{1}{2}\, \varepsilon a[\log 2 + C] + \ldots \ . \end{aligned}$$

For b = 0 these two formulas are in agreement with the values given by (20.69) and (20.70), which were derived from the explicit expressions (20.61) and (20.64).

22. Rigorous Approach to the Connection Problem

In this section we shall outline an approach to the connection problem which is based on a rigorously proved theorem. This approach is related to Langer's treatment of the turning point problem for an equation of the second order, which we shall discuss in Section 23.

We write the differential equation in the form

$$(22.1)\qquad \begin{cases} D_z u_1 = \rho z u_1 + Q_1 u \quad , \\ D_z u_2 = \qquad\quad Q_2 u \quad , \end{cases}$$

where

$$(22.2)\qquad Q_1 u = q_{11}u_1 + q_{12}u_2 \quad , \qquad Q_2 u = q_{21}u_1 + q_{22}u_2 \quad ,$$

and the $q_{\alpha\beta} = q_{\alpha\beta}(z,\varepsilon)$ are functions of z and ε regular at $z = \varepsilon = 0$. Without restriction we assume that

$$(22.3)\qquad q_{22} \equiv 0 \quad ,$$

for if this condition is not satisfied we need only replace $u(z)$ by $u(z)\exp\int_0^z q_{22}(z')dz'$ in order to obtain it.

Let $\overset{1}{u}(z,\rho)$ be a solution of (22.1) which is balanced and recessive in the sector $\mathcal{S}_1$. Let z_0 be a point in $\mathcal{S}_1$, and set

$$(22.4)\qquad \overset{1}{u}(z_0,\rho) = \omega(\varepsilon) = \omega = \{\omega_1, \omega_2\} \quad .$$

The solution $u(z) = \overset{1}{u}(z,\rho)$ is then the solution of the integral equation

$$(22.5)\qquad \begin{cases} u_1(z) = \omega_1 + F_1 u(z) \quad , \\ u_2(z) = \omega_2 + F_2 u(z) \quad , \end{cases}$$

with

$$F_1u(z) = \int_{z_0}^{z} e^{\frac{1}{2}\rho(z^2-\alpha^2)} Q_1u(\alpha)d\alpha \quad ,$$

(22.6)

$$F_2u(z) = \int_{z_0}^{z} Q_2u(\alpha)d\alpha \quad .$$

From this relation we shall derive estimates which are independent of ε if ε is sufficiently small, and are valid in the sectors $\mathcal{S}_1 + \mathcal{S}_i + \mathcal{S}_{-i}$, including the Stokes lines and the turning point.

For simplicity we assume that $z_0 = x_0$ is real positive. Further we first restrict ourselves to positive real values $z = x$ of z, assuming

(22.7) $$0 \leq x \leq x_0 \quad .$$

We introduce the norms

(22.8) $$\|u_1\| = \max_{0\leq x\leq x_0} |u_1(x)| \quad ,$$

(22.9) $$\|u_2\| = \max_{0\leq x\leq x_0} |u_2(x)| \quad .$$

We further set

(22.10) $$\|Q\| = \max_{\alpha,\beta} \max_{0\leq x\leq x_0} |q_{\alpha\beta}(z)| \quad .$$

We then find

(22.11) $$|F_1u(x)| \leq \|Q\| \left\{\|u_1\| + \|u_2\|\right\} \int_{x}^{x_0} e^{\frac{1}{2}\rho(x^2-\alpha^2)} d\alpha \quad .$$

Since

$$(22.12)\quad \int_x^{x_0} e^{\frac{1}{2}\rho(x^2-\alpha^2)}\,d\alpha \le e^{\frac{1}{2}\rho x^2}\int_x^{\infty} e^{-\frac{1}{2}\rho\alpha^2}\,d\alpha$$

$$= e^{\frac{1}{2}\rho x^2}\int_0^{\infty} e^{-\frac{1}{2}\rho(x+\beta)^2}\,d\beta$$

$$= \int_0^{\infty} e^{-\frac{1}{2}\rho\beta^2-\rho\beta x}\,d\beta \le \int_0^{\infty} e^{-\frac{1}{2}\rho\beta^2}\,d\beta \le 2\sqrt{\varepsilon} \quad ,$$

we have

$$(22.13)\qquad \|F_1 u\| \le 2\sqrt{\varepsilon}\,\|Q\|\left\{\|u_1\|+\|u_2\|\right\} \quad .$$

Further, because of (22.3), we have

$$(22.14)\qquad \|F_2 u\| \le x_0\|Q\|\,\|u_1\| \quad .$$

To combine these formulas we introduce the norm

$$(22.15)\qquad \|u\| = \sqrt[4]{\rho}\,\sqrt{x_0}\,\|u_1\| + \|u_2\| \quad .$$

Restricting ε by

$$(22.16)\qquad \varepsilon \le x_0^2 \quad ,$$

we then have

$$(22.17)\quad \|Fu\| \le \left[2\sqrt[4]{\varepsilon}\sqrt{x_0}+x_0\right]\|Q\|\,\|u_1\| + 2\sqrt[4]{\varepsilon}\sqrt{x_0}\,\|Q\|\,\|u_2\|$$

$$\le \|Q\|\left[3x_0\,\|u_1\| + 2\sqrt[4]{\varepsilon}\,\sqrt{x_0}\,\|u_2\|\right] \quad .$$

From this, setting

$$(22.18)\qquad 3\|Q\|\sqrt{x_0} = \gamma \quad ,$$

we obtain

$$(22.19)\qquad \|Fu\| \le \sqrt[4]{\varepsilon}\,\gamma\,\|u\| \quad .$$

Note that the initial value ω, given by (22.4), satisfies inequalities

(22.20) $$|\omega_1| \leq c_1\varepsilon \quad , \quad |\omega_2| \leq c_2$$

with appropriate constants c_1, c_2, as may be inferred from the asymptotic expansion of $\overset{1}{u}(z,\rho)$. Hence there is a finite constant c_o such that

(22.21) $$\|\omega\| \leq c_o \quad ,$$

independently of ε. From (22.19) therefore we may conclude that

(22.22) $$\|F^r \omega\| \leq \left(\sqrt[4]{\varepsilon}\ \gamma\right)^r c_o \quad ,$$

where F^r stands for the r-times iterated integral operator F. Thus it is seen that for

(22.23) $$0 \leq \varepsilon \leq \theta\gamma^{-4} \quad , \quad 0 < \theta < 1 \quad ,$$

the series

(22.24) $$\sum_{r=0}^{\infty} F^r \omega(\varepsilon)$$

converges uniformly in ε and uniformly in $0 \leq x \leq x_o$. Evidently, the sum of this series satisfies equation (22.5), so that

(22.25) $$\sum_{r=0}^{\infty} F^r \omega(\varepsilon) = \overset{1}{u}(x,\rho) \quad .$$

In particular, the value $\overset{1}{u}(0,\rho)$ of $\overset{1}{u}(z,\rho)$ at $z = 0$ is given by a convergent series of terms which vanish as $\varepsilon \longrightarrow 0$ at least as fast as $\varepsilon^{r/4}$.

To complete the argument, it should be shown that each of these terms admits an asymptotic expansion with respect to ε. It should not be difficult to do so, since these terms are explicitly given by integrals involving the coefficients $q_{\alpha\beta}(x)$ and the functions $e^{\pm\frac{1}{2}\rho x^2}$. Once this is done, the asymptotic expansion of the value $\overset{1}{u}(0,\rho)$ is found and the connection problem is then solved.

Further, it could be shown that the results of this rigorous procedure agree with the results of the formal procedure outlined in Section 21.

In the preceding discussion we have restricted the point z to lie on the positive real axis. We may remove this restriction and allow z to lie on one of the Stokes lines $z = |z|e^{\pm 3i\pi/4}$. Since $\left|e^{\pm\frac{1}{2}\rho z^2}\right| = 1$ for such values of z, estimates similar to those derived in this section hold. In this way it would be possible to determine the Stokes multipliers directly and thus solve the continuation problem.

23. Singular Turning Point Problems

Investigations of the turning point problem in the literature have been mostly concerned with the differential equation

$$D_z^2 w = [\rho^2 \chi(z) + \rho\chi_1(z,\rho)]w \quad , \tag{23.1}$$

in which the function $\chi(z)$ vanishes at $z = 0$ while $\chi_1(z,\rho)$ admits an expansion with respect to powers of $\varepsilon = \rho^{-1}$. For simplicity we assume $\chi_1(z)$ to be independent of ρ. We assume that the functions χ and χ_1 are analytic in the neighborhood of $z = 0$, and that $D_z\chi(0) \neq 0$. Without serious restriction we may even suppose that

(23.2) $$D_z \chi(0) = 1 \quad ,$$

in addition to

(23.3) $$\chi(0) = 0 \quad .$$

We may write equation (23.1) as a system

(23.4) $$\begin{cases} D_z(\varepsilon D_z w) = [\rho \chi + \chi_1] w \quad , \\ D_z w \qquad\quad = \rho(\varepsilon D_z w) \quad . \end{cases}$$

The eigenvalues of the leading matrix

(23.5) $$\begin{pmatrix} 0 & \chi \\ 1 & 0 \end{pmatrix}$$

are

(23.6) $$g(z) = \pm \sqrt{\chi(z)} \quad .$$

The functions

(23.7) $$h(z) = \pm \int^{z} \sqrt{\chi(\zeta)}\, d\zeta$$

are unique on a two-sheeted Riemann surface. From assumption (23.2), we have

(23.8) $$h(z) \sim \pm \frac{2}{3} z^{3/2} + \ldots$$

near $z = 0$; hence the "transition lines" $\operatorname{Re} h = 0$ enter the turning point $z = 0$ in directions $\theta = \arg z$ given by

(23.9) $$\theta = \pm\frac{\pi}{3}, \pm\pi, \pm\frac{5\pi}{3} \quad .$$

Evidently, the Riemann surface is divided into six sectors by these lines.

It follows from the general theory that to each of these sectors there is a solution which is recessive in that sector and dominant in the two adjacent sectors. Accordingly, there would be six such solutions. Considered as a function of z, however, a solution associated with one sector may at the same time be regarded as a solution of the opposite asymptotic type associated with the congruent sector in the other sheet of the Riemann surface. Thus in this sense there are three distinct solutions.

We note that the maximal domain of each of these solutions is a plane slit along one of the transition rays.

It is convenient to introduce a new variable $\tilde{z}$ in such a way that actually

$$h(z) = \pm \frac{2}{3} \tilde{z}^{3/2} \tag{23.10}$$

and

$$\left.\frac{d\tilde{z}}{dz}\right|_{z=0} = 1 \quad . \tag{23.11}$$

We also introduce the function

$$p = \tilde{z}^{-1/2} \sqrt{\chi} = \frac{d\tilde{z}}{dz} \quad , \tag{23.12}$$

considered as function of $\tilde{z}$; it is evidently regular at $\tilde{z} = 0$. Then we may write equation (23.1) in the form

$$D_{\tilde{z}}(pD_{\tilde{z}}w) = [\rho^2 p\tilde{z} + \rho p^{-1} \chi_1]w \quad . \tag{23.13}$$

From now on we will again write z in place of $\tilde{z}$. We then may write

$$\begin{cases} D_z(\varepsilon D_z w) = \rho z w + a(\varepsilon D_z w) + bw \quad , \\ D_z w = \rho(\varepsilon D_z w) \quad , \end{cases} \tag{23.14}$$

with

$$a = -p^{-1} D_z p \quad , \quad b = p^{-2} \chi \quad . \tag{23.15}$$

We diagonalize this system by setting

$$(23.16)\qquad \begin{aligned} u_1 &= \varepsilon D_z w + z^{1/2} w \quad , \\ u_2 &= \varepsilon D_z w - z^{1/2} w \quad . \end{aligned}$$

Then we obtain

$$(23.17)\qquad \begin{cases} D_z u_1 = \rho z^{1/2} u_1 + \frac{1}{2} a(u_1+u_2) + \frac{1}{2}[bz^{-1/2} + \frac{1}{2} z^{-1}][u_1-u_2], \\ D_z u_2 = -\rho z^{1/2} u_2 + \frac{1}{2} a(u_1+u_2) + \frac{1}{2}[bz^{-1/2} - \frac{1}{2} z^{-1}][u_1-u_2]. \end{cases}$$

We ask for solutions $u(z,\rho)$ with the expansion

$$(23.18)\qquad u \sim e^{-\frac{2}{3}\rho z^{3/2}} \sum_{\kappa=0}^{\infty} \varepsilon^{\kappa} u^{(\kappa)} \quad .$$

The terms $u^{(\kappa)}$ satisfy the equations

$$(23.19)\qquad \begin{aligned} 2z^{1/2} u_1^{(\kappa+1)} &= D_z u_1^{(\kappa)} - \tfrac{1}{2} a[u_1^{(\kappa)} + u_2^{(\kappa)}] \\ &\qquad - \tfrac{1}{2} [bz^{-1/2} + \tfrac{1}{2} z^{-1}][u_1^{(\kappa)} - u_2^{(\kappa)}] , \\ D_z u_2^{(\kappa)} &- \tfrac{1}{2} a[u_1^{(\kappa)} + u_2^{(\kappa)}] \\ &\qquad - \tfrac{1}{2} [bz^{-1/2} - \tfrac{1}{2} z^{-1}][u_1^{(\kappa)} - u_2^{(\kappa)}] = 0 \quad . \end{aligned}$$

For the first term $u^{(0)}$ we find

$$(23.20)\qquad \begin{aligned} u_1^{(0)}(z) &= 0 \quad , \\ u_2^{(0)}(z) &= c_2^{(0)} z^{1/4} \exp \tfrac{1}{2}\left[\int^z a(\zeta)d\zeta - \int^z b(\zeta)\zeta^{-1/2} d\zeta\right] \quad . \end{aligned}$$

Hence we have

$$(23.21) \quad w(z) \sim -\frac{1}{2} c_2^{(0)} z^{-1/4} \exp \frac{1}{2}\left[\int a(z)dz - \int b(z)z^{-1/2}dz\right] e^{-\frac{2}{3}\rho z^{3/2}} .$$

The subsequent terms could, of course, be determined easily by explicit integration.

In order to solve the continuation problem we could proceed as in the preceding sections. We could either solve the connection problem formally by solving a stretched differential equation, or we could approach the connection problem rigorously by solving an appropriate integral equation. Finally, we could use such an integral equation to treat the connection problem directly. The latter approach would essentially be that introduced by Langer [E] originally.

Under the specific circumstances which we have assumed here, one can proceed more simply. Consider a solution $\overset{o}{w}$ which is recessive in the sector $|\arg z| < \frac{\pi}{3}$, whose asymptotic expansion therefore carries the factor $e^{-\frac{2}{3}\rho z^{3/2}}$. To obtain the expansion of $\overset{o}{w}$ on the Stokes line $\arg z = \pm\pi$, we may express this solution in terms of a solution $\overset{1}{w}$ which is recessive for $|\arg z - \frac{2}{3}\pi| < \frac{\pi}{3}$ and a solution $\overset{2}{w}$, recessive for $|\arg z - \frac{4}{3}\pi| < \frac{\pi}{3}$. Since the latter solution is of the same asymptotic type as $\overset{o}{w}$, it may be chosen so as to have also the same asymptotic expansion. Hence we have

$$(23.22) \qquad \overset{o}{w}(z) = \overset{2}{w}(z) + \overset{o}{p}_1 \overset{1}{w}(z) .$$

Since the function $\overset{o}{w}(z)$ is one-valued, we may obtain the asymptotic expansion of $\overset{o}{w}(z)$ on $\arg z = \pm\pi$ just as well by expressing $\overset{o}{w}$ in terms of solutions $\overset{-1}{w}(z)$ and $\overset{-2}{w}(z)$ which are recessive in the sectors $|\arg z + \frac{2}{3}\pi| < \frac{\pi}{3}$ and $|\arg z + \frac{4}{3}\pi| < \frac{\pi}{3}$ respectively:

$$\overset{o}{w}(z) = \overset{-2}{w}(z) + \overset{o}{p}_{-1}\overset{-1}{w}(z) \quad . \tag{23.23}$$

Now, the functions $\overset{-2}{w}(z)$ and $\overset{2}{w}(z)$ are identical with multiples of $\overset{1}{w}(z)$ and $\overset{-1}{w}(z)$ respectively, for the exponential factor which $\overset{\pm 2}{w}(z)$ carry is given as $e^{-\frac{2}{3}\rho z^{3/2}}$ on the upper sheet $\pi < |\arg z| \leq 2\pi$ of the Riemann surface and hence as $e^{+\frac{2}{3}\rho z^{3/2}}$ on the lower sheet $|\arg z| < \pi$. Consequently,

$$\overset{o}{p}_1\overset{1}{w}(z) = \overset{-2}{w}(z) \quad \text{and} \quad \overset{o}{p}_{-1}\overset{-1}{w}(z) = \overset{2}{w}(z) \quad . \tag{23.24}$$

Accordingly, we have

$$\overset{o}{w}(z) = \overset{2}{w}(z) + \overset{-2}{w}(z) \quad . \tag{23.25}$$

Note that $\overset{2}{w}(z)$ has the same asymptotic expansion as $\overset{o}{w}(z)$ when the latter is continued in the upper half-plane, while $\overset{-2}{w}(z)$ has the same expansion as $\overset{o}{w}(z)$ when it is continued in the lower half-plane. Thus, <u>the asymptotic expansion of $\overset{o}{w}(z)$ on the Stokes line</u> $\arg z = \pm\pi$ <u>is obtained by continuing the expansion of $\overset{o}{w}(z)$ to</u> $\arg z = \pi$ <u>and</u> $\arg z = -\pi$ <u>and adding the results</u>.

Suppose, on the other hand, a solution $\overset{*}{w}(z)$ is given in neighborhood of $\arg z = \pm\pi$. Then one may write this solution in the form

$$\overset{*}{w}(z) = c_2\overset{2}{w}(z) + c_{-2}\overset{-2}{w}(z) \quad . \tag{23.26}$$

Now one may, for example, use the identity

$$\overset{-2}{w}(z) = \overset{o}{p}_1\overset{1}{w}(z) \tag{23.27}$$

and write

$$\overset{*}{w}(z) = c_2[\overset{2}{w}(z) + \overset{-2}{w}(z)] + [c_{-2} - c_2]\overset{o}{p}_1\overset{1}{w}(z) \quad . \tag{23.28}$$

The function

$$\overset{*}{w}(z) - c_2\overset{o}{w}(z) - [c_{-2} - c_2]\overset{o}{p}_1\overset{1}{w}(z) \tag{23.29}$$

is therefore asymptotically zero on the line arg $z = \pm\pi$. Since the exponents $\pm\rho z^{3/2}$ of the exponential factors are purely imaginary there, it is clear that any solution which is asymptotically zero on the line arg $z = \pm\pi$ is asymptotically zero in the whole neighborhood of $z = 0$. Accordingly, we have throughout

$$\overset{*}{w}(z) \sim c_2\overset{o}{w}(z) + [c_{-2} - c_2]\overset{o}{p}_1\overset{1}{w}(z) \quad . \tag{23.30}$$

Since the asymptotic expansions of $\overset{o}{w}(z)$ and $\overset{1}{w}(z)$ on arg $z = 0$ are known, <u>the expansion of</u> $\overset{*}{w}(z)$ <u>on the line</u> arg $z = 0$ <u>has been found</u>.

24. The Adiabatic Theorem

The problem of "adiabatic" transition in mechanics and other fields of physics is essentially a problem of asymptotic integration. Suppose a vibratory system which up to a certain time oscillates in one of its normal modes is from that time on slowly modified. Then its motion will be approximately a normal mode of the system at each time, provided the modification is sufficiently slow. In the limit of "infinitely slow", or "adiabatic" modification, the system passes successively through the normal modes which are associated with the system at each time. This statement is the "adiabatic theorem".

We shall describe this problem of adiabatic transition in connection with quantum mechanical motion, governed by Schrödinger's equation. For simplicity we assume the

Schrödinger function ψ to depend on a variable which may assume two values, 1 and 2; i.e. $\psi = \{\psi_1, \psi_2\}$. The Schrödinger equation,

$$iD_t\psi = H\psi \tag{24.1}$$

for the wave function $\psi = \psi(t)$ as function of the time t then involves the "Hamiltonian" H, a two-by-two matrix. The matrix itself is assumed to depend on the time t and, in addition, on a "slowness parameter" ρ, which may be chosen as the length of the time interval during which the Hamiltonian $H = H(t, \rho)$ changes from an "initial" Hamiltonian H_o to an "end" Hamiltonian H_1. If we denote the initial time by t_o, the end time is then $t_o + \rho$, and we then have

$$H(t_o, \rho) = H_o \quad , \quad H(t_o + \rho, \rho) = H_1 \quad . \tag{24.2}$$

Without serious restriction we may assume that H depends only on the ratio

$$\tau = (t - t_o)/\rho \quad , \tag{24.3}$$

i.e.

$$H = H(\tau) \quad , \tag{24.4}$$

so that

$$H(0) = H_o \quad , \quad H(1) = H_1 \quad . \tag{24.5}$$

Introducing τ instead of t as independent variable we write the differential equation (24.1) in the form

$$D_\tau \psi = -i\rho H(\tau)\psi \quad . \tag{24.6}$$

Having prescribed the initial value $\psi^{(o)}$ of $\psi(\tau, \rho)$ for $\tau = 0$,

$$\psi(0, \rho) = \psi^{(o)} \quad , \tag{24.7}$$

we are to find the end value

$$\psi^{(1)} = \psi(1,\rho) \tag{24.8}$$

for large values of ρ.

Since equation (24.6) is evidently of precisely the type considered in the previous sections, it is clear that the problem can be solved by the methods developed there.

Instead of a specific solution $\psi(\tau,\rho)$, we shall find a fundamental solution which we shall write as a matrix $\Psi(\tau) = \Psi(\tau,\rho)$, which then also satisfies the equation

$$D_\tau \Psi(\tau) = -i\rho H(\tau)\,\Psi(\tau) \quad . \tag{24.9}$$

Denoting the inverse of this matrix by $\Psi^{-1}(\tau)$, we may express $\psi(\tau) = \psi(\tau,\rho)$ as

$$\psi(\tau) = \Psi(\tau)\,\Psi^{-1}(0)\psi(0) \tag{24.10}$$

and hence $\psi^{(1)} = \psi^{(1)}(\rho)$ by

$$\psi^{(1)} = \Psi(1)\,\Psi^{-1}(0)\psi^{(0)} \quad . \tag{24.11}$$

The matrix $H(\tau)$ we assume to be Hermitian. It is then diagonizable for each value of τ. We assume that H depends analytically on τ. Then, as was proved by Rellich, this diagonalization can be performed with the aid of a unitary matrix $U(\tau)$ which itself depends analytically on τ. Denoting by $U^*(\tau)$ the inverse of $U(\tau)$ we may write $H(\tau)$ in the form

$$H(\tau) = U(\tau)\Omega(\tau)U^*(\tau) \quad , \tag{24.12}$$

where the matrix

$$\Omega(\tau) = \begin{pmatrix} \omega_+(\tau) & 0 \\ 0 & \omega_-(\tau) \end{pmatrix} \tag{24.13}$$

is diagonal. Since H was assumed Hermitian, the eigenvalues $\omega_{\pm}$ are real. Without restriction we may assume that

$$\omega_-(\tau) + \omega_+(\tau) = 0 \quad ; \tag{24.14}$$

for otherwise we may factor out from $\psi(\tau)$ the number

$$\exp\left\{-\tfrac{i}{2}\int [\omega_+(\tau) + \omega_-(\tau)]d\tau\right\} \tag{24.15}$$

to make this so. Omitting the argument τ, we set

$$\omega_+ = -\omega_- = \omega \quad . \tag{24.16}$$

Introducing the matrix

$$\eta = \begin{pmatrix} 1 & 0 \\ 0 & -1 \end{pmatrix}, \tag{24.17}$$

we write

$$\Omega = \omega\eta \quad . \tag{24.18}$$

The unitary matrix $U = U(\tau)$ can always be assumed to be of the form

$$U = \begin{pmatrix} \cos\phi & \sin\phi \\ -\sin\phi & \cos\phi \end{pmatrix}, \tag{24.19}$$

in which

$$\phi = \phi(\tau) \tag{24.20}$$

is an analytic function of τ.

Instead of the matrix Ψ we introduce the matrix

$$W = U^* \Psi \quad . \tag{24.21}$$

As a simple calculation shows, W satisfies the differential equation

$$D_\tau W = -i\rho\omega\eta W + \dot{\phi}\cdot\Theta W \tag{24.22}$$

in which Θ is the matrix

$$\Theta = \begin{pmatrix} 0 & -1 \\ 1 & 0 \end{pmatrix} \tag{24.23}$$

and

$$\dot{\phi}(\tau) = D_\tau\phi(\tau) \quad . \tag{24.24}$$

We could give the equation (24.22) precisely the form assumed in the previous sections by introducing a new variable such that

$$z\,dz = -i\omega\, d\tau \quad . \tag{24.25}$$

The results of the previous sections could then be applied. We prefer to proceed independently.

We introduce the quantity

$$k(\tau) = \int^{\tau} \omega(\tau')d\tau' + \text{constant}, \tag{24.26}$$

so that the quantity h employed in the previous sections is given by $h = -ik$. From the general theory we conclude that there are two asymptotic types of solutions, with asymptotic expansions of the form

$$\overset{\pm}{w}(\tau) = e^{\mp i\rho k(\tau)}\, \overset{\pm}{v}(\tau) \quad , \tag{24.27}$$

where

$$\overset{\pm}{v}(\tau) = \sum_{\kappa=0}^{\infty} \rho^{-\kappa}\, \overset{\pm}{v}{}^{(\kappa)}(\tau) \quad . \tag{24.28}$$

Here $\overset{+}{w}$ as well as $\overset{-}{w}$ is a column with the two components $\overset{+}{w}_{\pm}$ and $\overset{-}{w}_{\pm}$ respectively. Using two such solutions, we form the matrix

$$W = (\overset{+}{w},\overset{-}{w}) = \begin{pmatrix} \overset{+}{w}_+ & \overset{-}{w}_+ \\ \overset{+}{w}_- & \overset{-}{w}_- \end{pmatrix} , \tag{24.29}$$

and similarly

$$V = (\overset{+}{v},\overset{-}{v}) = \begin{pmatrix} \overset{+}{v}_+ & \overset{-}{v}_+ \\ \overset{+}{v}_- & \overset{-}{v}_- \end{pmatrix} . \tag{24.30}$$

Insertion of (24.27) into the equation (24.22) yields the equations

$$\begin{cases} D_\tau \overset{\pm}{v}_{\pm} = \mp \dot{\phi}\, \overset{\pm}{v}_{\mp} , \\ D_\tau \overset{\pm}{v}_{\mp} = \pm\, 2i\rho\omega \overset{\pm}{v}_{\mp} \pm \dot{\phi}\, \overset{\pm}{v}_{\pm} . \end{cases} \tag{24.31}$$

Of course, we could write these equations symbolically in the form

$$W = V \exp\{-i\rho k \eta\} , \tag{24.32}$$

$$D_\tau V = i\rho\omega[V\eta - \eta V] + \dot{\phi}\Theta V . \tag{24.33}$$

Using (24.31) we easily derive the terms of the expansion (24.28). We write down two terms, employing convenient constants of integration:

$$V^{(0)} = \begin{pmatrix} 1 & 0 \\ 0 & 1 \end{pmatrix} , \tag{24.34}$$

$$V^{(1)} = i \begin{pmatrix} -\int^{\tau} [2\omega]^{-1} \dot{\phi}^2 d\tau & [2\omega]^{-1} \dot{\phi} \\ [2\omega]^{-1} \dot{\phi} & \int^{\tau} [2\omega]^{-1} \dot{\phi}^2 d\tau \end{pmatrix} . \tag{24.35}$$

The matrix $V(\tau)$ can also be written asymptotically in the form

$$(24.36) \qquad V(\tau) \sim \exp \rho^{-1} V^{(1)}(\tau) \quad ,$$

which is unitary since $iV^{(1)}$ is Hermitian.

Let us choose two solutions $\overset{+}{w}(\tau)$ and $\overset{-}{w}(\tau)$ which at the initial point $\tau = 0$ have asymptotic expansions given by (24.27). Let us for the moment assume that there is no turning point in the interval $0 \leq \tau \leq 1$, i.e. that the eigenvalue $\omega(\tau)$ remains different from zero there. Then the asymptotic expansion (24.27) remains valid in this whole interval.

From (24.21), (24.32), (24.36), we then find

$$(24.37) \quad \Psi(\tau) = U(\tau)W(\tau) \sim U(\tau) \exp\{\rho^{-1}V^{(1)}(\tau)\} \exp\{-i\rho k(\tau)\eta\} \quad ;$$

by virtue of

$$(24.38) \qquad k(1) - k(0) = \int_0^1 \omega(\tau)d\tau \quad ,$$

cf. (24.26), we hence have

$$(24.39) \quad \Psi(1)\Psi^{-1}(0) = U(1)W(1)W^{-1}(0)U^*(0)$$
$$\sim U(1) \exp\{\rho^{-1}V^{(1)}(1)\} \exp\left\{-i\rho\left(\int_0^1 \omega(\tau)d\tau\right)\eta\right\}$$
$$\exp\{-\rho^{-1}V^{(1)}(0)\}\, U^*(0) \quad .$$

Disregarding the terms involving $\rho^{-1}V^{(1)}$, we find that in lowest order

$$(24.40) \quad \Psi(1)\Psi^{-1}(0) \sim U(1) \exp\left\{-i\rho\left(\int_0^1 \omega(\tau)d\tau\right)\eta\right\} U^*(0) \quad .$$

In order to interpret this formula we consider eigenfunctions of the operator $H(\tau)$ associated with the eigenvalues $\omega_{\pm}(\tau) = \pm\omega(\tau)$. We introduce the columns

(24.41) $$\xi^{+} = \begin{pmatrix} 1 \\ 0 \end{pmatrix} \quad \text{and} \quad \xi^{-} = \begin{pmatrix} 0 \\ 1 \end{pmatrix} ,$$

which by (24.17) satisfy the relation

(24.42) $$\eta \cdot \xi^{\pm} = \pm \xi^{\pm} ,$$

and hence also the relation

(24.43) $$\Omega(\tau)\xi^{\pm} = \pm\omega(\tau)\xi^{\pm} .$$

By virtue of (24.12), therefore, the functions $U(\tau)\xi^{\pm}$ satisfy the relations

(24.44) $$H(\tau)[U(\tau)\xi^{\pm}] = \pm\omega(\tau)[U(\tau)\xi^{\pm}]$$

and hence are eigenfunctions of the Hamiltonian $H(\tau)$.

Suppose now the initial function $\psi^{(0)}$ is an eigenfunction

(24.45) $$\psi^{(0)} = U(0)\cdot\xi^{\pm}$$

of the Hamiltonian at the initial time t_o. Then, since

(24.46) $$e^{a\eta}\,\xi^{\pm} = e^{\pm a}\,\xi^{\pm} ,$$

we have

(24.47) $$\exp\left\{-i\rho\left(\int_0^1 \omega(\tau)d\tau\right)\eta\right\} U^{*}(0)\psi^{(0)}$$

$$= \exp\left\{\mp i\rho \int_0^1 \omega(\tau)d\tau\right\}\xi^{\pm} .$$

Formulas (24.40) and (24.11) therefore give

$$(24.48) \qquad \psi^{(1)} \sim \exp\left\{ \mp i\rho \int_0^1 \omega(\tau)d\tau \right\} U(1)\xi^{\pm} \quad .$$

Thus it is seen that in first approximation the wave function ψ at the end time $t_o + \rho$ is an eigenfunction of the Hamiltonian at the end time. Since the end time was arbitrary we see that at each time the wave function--to first approximation--agrees with an eigenfunction of the Hamiltonian corresponding to that time. Thus the adiabatic theorem is demonstrated.

Indeed, formula (24.40) gives a refinement of this statement. We are satisfied with drawing one conclusion from this result, namely the following:

Assuming that at the initial time t_o the wave function was an eigenfunction of the Hamiltonian $H(0)$ with, say, the eigenvalue $+\omega(0)$, the probability that at the time $t_o + \rho$ the wave function is an eigenfunction of the Hamiltonian $H(1)$ with the corresponding eigenvalue $+\omega(1)$ differs from 1 by a term of order ρ^{-2}.

To verify that this is so we note that, according to the principles of quantum theory, the probability in question is given by the square of the absolute value of the upper left-hand element of the matrix

$$(24.49) \quad W(1)W^{-1}(0) \sim [1 + \rho^{-1}V^{(1)}(1)] \exp\left\{ -i\rho \left(\int_0^1 \omega(\tau)d\tau \right) \eta \right\} [1 + \rho^{-1}V^{(1)}(0)]^{-1} \quad ,$$

and observe that by (24.35) the deviation of this matrix from a diagonal unitary matrix is purely imaginary and of order ρ^{-1}.

Up to now we had assumed that on the interval $t_o \le t \le t_o + \rho$ the eigenvalues of the Hamiltonian are distinct. We proceed to discuss the case in which the eigenvalues coalesce at a certain time between t_o and $t_o + \rho$. For simplicity we assume that this happens at a time corresponding to $\tau = 0$, so that

(24.50) $$\omega(0) = 0 \quad ;$$

we also assume that

(24.50a) $$\dot{\omega}(0) = D_\tau \omega(0) > 0 \quad .$$

To do this we of course perform a translation of the τ-axis, so that the original τ-interval [0,1] now becomes the interval $[\tau_o, \tau_1]$, where

(24.51) $$\tau_o < 0 < \tau_1 \quad .$$

We may take

(24.52) $$k(0) = 0 \quad .$$

The transition lines $\mathrm{Im}\, k(\tau) = 0$ are then simply the real and imaginary axes. According to the general theory we may assign to each quadrant a solution which is recessive there and dominant, but of the same asymptotic type, in the two adjacent quadrants. The solutions which are associated with the two quadrants $\mathrm{Re}\, \tau < 0$ will be characterized by the subscript ℓ, those associated with the two quadrants $\mathrm{Re}\, \tau > 0$ by the subscript r. Specifically, we denote by $\overset{\pm}{w}_\ell(\tau)$ and $\overset{\pm}{w}_r(\tau)$ the solutions associated with the quadrants $\mathrm{Re}\, \tau < 0$, $\mathrm{Im}\, \tau \gtrless 0$ and $\mathrm{Re}\, \tau > 0$, $\mathrm{Im}\, \tau \lessgtr 0$ respectively.

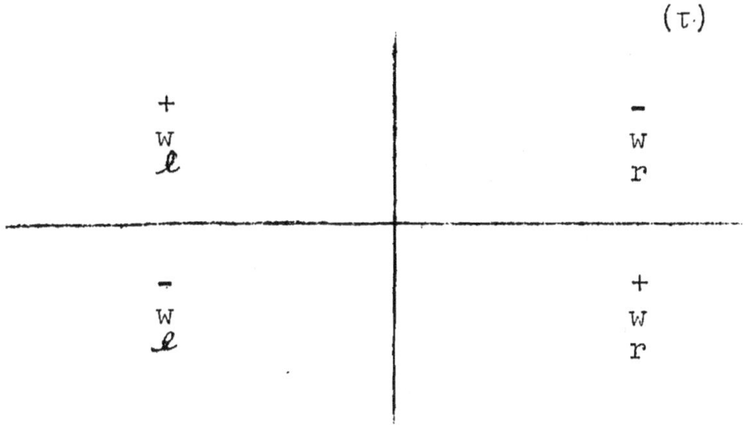

Figure 14

Sectors in which the w are recessive

Suppose we form the matrix W from the solutions $\overset{\pm}{w}_{\ell}(\tau)$:

(24.53) $$W(\tau) = W_{\ell}(\tau) = (\overset{+}{w}_{\ell}(\tau), \overset{-}{w}_{\ell}(\tau)) \quad .$$

Then we may use formula (24.37) for $\tau = \tau_0$, but not for $\tau = \tau_1$. In order to find the asymptotic description of the matrix $W(\tau)$ which is valid for $\tau = \tau_1$, we must express $\overset{+}{w}_{\ell}(\tau)$ in terms of $\overset{\pm}{w}_{r}(\tau)$. This can be done by employing a matrix $P = P(\varepsilon)$, such that

(24.54) $$W_{\ell} = W_{r} P \quad .$$

The diagonal terms of this matrix

(24.55) $$P = \begin{pmatrix} \overset{+}{p}_{+} & \overset{-}{p}_{+} \\ \overset{+}{p}_{-} & \overset{-}{p}_{-} \end{pmatrix}$$

can be found immediately up to second order from the matrices $V^{(0)}$, $V^{(1)}$ given by (24.24) and (24.35). These terms depend on the lower limits of the integrals occurring in the diagonal terms of $V_\ell^{(1)}$ and $V_r^{(1)}$. We take these lower limits as negative and positive real numbers $\tau_\ell < 0 < \tau_r$ respectively. Since $\omega(\tau)$ changes sign, we may take these numbers such that

$$(24.56) \qquad \int_{\tau_\ell}^{\tau_r} [2\omega]^{-1} \dot{\phi}^2 \, d\tau = 0$$

provided Cauchy's principal value of this integral is taken. The asymptotic expansions (24.28) of both functions $\overset{+}{v}_\ell(\tau)$ and $\overset{+}{v}_r(\tau)$ are valid in the quadrant Re $\tau > 0$, Im $\tau > 0$. For the first, "+", components of these functions these expansions are

$$(24.57) \qquad \overset{+}{v}_{\ell +}(\tau) = 1 - i\rho^{-1} \int_{\tau_\ell}^{\tau} [2\omega]^{-1} \dot{\phi}^2 \, d\tau \quad ,$$

$$(24.58) \qquad \overset{+}{v}_{r +}(\tau) = 1 - i\rho^{-1} \int_{\tau_r}^{\tau} [2\omega]^{-1} \dot{\phi}^2 \, d\tau \quad ,$$

where the path of integration is to run in the upper half-plane Im $\tau > 0$. Since

$$(24.59) \qquad \overset{+}{p}_- \; \overset{-}{v}_{r +}(\tau) = \overset{+}{v}_{\ell +}(\tau) - \overset{+}{p}_+ \; \overset{+}{v}_{r +}(\tau)$$

is the first component of a multiple of a solution $\overset{-}{v}_r(\tau)$ which is recessive in the quadrant Re $\tau > 0$, Im $\tau > 0$, we expect that the factor $\overset{+}{p}_+$ has an asymptotic expansion beginning as

$$(24.60) \qquad \overset{+}{p}_+ \sim 1 - i\rho^{-1} \int_{\tau_\ell}^{\tau_r} [2\omega]^{-1} \dot{\phi}^2 \, d\tau \quad .$$

By comparing the expansions of $\bar{v}_{\ell-}(\tau)$ and $\bar{v}_{r-}(\tau)$ in the quadrant Re $\tau > 0$, Im $\tau < 0$, we are similarly led to the expansion

$$(24.61) \qquad \bar{p}_- \sim 1 + i\rho^{-1} \int_{\tau_\ell}^{\tau_r} [2\omega]^{-1} \dot{\phi}^2 \, d\tau \quad .$$

Using the stipulation (24.56) and setting

$$(24.62) \qquad D_\tau \omega(0) = \dot{\omega}(0) \quad ,$$

we find

$$(24.63) \qquad \overset{+}{\bar{p}}_{\pm} \sim 1 - \pi\rho^{-1}[2\dot{\omega}(0)]^{-1} \dot{\phi}^2(0) \quad .$$

In order to determine the coefficients $\overset{+}{p}_-$ and $\bar{p}_+$, we make use of the reducibility of the continuation problem to the connection problem and solve the connection problem formally by solving a stretched differential equation, as explained in Section 21.

In order to carry out this procedure properly, one should introduce the quantity $[\rho k(\tau)]^{1/2}$ as new independent variable. For the determination of the terms of lowest order, however, it is sufficient to introduce the variable

$$(24.64) \qquad \zeta = \sqrt{\rho}\, \tau \quad .$$

The terms of lowest order of the differential equations (24.31) then become--with $\rho^{-1} = \varepsilon$--

$$(24.65) \qquad \begin{cases} D_\zeta \overset{+}{\bar{v}}_{\pm} \sim \mp \sqrt{\varepsilon}\, \dot{\phi}(0) \overset{+}{\bar{v}}_{\mp} \sim 0 \quad , \\ D_\zeta \overset{+}{\bar{v}}_{\mp} \sim \pm 2i\zeta \dot{\omega}(0) \overset{+}{\bar{v}}_{\mp} \pm \sqrt{\varepsilon}\, \dot{\phi}(0) \overset{+}{\bar{v}}_{\pm} \quad . \end{cases}$$

The solutions--to the lowest order--are

$$\overset{+}{\bar{v}}_{\underset{-}{+}} \sim 1 \quad ,$$

(24.66)

$$\overset{+}{\bar{v}}_{\underset{+}{-}} \sim \pm\sqrt{\varepsilon}\ \dot{\phi}(0) \int_{\infty}^{\zeta} e^{\pm i\dot{\omega}(0)(\zeta^2 - \xi^2)}\, d\xi \quad ,$$

whence follows--after re-introducing the variable τ --

$$\overset{+}{\bar{v}}_{\underset{+}{-}}(\tau) \sim \pm\ \dot{\phi}(0) \int_{\infty}^{\tau} e^{\pm i\rho\dot{\omega}(0)(\tau^2 - \hat{\tau}^2)}\, d\hat{\tau} \quad . \tag{24.67}$$

The lower limit ∞ is to be chosen in the quadrant in which the desired solution is recessive.

The asymptotic behavior of the expansions (24.66), (24.67) in the vicinity of $\tau = \infty$ should agree with the behavior of the asymptotic formula (24.36) at the turning point. This is evidently the case for $\overset{+}{\bar{v}}_{\underset{-}{+}}$ to lowest order.

Since as $\rho \longrightarrow \infty$

$$\pm \int_{\infty}^{\tau} e^{\pm i\rho\dot{\omega}(0)(\tau^2 - \hat{\tau}^2)}\, d\hat{\tau} \sim i\varepsilon/2\dot{\omega}(0)\tau \quad , \tag{24.68}$$

we find

$$\overset{+}{\bar{v}}_{\underset{+}{-}}(\tau) \sim i\varepsilon\dot{\phi}(0)/2\dot{\omega}(0)\tau \quad , \tag{24.69}$$

while from (24.35) we had

$$\overset{+}{\bar{v}}_{\underset{+}{-}}(\tau) \sim i\varepsilon\dot{\phi}(\tau)/2\dot{\omega}(\tau) \quad . \tag{24.70}$$

The behavior of the right member of (24.70) at the turning point $\tau = 0$ is evidently given by (24.69).

We now employ formulas (24.66) to obtain the behavior of the functions $\overset{+}{\bar{v}}(\tau)$ at the turning point $\tau = 0$, which corresponds to $\zeta = 0$. (Note that formula (24.69) gives the behavior of only the leading term of the asymptotic expansion of $\overset{+}{\bar{v}}_{\underset{+}{-}}(\tau)$ at the turning point.) We find

$$\overset{+}{\underset{\pm}{v}}(0) \sim 1 \quad , \tag{24.71}$$

$$\begin{aligned} \overset{+}{\underset{\ell\mp}{v_{-}}}(0) &\sim \mp \tfrac{1}{2}\sqrt{\varepsilon\pi/\dot{\omega}(0)}\;\dot{\phi}(0)e^{\pm 3\pi i/4} \quad , \\ \overset{+}{\underset{r\mp}{v_{-}}}(0) &\sim \mp \tfrac{1}{2}\sqrt{\varepsilon\pi/\dot{\omega}(0)}\;\dot{\phi}(0)e^{\mp\pi i/4} \quad . \end{aligned} \tag{24.72}$$

We may determine the matrix P by satisfying relation (24.54) at the origin. From (24.71), (24.72) we have

$$\underset{\ell}{W}(0) \sim \begin{pmatrix} 1 & -\tfrac{1}{2}\dot{\phi}(0)\sqrt{\varepsilon\pi/\dot{\omega}(0)}\;e^{\pi i/4} \\ \tfrac{1}{2}\dot{\phi}(0)\sqrt{\varepsilon\pi/\dot{\omega}(0)}\;e^{-\pi i/4} & 1 \end{pmatrix} \tag{24.73}$$

and

$$\underset{r}{W}(0) \sim \begin{pmatrix} 1 & \tfrac{1}{2}\dot{\phi}(0)\sqrt{\varepsilon\pi/\dot{\omega}(0)}\;e^{\pi i/4} \\ -\tfrac{1}{2}\dot{\phi}(0)\sqrt{\varepsilon\pi/\dot{\omega}(0)}\;e^{-\pi i/4} & 1 \end{pmatrix}. \tag{24.74}$$

From (24.54) we thus obtain the expression

$$P \sim \begin{pmatrix} 1 & -\dot{\phi}(0)\sqrt{\varepsilon\pi/\dot{\omega}(0)}\;e^{\pi i/4} \\ \dot{\phi}(0)\sqrt{\varepsilon\pi/\dot{\omega}(0)}\;e^{-\pi i/4} & 1 \end{pmatrix} \tag{24.75}$$

for the matrix P. We can make the right member unitary by setting

$$(24.76)\quad P \sim \begin{pmatrix} [1-\varepsilon\pi\dot{\phi}^2(0)/\dot{\omega}(0)]^{1/2} & -[\varepsilon\pi/\dot{\omega}(0)]^{1/2}\dot{\phi}(0)e^{\pi i/4} \\ [\varepsilon\pi/\dot{\omega}(0)]^{1/2}\dot{\phi}(0)e^{-\pi i/4} & [1-\varepsilon\pi\dot{\phi}^2(0)/\dot{\omega}(0)]^{1/2} \end{pmatrix}.$$

The first two terms in the expansion of the diagonal term in the latter expression evidently agree with (24.63).

Defining the matrix Z by the relation

$$(24.77)\quad \Psi(\tau_1)\Psi^{-1}(\tau_0) = U(\tau_1)ZU^*(\tau_0) \quad ,$$

we obtain by (24.21) and (24.54)

$$(24.78)\quad Z = W_{\ell}(\tau_1)W_{\ell}^{-1}(\tau_0) = W_r(\tau_1)PW_{\ell}^{-1}(\tau_0) \quad .$$

Hence by (24.32) and (24.34)

$$(24.79)\quad Z \sim \exp\left\{-i\rho k(\tau_1)\eta\right\} P \exp\left\{i\rho k(\tau_0)\right\} \quad ,$$

or

$$(24.80)\quad \begin{aligned} \overset{+}{Z}_{\overset{+}{-}} &\sim [1-\varepsilon\pi\dot{\phi}^2(0)/\dot{\omega}(0)]^{1/2} \exp\left\{\mp i\rho\int_{\tau_0}^{\tau_1}\omega(\tau)\,d\tau\right\} , \\ \overset{+}{Z}_{\overset{-}{+}} &\sim \pm[\varepsilon\pi/\dot{\omega}(0)]^{1/2}\dot{\phi}(0)e^{\mp\pi i/4}\exp\left\{\pm i\left[\int_{\tau_0}^{\tau_1}\omega(\tau)d\tau - \int_{\tau_0}^{0}\omega(\tau)d\tau\right]\right\} \end{aligned}$$

Of particular interest is the probability that an eigenfunction of the Hamiltonian $H(\tau_0)$ with the eigenvalue $\omega(\tau_0)$ goes over into an eigenfunction of the Hamiltonian $H(\tau_1)$ with the eigenvalue $-\omega(\tau_1)$. As mentioned above, this probability is given by $|\overset{-}{Z}_+|^2$. Asymptotically, it is therefore

$$(24.81)\quad |\overset{-}{Z}_+|^2 \sim \varepsilon\pi\dot{\phi}(0)/\dot{\omega}(0) \; .$$

Note that this probability vanishes like $\varepsilon = \rho^{-1}$, while the interchange probabilities in the case where the eigenvalues of H do not coalesce were seen above to be of order $\varepsilon^2 = \rho^{-2}$ and hence of lesser significance.

Of some interest is the special case in which the final set of eigenvalues $\pm\omega(\tau_1)$ is a permutation of the initial set of eigenvalues $\pm\omega(\tau_0)$:

$$\omega(\tau_1) = -\omega(\tau_0) \quad , \tag{24.82}$$

and in which, at the same time, the rotation $U(\tau)$ interchanges the principal axes:

$$U(\tau_1)\xi^{\pm} = \pm U(\tau_0)\xi^{\mp} \tag{24.83}$$

or

$$U(\tau_1)=U(\tau_0)\theta \quad . \tag{24.84}$$

In that case the final Hamiltonian agrees with the original one:

$$\begin{aligned} H(\tau_1) &= U(\tau_1)\Omega(\tau_1)U^*(\tau_1) \\ &= -U(\tau_0)\,\theta\,\Omega(\tau_0)\,\theta^{-1}U^*(\tau_0) \\ &= U(\tau_0)\,\Omega(\tau_0)U^*(\tau_0) = H(\tau_0) \quad . \end{aligned} \tag{24.85}$$

It is interesting that in this case there is a positive probability, given by (24.81), that, in spite of the interchange of eigenvalues, an initial eigenfunction will--except for a factor--go over into the same eigenfunction in the final state.

Reference for Section 23

[E] Langer, R. E.: The asymptotic solutions of ordinary linear differential equations of the second order, with special reference to Stokes phenomenon. Bulletin of the American Mathematical Society, vol. 40, pp. 545-582 (1934).

CPSIA information can be obtained
at www.ICGtesting.com
Printed in the USA
BVHW010917191120
593711BV00008B/386

9 781258 670566